State Formation through Emulation

Neither war nor preparations for war were the cause or effect of state formation in East Asia. Instead, emulation of China – the hegemon with a civilizational influence – drove the rapid formation of centralized, bureaucratically administered, territorial governments in Korea, Japan, and Vietnam. Furthermore, these countries engaged in state-building not to engage in conflict or to suppress revolt. In fact, war was relatively rare and there was no balance of power system with regular existential threats – the longevity of the East Asian dynasties is evidence of both the peacefulness of their neighborhood and their internal stability. We challenge the assumption that the European experience with war and state-making was universal. More importantly, we broaden the scope of state formation in East Asia beyond the study of China itself and show how countries in the region interacted and learned from each other and China to develop strong capacities and stable borders.

CHIN-HAO HUANG is associate professor of political science and head of studies for global affairs at Yale-NUS College in Singapore. His research and teaching focus on China's foreign relations, the international relations of East Asia, and international security. His books include *Power and Restraint in China's Rise* (2022) and *Identity in the Shadow of a Giant: How the Rise of China is Changing Taiwan* (2021).

DAVID C. KANG is Maria Crutcher Professor of International Relations at the University of Southern California, where he is also director of the USC Korean Studies Institute. He researches East Asian security, the international relations of historical East Asia, and Korean politics.

T0382461

State Formation through Emulation

The East Asian Model

CHIN-HAO HUANG
Yale-National University of Singapore College

DAVID C. KANG
University of Southern California

CAMBRIDGE
UNIVERSITY PRESS

University Printing House, Cambridge CB2 8BS, United Kingdom

One Liberty Plaza, 20th Floor, New York, NY 10006, USA

477 Williamstown Road, Port Melbourne, VIC 3207, Australia

314–321, 3rd Floor, Plot 3, Splendor Forum, Jasola District Centre,
New Delhi – 110025, India

103 Penang Road, #05–06/07, Visioncrest Commercial, Singapore 238467

Cambridge University Press is part of the University of Cambridge.

It furthers the University's mission by disseminating knowledge in the pursuit of
education, learning, and research at the highest international levels of excellence.

www.cambridge.org
Information on this title: www.cambridge.org/9781009098533
DOI: 10.1017/9781009089616

© Chin-Hao Huang and David C. Kang 2022

First published 2022

A catalogue record for this publication is available from the British Library

Library of Congress Cataloging-in-Publication Data
Names: Huang, Chin-Hao, author. | Kang, David C. (David Chan-oong), 1965- author.
Title: State formation through emulation : the East Asian model / Chin-Hao Huang, Yale-National
    University of Singapore College, David C. Kang, University of Southern California
Description: Cambridge, United Kingdom ; New York, NY : Cambridge University Press, 2022. |
    Includes bibliographical references and index.
Identifiers: LCCN 2021061924 (print) | LCCN 2021061925 (ebook) | ISBN 9781009098533
    (hardback) | ISBN 9781009096317 (paperback) | ISBN 9781009089616 (epub)
Subjects: LCSH: State, The. | East Asia–Politics and government. | Nation-building–East Asia. | East
    Asia–Foreign relations. | BISAC: SOCIAL SCIENCE / Sociology / General
Classification: LCC JC11 .H83 2022 (print) | LCC JC11 (ebook) | DDC 320.1–dc23/eng/20220304
LC record available at https://lccn.loc.gov/2021061924
LC ebook record available at https://lccn.loc.gov/2021061925

ISBN 978-1-009-09853-3 Hardback
ISBN 978-1-009-09631-7 Paperback

In memory of Ching-Chi Huang

– Chin-Hao Huang

In memory of Minqian Michelle Kang

– David C. Kang

Contents

Preface

This book began with an observation – an observation so obvious that it is usually overlooked or simply taken for granted: Korea, Japan, and Vietnam have copied an enormous amount from China. Over the years, and in conversations between the two of us, that observation slowly turned into an idea. That idea was turned into an actual research agenda at the prompting of Anna Grzymala-Busse, when she presented a paper as part of the USC (University of Southern California) Center for International Studies working paper series that Dave ran while he directed that center. Encouraged by her new approach to European state formation, we began to pursue our idea about state formation in East Asia. The result is this book.

Thanks to Didac Cerault, Ben Graham, Tanner Greer, Jacques Hymans, Pat James, Saori Katada, Ellen Kim, Sun Joo Kim, Na Young Lee, Jonathan Markowitz, Sebastian Mazzucca, Gerardo Munck, John Park, Kyuri Park, and Sixiang Wang for thoughtful comments on earlier drafts. Thanks to Hendrik Spruyt for his careful comments and for suggesting the title of this book. We particularly thank Anna Grzymala-Busse, R. Bin Wong, and all the participants of a manuscript review hosted by the USC Korean Studies Institute on January 8, 2021, for reading the entire manuscript and for so generously giving their time and energy to help make the final product better. We also thank the careful reviewers at Cambridge University Press, and John Haslam for his usual superb editorial advice on this project.

Shorter versions of the argument were presented at the EJIR (European Journal of International Relations) 25th anniversary workshop, Munk Center for International Studies, University of Toronto, March 26, 2019, and the USC Center for International Studies Working Paper Series, January 17, 2019. We are especially grateful to Jill Lin and Jackie Wong for superb Research Assistant work, including making many of the figures, and helping with all the footnotes and other important details. We thank David Cruickshank for superb editing help and Cynthia Col for her wonderful index.

Finally, we gratefully acknowledge the support of the Laboratory Program for Korean Studies through the Ministry of Education of the Republic of Korea and the Korean Studies Promotion Service of the Academy of Korean Studies (AKS-2015-LAB-2250002) and the JY Pillay Global Asia research fund at Yale-NUS College (IG19-SG117).

1 | Introduction

The East Asian Model of State Formation

The might and wealth of the Sui–Tang empires (618–907) at their peak deeply impressed China's neighbors. Japan, the Korean states, and even (briefly) Tibet imitated the Sui–Tang imperial model, and to a greater or lesser degree adopted the Chinese written language, Sui–Tang political institutions and laws, Confucian ideology, and the Buddhist religion. It was during this era that East Asia – a community of independent national states sharing a common civilization – took shape in forms that have endured down to modern times.

Richard von Glahn[1]

Korea, Japan, and Vietnam should not exist according to the dominant theories of state formation that were inductively derived from the European experience. Yet, by the eighth century CE, more than 7,000 men staffed the Japanese imperial bureaucracy.[2] This bureaucracy included a state council, eight ministries, and forty-six bureaus. A comprehensive administrative hierarchy of provinces, districts, and villages had been established throughout the empire. The court implemented a population census, a centralized tax system, a legal code, and a civil service examination, all based on Chinese Tang dynasty models.

Even by the thirteenth century, European state formation could not compare to that achieved a half millennium earlier in East Asia. The Catholic Church legal office, the Curia, was so advanced compared to thirteenth-century European royal courts that it was a "template for sophisticated administration";[3] others have observed that it "became

---

[1] Richard von Glahn, *The Economic History of China* (Cambridge: Cambridge University Press, 2016), 169.
[2] Patricia Ebrey and Anne Walthall, *Pre-Modern East Asia: To 1800: A Cultural, Social, and Political History* (Boston: Wadsworth Cengage Learning, 2014), 121.
[3] Anna Grzymala-Busse, "Beyond War and Contracts: The Medieval and Religious Roots of the European State," *Annual Review of Political Science*, 23, no. 1 (2020), 9.

the model for the beginnings of state bureaucracies."[4] Yet, the Curia had only 1,000 or so officials and was dwarfed by the complexity and size that the Japanese state bureaucracy had already achieved 500 years earlier. Further state formation in Europe was then driven by competition for territory and survival. As Philip Gorski and Vivek Sharma summarize the literature, "the bellicist paradigm makes war the underlying mechanism driving virtually all aspects of state formation [and] has become the standard narrative of state formation within the social sciences."[5]

What is often overlooked is the extent to which historical China, Korea, Japan, and Vietnam became fully functioning states. Each had attained centralized bureaucratic control defined over territory and the administrative capacity to tax their populations, field large militaries, and provide extensive public goods.[6] Moreover, three key institutional features of their engagement with state-building stand out: first, an examination for selecting civil servants on the basis of merit, not heredity; second, institutional organization both of the government itself into regular ministries and of the country into provinces and regions, with appointments controlled from the center; and third, formally negotiated borders as well as rules and norms and institutions for dealing with other states, recognized more widely as the Tribute System. By the tenth century CE, these four main political units in the region were centrally administered, bureaucratic organizations with power defined over a geographic area that conducted formal diplomatic relations with each other.

As well as overlooking the fact that state formation in China, Korea, Japan, and Vietnam had occurred 1,000 years earlier than in Europe, the well-known narrative of state formation in Europe often ignores that it occurred in East Asia for reasons of emulation, not bellicist competition. These countries did not engage in state-building in order to wage war or suppress revolt; in fact, war was relatively rare, and

---

[4] Michael Mitterauer, *Why Europe? The Medieval Origins of Its Special Path* (Chicago: University of Chicago Press, 2010), 150.

[5] Philip Gorski and Vivek Sharma, "Beyond the Tilly Thesis: 'Family Values' and State Formation in Latin Christendom," in Lars Kaspersen and Jeppe Strandsbjerg (eds.), *Does War Make States? Investigations of Charles Tilly's Historical Sociology* (New York: Cambridge University Press, 2017), 98.

[6] China emerged as a state beginning in the second century BCE, Korea and Japan emerged between the fifth and eighth centuries CE, and Vietnam in the tenth century.

there was no balance-of-power system with regular existential threats: The longevity of the East Asian dynasties is evidence of both the peacefulness of their neighborhood and their internal stability. Despite Charles Tilly's famous dictum that "war made the state, and the state made war,"[7] neither war nor preparations for war were the cause or effect of state formation in Korea, Japan, or Vietnam. Instead, emulation of China – the hegemon, which had a civilizational influence across the known world – drove the rapid formation of centralized, bureaucratically administered, territorial governments in Korea, Japan, and Vietnam. However, scholars of international relations have not sufficiently investigated how the system affects the units, and, in particular, how hegemonic systems may differ from balance-of-power systems. Moreover, how small, weaker actors support or resist large hegemons has been largely undertheorized in the study of authority relations, power, and legitimacy in the extant literature.[8]

In the chapters to follow, we provide historical evidence of Korean, Japanese, and Vietnamese emulation of Chinese civilization, which centrally included state formation. We show how extensively Korea, Japan, and Vietnam borrowed from China from the fifth to tenth centuries and why local elites adopted Chinese models for reasons of prestige and domestic legitimacy. We show that this occurred through conscious, intentional emulation and learning; and that a regionwide epistemic community existed, composed mainly of Confucian scholars as well as Buddhist monks, who interacted, traveled, and learned from each other. So intertwined is the history of China with its neighbors that Charles Holcombe concludes that "the early histories of both Korea and Japan would be incomprehensible except as parts of a larger East Asian community."[9] In his magisterial history of Vietnam, Keith Taylor concludes that "Vietnamese history as we know it today could not exist without Chinese history. The manner in which Vietnamese history overlaps with and is distinguished from Chinese history presents a singular example of experience in organizing and governing

[7] Charles Tilly, *The Formation of National States in Western Europe* (Princeton: Princeton University Press, 1975), 42.
[8] Chin-Hao Huang, *Power and Restraint in China's Rise* (New York: Columbia University Press, 2022).
[9] Charles Holcombe, *A History of East Asia: From the Origins of Civilization to the Twenty-First Century* (Cambridge: Cambridge University Press, 2011), 109.

human society within the orbit of Sinic civilization that can be compared with Korean and Japanese history."[10]

We also show why and how some societies on the Central Asian steppe resisted Chinese influence. Indeed, the fighting that occurred was mostly between different types of political unit, not similar ones. These societies were also free of the competitive pressures that pushed institutional conformity in East Asia up until the nineteenth century. War did not make states on the Central Asian steppe. Rather, China and the peoples of the Central Asian steppe were quite aware of their differences and determined to preserve them as long as possible for opportunistic reasons. Some would even argue that there was a unique symbiotic interaction between Chinese dynasties and those who lived in the Central Asian steppe. Hendrik Spruyt points out, "A unified and prosperous China provided trading opportunities for the steppe tribes or booty by raiding, thereby making unified action by the otherwise loosely organized tribal federation possible. When China was racked by turmoil and civil war, the lack of economic benefits for unified action decreased in the steppe as well."[11] In other words, while confrontation and conflict were frequent, the genuine interest of the steppe nomads in competing against Chinese governance models or seeking to replace Chinese ideas – let alone the "territorial conquest of China proper" – was limited.[12]

1.1 East Asian History and Western Social Science Theory

Why is this important? The research presented here leads to new insights about state formation in all societies, not just those in East Asia. It moves the study of state formation beyond both Eurocentric and Sinocentric preoccupations to become truly comparative in nature. This research casts doubt on whether the bellicist thesis is a universal truth with explanatory power outside the European region in which it was inductively derived. If we are right, the bellicist approach is just one possible causal mechanism that is often applied as a partial

[10] Keith Taylor, *A History of the Vietnamese* (Cambridge: Cambridge University Press, 2013), 4.
[11] Hendrik Spruyt, *The World Imagined: Collective Beliefs and Political Order in the Sinocentric, Islamic and Southeast Asian International Societies* (Cambridge: Cambridge University Press, 2020), 101.
[12] Spruyt, *The World Imagined*, 101.

narrative about a particular time and place. Further examination of East Asian history would likely generate different assumptions and theories about international relations, which would probably lead to different conclusions about how politics work and societies are organized in all regions of the world.[13]

Indeed, our work suggests that emulation was likely more important even in European state formation than is commonly recognized, as scholars such as Anna Grzymala-Busse and Philip Gorski are pointing out.[14] It is quite likely that emulation and diffusion were central causal factors in state formation in Europe, Latin America, and other regions; and that the bellicist thesis was less prevalent than has been commonly acknowledged.

Victoria Hui compellingly argues that scholars should "set aside universal theories" and be aware that "competing causal mechanisms and strategic interactions generate multiple equilibria," which are "sensitive to historically contingent conditions."[15] This is especially the case when assuming that the European experience is universal across time and space. The willingness to acknowledge the Eurocentric origins of much of international relations theory is not new since "the median American scholar of IR is deeply comfortable with European examples and analogies and has almost no exposure to Asian examples and history. Thus, when faced with Asian examples, they are considered within the context they are taught: through the European lens."[16] What is new in this book is the deep and extensive empirical evidence we bring to bear that shows that the Eurocentric theories are not universal and, furthermore, a new argument about the causes of state formation that marks a positive theoretical advance.

J. C. Sharman explains how understanding historical Asian polities might help change our long-held assumptions about developments in Europe.

[13] Yuen Foong Khong, "The American Tributary System," *Chinese Journal of International Politics*, 6, no. 1 (2013), 1–47.

[14] Grzymala-Busse, "Beyond War and Contracts"; and Philip S. Gorski, *The Disciplinary Revolution: Calvinism and the Rise of the State in Early Modern Europe* (Chicago: University of Chicago Press, 2003).

[15] Victoria Hui, *War and State Formation in Ancient China and Early Modern Europe* (Cambridge: Cambridge University Press, 2005), 2–34.

[16] David C. Kang and Alex Yu-Ting Lin, "US Bias in the Study of Asian Security: Using Europe to Study Asia," *Journal of Global Security Studies*, 4, no. 3 (2019), 393.

First, it disconfirms the idea of a single path to military effectiveness, of sequences of necessary and sufficient causes, either technological or tactical, by which war makes states. Second, it undermines stereotypes according to which relatively transient successes by small European polities are too often portrayed as epochal triumphs, whereas mighty, long lived Asian empires are characterized as merely failures waiting to happen.[17]

Shifting the lens through which we view the past of state formation can thus have a significant impact on changing and informing our understanding of how interstate relations work across time and space.

In contrast to the extensive literature on European state formation, there is comparatively less scholarship in the social science literature on state formation in East Asia. Most scholarship on East Asian state formation focuses on what can be called Phase I: the emergence of unified China during and after the Warring States period (475–221 BCE).[18] Yet, this scholarship suffers from two main limitations: temporal and geographic. Temporally, it ignores almost all of East Asian history and focuses on the emergence of China 2,000 years ago as if it were the only event of consequence. This is as if scholars explored the rise of the Roman Empire in the third to first centuries BCE and concluded that nothing of significance then happened in European history until the end of the Holy Roman Empire in 1806. In short, there is an overused stereotype of stagnant and endless dynastic Chinese cycles that should have been excised long ago from any serious scholarship on East Asia. Most state formation in East Asia occurred centuries after the initial emergence of centralized Chinese rule.

Geographically, much of the scholarship treats China as equivalent to all of East Asia and barely acknowledges the existence of any other political units in the region. This overemphasizes the role of China in the system. Yet Korea and Japan (and later Vietnam and elsewhere) emerged as states over 1,000 years ago, beginning in the fifth to eighth centuries CE, which can be called Phase II, and they often interacted

---

[17] J. C. Sharman, *Empires of the Weak: The Real Story of European Expansion and the Creation of the New World Order* (Princeton, NJ: Princeton University Press, 2019), 6.

[18] Edgar Kiser and Yong Cai, "War and Bureaucratization in Qin China: Exploring an Anomalous Case," *American Sociological Review*, 68, no. 4 (2003), 513; Dingxin Zhao, "Spurious Causation in a Historical Process: War and Bureaucratization in Early China," *American Sociological Review*, 69, no. 4 (2004), 603–607; and Hui, *War and State Formation*.

with each other without paying any attention to China (Figure 1.1). It may seem odd to suggest *not* focusing on the hegemon. Our point, however, is that more emphasis needs to be placed on the agency that existed across the entire East Asian region. This is all the more necessary if the discipline of international relations is going to widen its inquiry beyond China and Phase I, and address state formation across the breadth of historical East Asia throughout the 1,700 years that encompass Phase II and beyond.

There are notable exceptions to these observations, of course, and we do not mean to be too blunt or sweeping in our claims. Indeed, much of this book builds directly on the insights of scholars who have examined China over time or compared countries in East Asia with each other. Perhaps the most influential among the former category are Dingxin Zhao and R. Bin Wong, both of whom make powerful arguments about how the Chinese state evolved over 2,000 years.[19] In the latter category, Victor Lieberman and Alexander Woodside have written groundbreaking books: Lieberman exploring the sweep of both Southeast Asian state formation, and Woodside reminding us of the "lost modernities" of China, Korea, and Vietnam.[20]

1.2 A Disclaimer and a Defense

This book explores state formation in East Asia across an immense span of time and across an immense geographic region. In so doing, we are mindful of a common criticism (and outdated view) that Korea, Japan, and Vietnam are seen as "little Chinas."[21] Historians such as

---

[19] Dingxin Zhao, *The Confucian-Legalist State: A New Theory of Chinese History* (Oxford: Oxford University Press, 2015); and R. Bin Wong, *China Transformed: Historical Change and the Limits of European Experience* (Ithaca, NY: Cornell University Press, 1997).

[20] Victor Lieberman, *Strange Parallels: Southeast Asia in Global Context*, c. 800–1830, vol. 1, *Integration on the Mainland* (Cambridge: Cambridge University Press, 2003); Victor Lieberman, *Strange Parallels: Southeast Asia in Global Context*, c. 800–1830, vol. 2, *Mainland Mirrors: Europe, Japan, China, South Asia, and the Islands* (Cambridge: Cambridge University Press, 2009); and Alexander Woodside, *Lost Modernities: China, Vietnam, Korea, and the Hazards of World History* (Cambridge, MA: Harvard University Press, 2006).

[21] See, for example, Benjamin Elman, John Duncan, and Hermann Ooms (eds.), *Rethinking Confucianism: Past and Present in China, Japan, Korea, and Vietnam* (Los Angeles: University of California, 2002), iii.

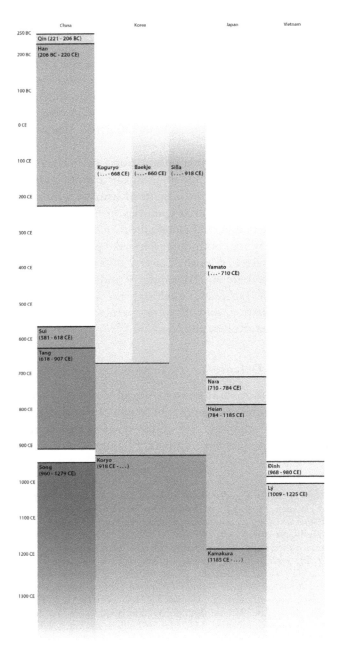

Figure 1.1 East Asian state formation, 200 BCE–1200 CE

Shawn McHale have argued that, even though "it is clear that we can find evidence suggesting that Vietnam fit neatly within the East Asian Confucian world ... the influence of Confucianism in Vietnam has been exaggerated and misconceived."[22] Our purpose here is to neither contest nor ignore the considerable subtlety and difference and individuality of each country in East Asia. These countries are all unique, all retain a large degree of agency, and all have their own particular histories, interactions with each other, and cultures. As R. Bin Wong put it years ago, "A book of this scale unavoidably contains descriptions and assessments that some readers will consider incomplete or misleading ... differences and similarities are a basis for comparison."[23]

Rather, our purpose here is different: to compare the broad similarities within the region and to contrast that with the major differences in the European region. It is fully possible to both recognize that there were differences among China, Korea, Japan, and Vietnam and, at the same time, to acknowledge clear similarities and shared influences across them. For the purposes of exploring over 1,000 years of history in four countries, we will inevitably miss much nuance – and further research should explore each of these countries in depth, with much greater detail and specificity than we could hope to do in one monograph. This book is clearly a work of social science, not history: We are concerned primarily with engaging a major theoretical literature about state formation by bringing new empirical evidence to the discussion. As such, we draw broad patterns and explore systematic differences across regions and across time, while realizing that we are perhaps overlooking particular nuance within the cases that we group together.

This is a relatively understudied area of research, but the findings relayed in this book offer a positive theoretical advance with a new argument about the causes of state formation that has central implications for some of the most fundamental theories of the political science and international relations disciplines. Emulation was likely as

---

[22] Shawn McHale, "Mapping a Vietnamese Confucian Past and Its Transition to Modernity," in Elman et al. (eds.), *Rethinking Confucianism*, 397.
[23] Wong, *China Transformed*, 7.

important in European state formation as was bellicist competition. Indeed, around the world, more attention should be paid to emulation as a key element of state formation. We hope this book is one contribution to widening our understanding of state formation in all regions and across all epochs, not just East Asia.

2 | Theories of State Formation and Diffusion

This book principally focuses on examining and assessing the bellicist thesis as it applies to state-building in East Asia and on providing an alternative explanation that emphasizes emulation as the key causal factor. We take the conventional definition for what constitutes a state: Most centrally, a state is composed of an administrative bureaucracy. Anthony Giddens defines a state as "a political apparatus (governmental institutions, such as court, plus civil-service officials), ruling over a given territory, whose authority is backed by a legal system and the capacity to use force."[1] Hui defines the state as "monopolization of the means of coercion, nationalization of taxation, and bureaucratization of administration."[2] Tuong Vu argues that "centralized bureaucracy is perhaps the most important institution in the structure of any state."[3]

Why and when states emerge has been a central and enduring question for social scientists. In this chapter, we explore the bellicist thesis, showing that it is inductively derived from the European experience; indeed, we show that it is perhaps more a narrative about a specific context than a theory. We also discuss the scant literature on East Asian state formation, which mostly focuses on the emergence of the Qin and Han dynasties in the second century BCE. Neither literature addresses how state formation actually spreads and diffuses, often simply taking for granted that competition or market selection is the causal mechanism. However, although ideas sometimes spread through competition, as the bellicist thesis suggests, they also diffuse through emulation. As a more precise way of differentiating the bellicist thesis from other explanations, in the final section of this chapter

---

[1] Anthony Giddens, *Sociology* (Cambridge: Polity Press, 1989), 301.
[2] Victoria Hui, "Toward a Dynamic Theory of International Politics: Insights from Comparing Ancient China and Early Modern Europe," *International Organization*, 58, no.1 (2004), 181.
[3] Tuong Vu, "Studying the State through State Formation," *World Politics*, 62, no. 1 (2010), 152.

we discuss theories of diffusion. Most theories of state formation simply posit a mechanism of diffusion without truly addressing it: We show that there are ways to distinguish among competition, emulation, and learning as drivers of the diffusion of ideas across different countries.

2.1 The Bellicist Thesis for European State Formation

The bellicist causal arguments are clear: War and preparation for war lead to the creation of a bureaucratic administration aimed at extracting resources from society; and this outlasts any particular war that the state may fight.[4] This approach argues that the threat of war led to consolidation and centralization of European states;[5] and Samuel Huntington's famous argument was that "War was the great stimulus to state building."[6] As Tilly describes it, bureaucracy, courts, parliaments, and other institutions are simply the by-products of preparations for war.[7] Furthermore, those states with the best administration and resource extraction were more likely to survive. That is, war made the state, and then the state made more war; if it survived, the state was even more state-like and even more warlike.[8] Gorski and Sharma describe the dominant orthodoxy "as neo-Darwinian [where] natural selection on military capacity is the fundamental law of state formation."[9]

This belief that Europe is the source and measure of all things is deeply rooted in our profession. For example, Jordan Branch has claimed that the European "treatment of political authority exclusively in terms of homogenous territorial areas separated by discrete

---

[4] Charles Tilly, *Coercion, Capital, and European States, A.D. 990–1990* (Cambridge: Blackwell Publishing, 1992), 20–21.

[5] Jeffrey Herbst, "War and the State in Africa," *International Security*, 14, no. 4 (1990), 117–139.

[6] Samuel P. Huntington, *Political Order in Changing Societies* (New Haven, CT: Yale University Press, 1968), 123.

[7] Tilly, *Coercion, Capital, and European States*, 75–117.

[8] This evolutionary selection or competition metaphor has been widely critiqued. See, for example, Hendrik Spruyt, "Diversity or Uniformity in the Modern World? Answers from Evolutionary Theory, Learning, and Social Adaptation," in William Thompson (ed.), *Evolutionary Interpretations of World Politics* (New York: Routledge, 2001), 110–132.

[9] Gorski and Sharma, "Beyond the Tilly Thesis," 98.

boundary lines ... is unique to the modern state system."[10] But this claim is nothing more than an observation about developments in Europe. Whether it applies to other regions is certainly contestable. As this book will show, there is considerable evidence that the East Asian countries developed national states with immense administrative power centuries before it was even conceivable in Europe. Furthermore, these were clearly territorial polities with defined and negotiated borders.

A subset of the bellicist literature on state formation in Europe emphasizes bargaining between the ruler and powerful domestic actors under the shadow of war. According to these "contractualist" scholars, the development of states and their institutional configurations was the result of a series of contracts between rulers and society. They argue that the rulers needed to extract resources from society in order to wage war. This indirectly caused dilution of political authority as powerful rivals exerted domestic constraints on the ruler: In order to raise taxes or borrow money, the sovereign had to bargain with politically powerful societal actors who demanded concessions in return, such as representative institutions. The protection of individual and property rights was then crafted in order for the state to have steady revenue. This contractualist literature thus uses the unintended emergence of representative institutions to explain the further unintended consequence of economic growth.[11]

This approach sees institutional configurations beginning as a series of contracts between rulers and powerful domestic actors, which ultimately become institutionalized.[12] Douglass North and Barry Weingast focus specifically on the rise of independent central banks, which first appeared in Europe in the seventeenth century. They argue that because central banks were more efficient for raising revenue and

---

[10] Jordan Branch, "'Colonial Reflection' and Territoriality: The Peripheral Origins of Sovereign Statehood," *European Journal of International Relations*, 18, no. 2 (2011), 2.

[11] Douglass C. North, *Structure and Change in Economic History* (New York: W. W. Norton & Company, 1981); Douglass C. North and Barry Weingast, "Constitutions and Commitment: The Evolution of Institutions Governing Public Choice in Seventeenth-Century England," *Journal of Economic History*, 49, no. 4 (1989), 803–832; and Margaret Levi, *Of Rule and Revenue* (Berkeley: University of California Press, 1988).

[12] Hendrik Spruyt, *The Sovereign State and Its Competitors: An Analysis of Systems Change* (Princeton, NJ: Princeton University Press, 1996).

hence for making war than other forms of finance, England in particular was able to achieve predominance. They write that "Thus were the institutional foundations of modern capital markets laid in England. These institutional changes were more successful than their originators had hoped ... the ability of the new government to finance a war at unprecedented levels played a critical role in defeating France."[13]

Margaret Levi argues that these internal rivals can limit the ability of the ruler to simply predate and extract resources from society.[14] Internal rivals reduce the tax-extraction ability of the state.[15] Close substitutes to the ruler (internal rivals, or even external) can also reduce the leverage of the ruler or state in extracting income from society. Groups closer to a border or with other lower opportunity costs of switching to a rival will face less predation: Those with more access to substitutes will be taxed less than those with fewer alternatives.[16]

Although the bellicist thesis in all its variants may explain part of the European experience, it is clearly not universal. For example, North and Weingast's argument about independent banks is in reality a *post hoc* story about England; it is certainly not an *ex ante* theory that can explain why and when some states develop independent financial institutions and others do not. Indeed, as subsequent chapters will address in detail, from antiquity up until the modern era, East Asian states financed all their operations from tax revenues. Independent banks and finance were totally absent. Jean-Laurent Rosenthal and R. Bin Wong have addressed this contractualist literature directly in their work on the ancient Chinese economy. They note that the power of the state did not devolve into corruption or predation in historical China, writing

the history of the Qing offers a caution against the theses of North, and North, Wallis, and Weingast discussed earlier that representative government is necessary for broad security of property rights. The Chinese emperor,

[13] North and Weingast, "Constitutions and Commitment," 821–824.
[14] Levi, *Of Rule and Revenue*, 17–33.
[15] Cameron Thies, "War, Rivalry, and State Building in Latin America," *American Journal of Political Science*, 49, no. 3 (2005), 4551–4465.
[16] Cameron Thies, "State Building, Interstate and Intrastate Rivalry: A Study of Post-Colonial Developing Country Extractive Efforts, 1975–2000," *International Studies Quarterly*, 48, no. 1 (2004), 55.

unless compelled by very serious challenges, did not undertake policies of confiscation nor did he distort markets for personal gain.[17]

Indeed, the lack of predation in East Asia was clear and remarkable, given the concerns consistently raised in the scholarly literature derived from Europe about the dangers of an unconstrained sovereign.[18] As Rosenthal and Wong point out, "China is striking; its emperors never faced formal limits in fiscal policy."[19] As this book will show, for literally centuries, East Asian states financed massive state bureaucracies and militaries that dwarfed those of contemporaneous Europe, were more extensive, and had more comprehensive administrative operations. And they did this using only tax revenues, with none of the bargaining between ruler and elites over loans and finance that existed in Europe.

The bellicist thesis in all its variants actually appears to reflect a limited understanding or attention to other regions and civilizations, not least East Asia. This key point will become clearer in the rest of this book, and we will revisit and expound on it in the conclusion. Based on the discussion and critique thus far, one of the main problems with the contractualist literature on European state formation in all its various forms should be evident: It relies on a presumption that because Europe in the nineteenth century experienced a rise in economic and military power, the experience in Europe *must therefore have* been somehow efficient; and it then crafts a story via backwards induction to explain why it must have been the main purpose of the state; and if better financing gave states a comparative advantage in war; and if central banks gave states a comparative advantage in financing; then the question is not what England did, but why and when did some states create central banks but others did not? Why was England the exception and not the rule? Why did East Asian states not develop independent financial systems until the twentieth century? As this book will show, East Asian states used fundamentally different fiscal and monetary policies precisely because of their better developed ability to tax and to implement fiscal policy.

---

[17] Jean-Laurent Rosenthal and R. Bin Wong, *Before and beyond Divergence: The Politics of Economic Change in China and Europe* (Cambridge, MA: Harvard University Press, 2011), 163.

[18] Levi, *Of Rule and Revenue.*

[19] Rosenthal and Wong, *Before and beyond Divergence*, 167.

In fact, there are compelling reasons to think that much of the bellicist literature is actually sophisticated stories about Europe, not deductive theories. The bellicist argument is, in fact, a complex set of ad hoc and coincidental factors specific to Europe that over the centuries appeared in an uneven process that eventually resulted in the emergence of the eighteenth-century state. As Sharman puts it: "Many claims about supposedly unique European achievements have turned out to reflect ignorance about the rest of the world. Any example looks unique if you ignore all the rest. Although this imbalance is far from rectified, new studies of other regions have increasingly debunked claims of European exceptionalism."[20]

Consider, as an alternative, the role of religion in the long history of Europe. The occasional mention of the role of "the clergy" by scholars such as Tilly is not enough. The clergy were not simply another interest group: The substance of religious beliefs and influence was central to European state formation. As Grzymala-Busse argues about Europe, "the Church had the wealth, spiritual authority, and expertise to fundamentally mold politics [It] wielded doctrine, law, literacy, and administrative innovations to shape nascent states ... the struggle between the papacy and the rulers [was] unrelenting."[21]

Imagine, for example, that Buddhism had been the dominant religious practice in medieval Europe, not Catholicism. The substance of Buddhist beliefs, as well as the institutional forms of Buddhism as a religious philosophy, are quite different from those of European Christendom. This would have led to systematic differences in how Buddhism would have interacted with politics compared to Christianity.[22] It is unlikely that war or state formation in a Buddhist Europe would have been the same. Yet we still treat approaches like the bellicist argument as objective, universal, and deductive theories, rather than the stories they really are.

Indeed, the particular type and substance of European religions had a fundamental impact on patterns of both war and state formation in Europe. The Holy Roman Empire, the Pope, crusades, inquisitions, pogroms, and the extraordinary sectarian violence between Catholics and Protestants were all elements unique to Europe. There is a small

[20] Sharman, *Empires of the Weak*, 13.
[21] Grzymala-Busse, "Beyond War and Contracts," 24.
[22] David C. Kang, "Why Was There no Religious War in East Asian History?" *European Journal of International Relations*, 20, no. 4 (2014), 965–986.

but growing literature that argues that religion was central in explaining the contours and substance of European state formation. Daniel Philpott argues that "a crucial spring of our state system was the Protestant Reformation ... no Reformation, no Westphalia" and that without the Reformation "the substantive powers of the Holy Roman Empire and its emperor, the formidable temporal powers of the church, religious uniformity, truncations of the sovereign powers of secular rulers, Spain's control of the Netherlands ... would not have disappeared when they did, to make way for the system of sovereign states."[23] Similarly, Grzymala-Busse writes that "one of the most powerful political and social actors through both the Carolingian era and for long afterwards was the Roman Catholic Church – a transnational, hierarchical, coherent political organization, with extensive resources, administrative capacities – and, above all, claims on authority both divine and worldly."[24] Daniel Nexon argues that "the Protestant Reformations led to a crisis in European politics, because they triggered specific mechanisms and processes embedded in the structure of early modern composite states."[25]

Furthermore, as noted in Chapter 1, some scholars have also argued that there were processes of emulation in Europe in addition to bellicist competition. Ideational and institutional pressures pushed Europe toward cultural conformity. Gorski, for example, emphasizes the impact of Reformation ideas in driving a redefinition of the purposes of rulers and the institutions of statehood, in ways that helped drive European cultural conformity.[26] Grzymala-Busse also emphasizes emulation of religious institutions in European state-building, writing "the Church was a template for sophisticated administration ... The division of labor in the royal courts mirrored that of the papal administration, with distinct offices in charge of finances, judicial tasks, and correspondence that first arose in the eleventh century – and the same template was adopted across Europe."[27] Indeed, the conventional

---

[23] Daniel Philpott, "The Religious Roots of Modern International Relations," *World Politics*, 52, no. 2 (2000), 206–214.

[24] Anna Grzymala-Busse, "Strangled at Birth? How the Catholic Church Shaped State Formation in Europe," Manuscript, Stanford University (2018), 7.

[25] Daniel H. Nexon, *The Struggle for Power in Early Modern Europe: Religious Conflict, Dynastic Empires, and International Change* (Princeton, NJ: Princeton University Press, 2009), 265.

[26] Gorski, *The Disciplinary Revolution*.

[27] Grzymala-Busse, "Beyond War and Contracts," 27.

wisdom – the bellicist and contractualist theses – was inductively derived from, and then tested on, the European experience.[28]

Despite the continued debate about the European experience, the bellicist thesis has become widely accepted and enormously influential in scholarship. A large body of literature extrapolates the European experience as universal and, with various modifications, asserts that the demands of war drive states to create institutions that can extract resources from society.[29] There is a small but significant literature that explores state formation in Latin America.[30] Miguel Centeno defines bureaucratization as the key institutional component of a state, arguing that the lack of "total wars" in Latin America stunted the growth of the bureaucratic state in the region.[31] Fernando Lopez-Alves finds that Latin American guerilla insurgencies delayed consolidation of the state and "state makers had to make important tax concessions to the landed elite and traders, especially in regions of high rural mobilization."[32] Writing about East Asia in the twentieth century, Enze Han and Cameron Thies disagree, concluding that "studies on the effect on state building of internal challenges have not reached much consensus ... the effects of civil conflicts on state capacity in [contemporary] East Asia seem mixed."[33]

2.2 State Formation in East Asia

In contrast to the extensive literature on European state formation, there is comparatively less scholarship in the social science literature on

---

[28] Hendrik Spruyt, "War and State Formation: Amending the Bellicist Theory of State Making," in Lars Kaspersen and Jeppe Strandsbjerg (eds.), *Does War Make States? Investigations of Charles Tilly's Historical Sociology* (New York: Cambridge University Press, 2017), 73–97.

[29] Miguel Centeno, *Blood and Debt: War and the Nation State in Latin America* (University Park, PA: Penn State University Press, 2003); Enze Han and Cameron Thies, "External Threats, Internal Challenges, and State Building in East Asia," *Journal of East Asian Studies*, 19, no. 3 (2019), 339–360; and Thies, "War, Rivalry, and State Building in Latin America."

[30] Thies, "State Building, Interstate and Intrastate Rivalry"; Thies, "War, Rivalry, and State in Building Latin America"; and Centeno, *Blood and Debt*.

[31] Centeno, *Blood and Debt*, 23.

[32] Fernando Lopez-Alves, "The Transatlantic Bridge: Mirrors, Charles Tilly, and State Formation in the River Plate," in Miguel Antonio Centeno and Fernando Lopez-Alves (eds.), *The Other Mirror: Grand Theory through the Lens of Latin America* (Princeton, NJ: Princeton University Press, 2001), 169.

[33] Han and Thies, "External Threats," 342–343.

state formation in East Asia. As discussed in Chapter 1, most scholarship on East Asian state formation focuses on Phase I – the emergence of unified China during and after the Warring States period (475–221 BCE). Edgar Kiser and Yong Cai argue that a partially bureaucratized state developed in Qin China (221–206 BCE), and that war was a main cause of that bureaucratization: "war was more frequent and severe in China, and ... Qin China was more bureaucratic than other historical states."[34] Dingxin Zhao disagrees, arguing that "during the entire Spring–Autumn period, almost all the wars were small and brief ... since bureaucratization *predated* the large-scale warfare, such wars were more likely the consequence than the cause of bureaucratization."[35]

A major attempt to explain Chinese state formation comes from Victoria Hui's scholarship.[36] Hui contrasts a logic of balancing in Europe with the logic of hegemony that eventually emerged in ancient China. Hui argues that "war made the state through self-strengthening reforms in ancient China, [and] war in fact deformed the state through self-weakening expedients in early modern Europe."[37] She concludes that "in ancient China, self-strengthening reforms ... culminated in the triumph of the universal Leviathan. In early modern Europe, self-weakening expedients weakened the logic of domination, allowing the logic of balancing to maintain rough parity in both international and domestic realms."[38] Hui argues that "self-strengthening reforms" – defined as mass infantry composed of peasant-soldiers and an elite professional standing army, tax exemptions for agricultural production, large-scale irrigation projects, and inducements for immigration – were the sources of the eventual Qin unification of central China.[39]

Explaining why Chinese rulers systematically made self-strengthening reforms that did not occur in Europe is central to Hui's discussion of why some states succeeded but others failed. While Hui has rightly forged an interesting discussion contrasting East Asian and European rationales for state formation, further theorizing is needed to address a number of pertinent follow-on questions: Why did Chinese

---

[34] Kiser and Cai, "War and Bureaucratization in Qin China," 513.
[35] Zhao, "Spurious Causation in a Historical Process," 605.
[36] Hui, "Toward a Dynamic Theory of International Politics;" and Hui, *War and State Formation.*
[37] Hui, *War and State Formation*, 49.   [38] Hui, *War and State Formation*, 50.
[39] Hui, *War and State Formation*, 79–84.

rulers consistently make good choices? Why did European rulers consistently make poor choices?

Hui argues that "strategic interaction generates multiple equilibria
which are unpredictable a priori."[40] Paying close attention to the limits
of any ostensibly universal theory, Hui writes that "timing matters ...
by the turn of the 3rd century BCE, all other Warring States had
pursued some variant of self-strengthening reforms [but] there may
be a disjuncture between motivation and capability."[41] In other words,
at times states make self-strengthening reforms, while at other times
they follow self-weakening expedients. Hui argues that "one should
not push such 'predictions' too far ... the outcome of balance of power
versus universal domination is not predictable a priori."[42]

Ultimately, Hui's powerful argument is more about the emergence of
hegemony in China than about Europe. Even in Hui's formulation,
state formation was a consequence of the emergence of hegemony, not
its cause, as will be elaborated further in Chapter 3. Equally, if not
more important, Hui's scholarship leads to a clear question: Beyond
China, what about other countries' experiences with state formation in
East Asia? What happened after this initial, nascent state-building in
200 BCE?

Another powerful contribution to the literature on Chinese state
formation comes from Dingxin Zhao. In a groundbreaking work of
scholarship, Zhao argues that China developed a

Confucian-Legalist state, a system of government that merged political and
ideological power, harnessed military power, and marginalized economic
power. In the Confucian-Legalist state, the emperors accepted
Confucianism as a ruling ideology and subjected themselves to the control
of a Confucian bureaucracy; while Confucian scholars both in and out of the
bureaucracy supported the regime and supplied meritocratically selected
officials who administrated the country using an amalgam of Confucian
ethics and Legalist regulations and techniques. This symbiotic relationship
between the ruling house and Confucian scholars gave birth to what is by
premodern standards a powerful political system – a system so resilient and
adaptive that it survived numerous challenges and persisted up until the
Republican Revolution of 1911.[43]

---

[40] Hui, *War and State Formation*, 34.
[41] Hui, *War and State Formation*, 85–86.
[42] Hui, "Toward a Dynamic Theory of International Politics," 183–200.
[43] Zhao, *The Confucian-Legalist State*, 14.

Zhao argues that, early on, military power became subordinate to political interests, writing that the "amalgam of political and ideological power curbed military power. In the Confucian-Legalist state, generals had no legitimate position in politics and were subordinate to civilian officials."[44] Zhao – like Hui – reminds us that "Historical development is nonlinear and largely unpredictable."[45] Zhao is also resolutely focused on China itself. This is fine as far as it goes: China is clearly the most vivid and important element of the East Asian model. Our contribution, however, is to firmly bring the countries surrounding China to equal scholarly attention and to take a regionwide view of state formation across the centuries. Many of the factors that scholars such as Zhao attribute to Chinese state formation are generalizable across the region, but for different reasons.

2.3 East Asia as a Region More Than China

In fact, important and probative as the literature on Phase I is, it suffers from two additional limitations, one temporal and one geographic. Temporally, it ignores almost all of East Asian history and focuses on the emergence of China two millennia ago as if it were the only event of consequence. Most of the literature stops the analysis in 221 BCE – as if state formation had ended, rather than simply began to emerge. In reality, state-building had only begun at that time.

There is also the overused, and long redundant, stereotype of stagnant and endless dynastic cycles in East Asian history. Scant scholarship covers the state formation that occurred centuries after the initial emergence of centralized Chinese rule. In fact, there was arguably no enduring Chinese state in this period. James Millward critiques arguments of continuity, writing that "the model of the Traditional Chinese World Order (a term coined by John King Fairbank) ... inaccurately, but influentially, assumed an unchanging, continuous China-centered international order and uniform Chinese diversity regime that functioned from antiquity through the nineteenth century."[46] Hui has also

---

[44] Zhao, *The Confucian-Legalist State*, 15.
[45] Zhao, *The Confucian-Legalist State*, 10.
[46] James Millward, "Qing and Twentieth-Century Chinese Diversity Regimes," in Andrew Phillips and Christian Reus-Smit (eds.), *Culture and Order in World Politics* (New York: Cambridge University Press, 2020), 73.

criticized scholars who believe in "China's supposedly timeless cultural and political unity."[47]

As this book will show, East Asian history was far more vibrant, creative, and contingent. The region grew, changed, evolved, and innovated as much or more than any other place on the planet, and scholarship on state formation should reflect that historical reality. To that end, our argument is complementary with that of Victor Lieberman, who argues that administrative cycles, although roughly corresponding to integration and disintegration, are not cyclical, but linear: "each reintegrated state is stronger than its predecessor."[48]

Even in China itself, most of the ostensible ideas and institutions of state formation had only begun to emerge in Phase I. Two central works on China over the millennia are by Dingxin Zhao and R. Bin Wong. Zhao researches the sweep of Chinese history, but his book is actually mainly focused on the first millennium BCE. Wong has worked assiduously to produce scholarship that takes China on its own terms. As he points out, "The collective weight of different traditions often crushes the Chinese experience into a form that fits Western expectations more closely than Chinese realities."[49] He then argues that

China's early empire left an institutional and ideological legacy upon the basis of which another empire was created which could claim legitimate succession from the earlier governments ... the Holy Roman Empire kept alive the idea of universal empire and assigned the Church a central role in establishing a civilizational unity, but there was no administrative infrastructure to sustain empire as a political reality.[50]

As with Zhao, Wong emphasizes ideational factors as central to the creation of the Chinese state: "The state's authority rested upon a mandate conferred by Heaven and revokable upon strong evidence of misrule ... the basic idea of legitimacy was premised upon supporting the people and regulating their livelihoods."[51]

[47] Victoria Hui, "Cultural Diversity and Coercive Cultural Homogenization in Chinese History," in Andrew Phillips and Christian Reus-Smit (eds.), *Culture and Order in World Politics* (New York: Cambridge University Press, 2020), 93.
[48] Lieberman, *Strange Parallels*, vol. 1, as described by Peter Perdue, "Strange Parallels across Eurasia," *Social Science*, 32, no. 2 (2008), 266.
[49] Wong, *China Transformed*, 71.   [50] Wong, *China Transformed*, 77.
[51] Wong, *China Transformed*, 92–93.

Other historians, such as Richard von Glahn and Alexander Woodside, posit Phase II – coinciding with the rise of the Tang dynasty (618–907 CE) – as the real era of state- and institution-building that became the historical "Chinese" state.[52] As Woodside points out,

The eighth century, indeed, would make a good choice as the first century in world history of the politically "early modern." It was in this century that the Chinese court first gained what it thought was a capacity to impose massive, consolidating, central tax reforms from the top down, which few European monarchies would have thought possible before the French revolution, given their privileged towns, provinces, nobles, and clergy.[53]

This book puts a sharper focus on precisely this period, Phase II, as a key era to explain state formation across East Asia.

Another potential blind spot of the scholarship on state formation in ancient China is that it focuses only on ancient China. Scholars sometimes write about East Asia as if China were the only participant in the system and contrast Europe and China, rather than Europe and East Asia. Geographically, the extant literature is Sinocentric to the point of ignoring – much less addressing in any serious manner – the experience of other countries in the region. It tends to treat China as the equivalent of the region and barely acknowledges the existence of any other political units in East Asia. This overemphasizes the role of China in the system. In fact, Phase II was far more consequential for state-building. Phase II – roughly from the fifth to the eighth centuries CE – occurred when the Tang unified China after three centuries of disunity, and also when states began to emerge on China's periphery in Korea, Japan, and later in Vietnam. It is precisely this failure to take the totality of East Asia seriously that keeps scholarship so narrowly confined by either Eurocentric or Sinocentric preoccupations. It is only by taking the region as a whole in all its diversity that we can truly begin to craft accounts of state formation that reflect the reality on the ground.

As odd as it may seem to call for *not* focusing on the hegemon, our point is that we need to place more emphasis on the agency that existed across the entire East Asian region. This is all the more necessary if the discipline of international relations is going to widen its inquiry beyond China and Phase I, and address state formation across the breadth of

[52] Woodside, *Lost Modernities.*   [53] Woodside, *Lost Modernities*, 1.

historical East Asia throughout the almost two millennia that encompass Phase II and beyond.

Two important scholars who engage in precisely the type of region-wide analysis that we call for here are Victor Lieberman and Alexander Woodside. Lieberman's ambitious and fascinating two-volume study discusses patterns of political, economic, and cultural change and integration in Southeast Asia from Burma to Vietnam; and then how those patterns have appeared around the globe over the past 1,000 years.[54] We largely mirror many of the arguments he makes, with more focus on East Asia itself. This book is consonant with Lieberman, who argues that "the crucial elements of modernity are the organizational and cultural configurations of the national bureaucratic-administrative state, as opposed to the loose autarchy of shifting regional polities of the punctuated equilibrium of vast and periodically conquered empires."[55] Although Lieberman identifies common factors around the globe, he focuses first on the various countries in Southeast Asia, noting the role of ideology, religion, and culture. Regarding Vietnam, for example, he writes that Confucianism "prescribed an aggressive program of moral, social, and economic, no less than administrative transformation."[56] Woodside, for his part, powerfully shows that, in China, Korea, and Vietnam "the monarch … largely governed through texts composed for them by Mandarins, rather than by more personal (and perhaps more feudal) means of persuasive human contact … The 'presented scholar' degree based on examinations … created a set of civil servants responsible to the throne, unencumbered (mostly) of aristocratic claims."[57] Woodside's focus on the meritocratic civil service examinations across East Asia is a central element of state formation. Indeed, Woodside's argument that it was East Asia – not Europe – that first became "modern" is also a central element of our argument.

It is perhaps more apt to characterize Phase I and the emergence of the Qin–Han dynasties as the emergence of hegemony, rather than

---

[54] Lieberman, *Strange Parallels*, vols 1 and 2.
[55] As described in Jack Goldstone, "New Patterns in Global History: A Review Essay on *Strange Parallels* by Victor Lieberman," *Cliodynamics*, 1, no. 1 (2010), 99.
[56] Victor Lieberman (ed.), *Beyond Binary Histories: Re-imagining Eurasia to c. 1830* (Ann Arbor: University of Michigan Press, 1999), 77.
[57] Woodside, *Lost Modernities*, 6.

state formation. Viewed this way, much of the extant literature is unable to answer or even address the most important questions: Why did hegemony arise in East Asia at all? How and why did the idea of hegemony and the idea of a unified China survive and continue to exist, even when the Han collapsed? Why did China reunify later and not remain broken apart?

In the empirical chapters to follow, we explain that state-building was an effort by the court to curb nobles' power. One way to curb the power of the nobles and to channel their ambitions is to create a state with institutions and administration. Rather than nobles building limits on the sovereign, it is also possible that the sovereign builds a state to limit the power of the noble class. As appears to be the case in historical East Asia, many of the reforms were undertaken to strengthen the court against an aristocracy. As Vu notes, in ancient East Asia, and in contrast to Levi's claims about ancient Europe, "states dominated society but were not predatory."[58] In a stark contrast from the bellicist thesis, institutional and bureaucratic control in East Asian states were born for reasons of prestige and domestic legitimacy in the competition between the court and the nobility. To further explain this causal argument for state formation in historical East Asia, we turn to the role of emulation.

2.4 Diffusion: Competition or Emulation

Much of the bellicist literature does not directly address the question of how the process of diffusion works. Instead, it simply implies that state formation was diffused through war, competition, or market forces: Those units that adapted best survived, and those that did not were "winnowed." In the case of East Asia, there was clearly diffusion from core to periphery, but a key question is how to explain it. In both the bellicist literature and the extant literature on Phase I of East Asian state formation, it is simply assumed that competition among rival states was the main cause of state formation. However, as Etel Solingen notes, "diffusion processes remain a focal point of contemporary international studies. Yet we have often paid less attention to

---

[58] Vu, "Studying the State through State Formation," 159; and Levi, *Of Rule and Revenue*, 17–33.

conceptualizing diffusion itself."[59] The main focus of diffusion has been on the spread of international norms or economic policies, although our concern here is broader.

Beth Simmons et al. identify four distinct causal mechanisms through which diffusion can take place: coercion, competition, rational learning, and emulation.[60] As Mireya Solis and Saori Katada describe them: (1) coercion exists when strong actors intentionally force weaker actors to adopt practices; (2) competition is a horizontal process where polities try to increase their competitiveness relative to peers; (3) rational learning occurs when states assess costs and benefits; and (4) emulation is where actors adopt policies or ideas that they deem to be appropriate from a sociocultural perspective.[61]

These causal processes are not mutually exclusive, even if the bellicist literature treats a particular kind of competition – interstate war – as monocausal in the European case. Coercion from China was absent in the historical era under study. Generally, studies of hegemons begin with material power and their goals and intentions. Even Daniel Nexon and Iver Neumann argue that "hegemons achieve preponderance in military and economic fields, and this enables them to shape and even create other fields ... diplomacy, finance, and sports."[62] However, this was not the case in fifth to eighth century East Asia. Indeed, during some of this period, even when China was divided and militarily weak, its ideas and civilization were powerful and enduring and eagerly sought, and the *idea* of a unified China remained very powerful.[63] While the conventional bellicist literature implies that competition over territory and survival was the key causal mechanism

---

[59] Etel Solingen, "Of Dominos and Firewalls: The Domestic, Regional, and Global Politics of International Diffusion," *International Studies Quarterly*, 56, no. 4 (2012), 631.

[60] Beth Simmons, Frank Dobbin, and Geoffrey Garrett, "The International Diffusion of Liberalism," *International Organization*, 60, no. 4 (2006), 781–810.

[61] Mireya Solis and Saori N. Katada, "Unlikely Pivotal States in Competitive Free Trade Agreement Diffusion: The Effect of Japan's Trans-Pacific Partnership Participation on Asia-Pacific Regional Integration," *New Political Economy*, 20, no. 2 (2015), 157.

[62] Daniel H. Nexon and Iver B. Neumann, "Hegemonic-Order Theory: A Field-Theoretic Account," *European Journal of International Relations*, 24, no. 3 (2017), 663.

[63] Yuri Pines, *The Everlasting Empire: The Political Culture of Ancient China and Its Imperial Legacy* (Princeton, NJ: Princeton University Press, 2012).

in diffusion, the main means in East Asia were emulation and learning. Perhaps they even played a larger role in the European state-building experience than the bellicists credit them.[64]

In the case of competition, states can compete with each other in different areas: For capital and export-market share in the contemporary world, or for territory and prestige as in historical Europe. While this process also may involve intentional copying (through learning or emulation), it is more of a selection process in which states that develop strong institutions survive, while others are selected out. Simmons et al. argue that "it is possible for governments to determine which countries compete with each other, in which markets, and how intense the competition is."[65] The conventional bellicist literature implies that competition over territory and survival was the key causal mechanism in diffusion.

As alternatives to competition, learning and emulation are similar causal mechanisms. The former is distinguished by the logic of consequences and the latter by the logic of appropriateness.[66]

Learning involves answering two questions of different levels: A simple tactical question of "How do we better achieve a particular goal?" and a deeper question of "What goals should we pursue?"[67] Learning is intentional and conscious, best recognized "when we see a highly successful policy change in country A, followed by similar changes in countries B and C."[68] Learning is based on a decision, after cost–benefit analysis, that one behavior works better than another. Often described as Bayesian updating, Frank Dobbin et al. define learning as "when new evidence changes our beliefs," and "people

---

[64] John Meyer, John Boli, George Thomas, and Francisco Ramirez, "World Society and the Nation-State," *American Journal of Sociology*, 103, no. 1 (1997), 144–181; and Walter Powell and Paul DiMaggio (eds.), *New Institutionalism and Organizational Analysis* (Chicago: University of Chicago Press, 1991).

[65] Simmons et al., "The International Diffusion of Liberalism," 793.

[66] James March and Johan Olsen, "The Logic of Appropriateness," in Robert E. Goodin (ed.), *The Oxford Handbook of Political Science* (Oxford: Oxford University Press, July 2011).

[67] Simmons et al., "The International Diffusion of Liberalism," 795.

[68] Simmons et al., "The International Diffusion of Liberalism," 798.

add new data to prior knowledge and beliefs to revise their assessment of that knowledge."[69]

Emulation reflects a similar process but focuses more on how actors aspire to and copy from others that they respect or admire. This is a "focus on the intersubjectivity of meaning – both legitimate ends and appropriate means are considered social constructs [where] there is a broad consensus on a set of appropriate social actors, appropriate societal goals, and means for achieving those goals."[70] In the contemporary era, John Boli-Bennett and John Meyer argue that what is "appropriate in terms of actors, goals, and policy means" has diffused around the world.[71] This focus on emulation is similar to the "practice turn" in international relations, which has focused on the "socially meaningful patterns of action which, in being performed more or less competently, simultaneously embody, act out, and possibly reify background knowledge and discourse in and on the material world."[72] Rather than being based on cost–benefit calculations, emulation is more aspirational. Simmons et al. note that "countries embrace new norms for symbolic reasons, even when they cannot begin to put them into practice."[73] Failure of emulation is not necessarily rejection but rather inability. Alastair Johnston, for example, sees emulation as coping and adaptation, and as particularly relevant for a country in a novel, unfamiliar environment.[74]

Amitav Acharya has argued that diffusion of a new idea is more likely when it works within, not against, an accepted identity. He writes "ideas that could be constructed to fit indigenous traditions were better received than those that did not have such potential ... without

---

[69] Frank Dobbin, Beth Simmons, and Geoffrey Garrett, "The Global Diffusion of Public Policies: Social Construction, Coercion, Competition, or Learning?" *Annual Review of Sociology*, 33, no. 1 (2007), 460.

[70] Simmons et al., "The International Diffusion of Liberalism," 799.

[71] John Boli-Bennett and John W. Meyer, "The Ideology of Childhood and the State: Rules Distinguishing Children in National Constitutions, 1870–1970," *American Sociological Review*, 43, no. 6 (1978), 797–812.

[72] Emanuel Adler and Vincent Pouliot, "International Practices," *International Theory*, 3, no. 1 (2011), 7.

[73] Simmons et al., "The International Diffusion of Liberalism," 800.

[74] Alastair Iain Johnston, *Social States: China in International Institutions, 1980–2000* (Princeton, NJ: Princeton University Press, 2008).

fundamentally altering their existing social identity."[75] Similarly, Stacie Goddard observes that "whether an actor's claim is legitimate depends on whether it resonates with existing social and cultural networks."[76] This is true, perhaps, in situations in which structure, order, and social identity itself are relatively stable and there is a fairly coherent social identity. But the goal itself may be change in social identity, or the situation and context may be fluid. In the case of state formation in Phase II of East Asia, we are concerned with wholesale creation and transformation of social identity.

Distinguishing between learning and emulation can be difficult because they are outwardly similar processes. Solingen points out that "mechanisms often operate in tandem and interactively and are hard to disentangle from each other" and that "learning and emulation [are] arguably separated by the extent to which alternatives are thoroughly considered and lessons 'rationally' learned, as opposed to merely imitated."[77] Experimental research in the natural sciences finds it challenging to neatly distinguish emulation and learning among chimpanzees and other primates.[78] Drawing on the parallel ideas of authority and coercion, David Lake recognizes the analytical challenges of distinguishing them in practice, explaining that "there is no 'bright line' separating these two analytic concepts, and I offer none here."[79]

In fact, as noted previously, many of the causal mechanisms for policy diffusion could be present at the same time: They are not mutually exclusive. In particular, while learning is an assessment of costs and benefits – and, empirically, there should be Bayesian updating that leads to changes in practices – it only takes place with agreement about what is desirable. As Simmons et al. put it, learning "is fostered by a cluster of intersubjectively defined conditions: Shared

---

[75] Amitav Acharya, "How Ideas Spread: Whose Norms Matter? Norm Localization and Institutional Change in Asian Regionalism," *International Organization*, 58, no. 2 (2004), 248.

[76] Stacie Goddard, *Indivisible Territory and the Politics of Legitimacy: Jerusalem and Northern Ireland* (Cambridge: Cambridge University Press, 2010), 24.

[77] Solingen, "Of Dominos and Firewalls," 634.

[78] Josep Call, Malinda Carpenter, and Michael Tomasello, "Copying Results and Copying Actions in the Process of Social Learning: Chimpanzees (*Pan troglodytes*) and Human Children (*Homo sapiens*)," *Animal Cognition*, 8, no. 3 (2005), 151–163.

[79] David Lake, "Escape from the State of Nature: Authority and Hierarchy in World Politics," *International Security*, 32, no. 1 (2007), 47–79.

norms, beliefs, and notion of evidentiary validity."[80] In contrast, pure copying or mimicking is a sign of emulation. In emulation, "followers may copy almost anything, and they may copy ritualistically. Evidence of ritualistic copying of policies suggests an effort to mimic the success of leading states without fully comprehending the roots of that success."[81] Writing about the contemporary era, Dobbin et al. observe that "evidence of the power of new policy norms is that countries often sign on when they have no real hope of putting new policies into practice."[82] In sum, it is probably impossible to definitively differentiate between emulation and learning.

2.5 Conclusion

State formation occurred in East Asia across many centuries, not just in Phase I, but also in particular in Phase II. An assessment of the bellicist thesis of state formation shows that its institutional and contractualist logics do not easily apply in East Asian state-building. Rather than bellicist competition, diffusion through emulation is an alternative, more convincing, causal mechanism.

---

[80] Simmons et al., "The International Diffusion of Liberalism," 795.
[81] Dobbin et al., "The Global Diffusion of Public Policies," 452.
[82] Dobbin et al., "The Global Diffusion of Public Policies," 453.

3 | *Phase I and Onwards*
Hegemony, Bureaucracy, and Confucianism

East Asia has perhaps the longest continuous history of centralized territorial rule in the world; states that had national control emanating from the center, and that projected ideas about nations and nationalism to their people. Emerging over 2,000 years ago, China as hegemon – and its main religious and political philosophies, Buddhism and Confucianism – had a powerful effect on the rest of East Asian domestic and international politics, even while what it meant to be Chinese and how best to organize society and government were continually modified and debated within China itself. Chinese civilization in the region was inescapable, and most states and societies were forced to deal with China in their own way. Domestically within each state, China influenced state formation and societal practices, from language and religion to political institutions and economic activity.

The elites of Korea, Japan, and Vietnam consciously copied Chinese institutional, normative, philosophical, and discursive practices to emulate China, not to challenge it. These three states, along with China, comprised a Confucian society where values, goals, and standing were mutually shared and recognized. Chinese civilization had an enduring impact on all the political units in the region, and examining the range of societies and states provides a better understanding of its effect and the consequences of Chinese civilization. China stood at the top of the hierarchy, and there was no intellectual challenge to the idea of what constituted civilization until the nineteenth century and the arrival of the Western powers.

This chapter examines Phase I of state formation in East Asia, which can be defined as the era of the Qin (221–206 BCE) and Han (206 BCE–220 CE) dynasties. We examine the emergence of hegemony and discuss the beginnings of state formation. We will show in particular that state formation followed hegemony, rather than led it. We also explore the enduring intellectual and philosophical sources of rule in East Asia, in particular the Mandate of Heaven, the responsibility of rule, and the unquestioned principle of hierarchy in domestic and international relations.

3.1 The Emergence of Hegemony in East Asia

The East Asian experiment with governance began quite early, with the emergence of China and its main philosophy of Confucianism during the Axial age (800–200 BCE). For four centuries, what is now central China was characterized by numerous small countries that occasionally fought with each other. Known as the Warring States period (475–221 BCE), this era was brought to a close by the Qin conquest of all other states in 221 BCE. Hegemony emerged in China with the Qin and Han dynasties. From then on, although Chinese power waxed and waned over the centuries, East Asia was a hegemonic system. Numerous scholars have attempted to explain why China emerged whereas in Europe there was no true hegemon for any significant length of time, but that is not our task.[1] Our task is different, to explain how the various units within this hegemonic system chose to order themselves, organize their societies, and interact with each other.

People within what is today known as China used the term "manifest civility" or "civilization" as early as 2,000 years ago and, as Charles Keyes notes, "from Han times on ... those who lived on the frontiers of the empire were considered to be barbarians ... that is, they had not yet accepted the order presided over by the emperor or the authority of a literature written in Chinese."[2] Throughout the next two millennia, the concepts of "Chinese" and "barbarian" were subject to debate and interpretation, and there was never a fixed definition.[3] But the ideas have been present throughout Chinese history, and Mark Strange notes that

---

[1] Kenneth Pomeranz, *The Great Divergence: China, Europe, and the Making of the Modern World Economy* (Princeton, NJ: Princeton University Press, 2001).

[2] Charles Keyes, "The Peoples of Asia: Science and Politics in the Classification of Ethnic Groups in Thailand, China, and Vietnam," *Journal of Asian Studies*, 61, no. 4 (2002), 1171.

[3] Charles Giersch, "'A Motley Throng': Social Change on Southwest China's Early Modern Frontier, 1700–1880," *Journal of Asian Studies*, 60, no. 1 (2001), 67–94; Erica Fox Brindley, "Barbarians or Not? Ethnicity and Changing Conceptions of the Ancient Yue (Viet) Peoples (~400–50 B.C.)," *Asia Major*, 16, no. 1 (2003), 1–32; and Marc S. Abramson, *Ethnic Identity in Tang China* (Philadelphia: University of Pennsylvania Press, 2008).

running through the periods (and surviving even to the present day) are a core set of defining concepts: that China is a unified sovereign state; that the Chinese polity draws legitimacy from a dominant cultural tradition, which founds itself on the value system of a core canon of authoritative texts; and that this cultural and moral tradition has close associations with an ethnic identity.[4]

As Zhao notes, "China was the only place in the world where a consistent imperial system persisted most of the time for over two millennia."[5]

In Chapter 2, we criticized scholars who view Chinese history as a continuous, uninterrupted set of stagnant dynasties running from antiquity to the twentieth century. What is China today experienced both centuries where central rule broke down and considerable evolution in the political, economic, social, and cultural spheres over 2,000 years. Chinese history was more contingent than inevitable. Yet, at the same time, what was remarkable about Chinese history is the idea of China itself, and its ability to re-form after collapse. For example, Mark Lewis notes, "China owes its ability to endure across time, and to re-form itself again and again after periods of disunity, to a fundamental reshaping of Chinese culture by the earliest dynasties, the Qin and the Han."[6] Naomi Standen notes that "we should not doubt, however, that many people in the tenth century did have a clear sense of belonging within a particular cultural nexus."[7] As Brantly Womack writes, "the Mongols and the Manchus conquered China, but Mongolia and Manchuria did not become the new centers of Asia, nor did they obliterate the old one."[8]

East Asia historically has been a hierarchical and hegemonic order since the second century BCE, and it is important to underline the persistence of this order. As Yuri Pines writes, choosing particular starting and end points

---

[4] Mark Strange, "An Eleventh-Century View of Chinese Ethnic Policy: Sima Guang on the Fall of Western Jin," *Journal of Historical Sociology*, 20, no. 3 (2007), 237.

[5] Zhao, *The Confucian-Legalist State*, 8.

[6] Mark Edward Lewis, *The Early Chinese Empires* (Boston: Harvard University Press, 2007), 1.

[7] Naomi Standen, *Unbounded Loyalty: Frontier Crossing in Liao China* (Honolulu: University of Hawai'i, 2007), 30.

[8] Brantly Womack, *China among Unequals: Asymmetric Foreign Relations in Asia* (Singapore: World Scientific, 2010), 154.

The Chinese empire was established in 221 BCE, when the state of Qin unified the Chinese world ... the Chinese empire ended in 1912 ... for 2,132 years, we may discern striking similarities in institutional, sociopolitical, and cultural spheres throughout the imperial millennia. The Chinese empire was an extraordinarily powerful ideological construct. The peculiar historical trajectory of the Chinese empire was not its indestructability ... but rather its repeated resurrection in more or less the same territory and with a functional structure similar to that of the preturmoil period.[9]

Similarly, Joseph MacKay observes,

For more than two millennia ... a relatively consistent idea persisted of what Imperial China was or should be. When China was ascendant, as during the Han and Ming dynasties, this identity justified Chinese regional dominance. When China was in decline, it provided a source of aspiration. When foreigners occupied the country, as did the Mongols under the Yuan dynasty and the Manchus under the Qing dynasty, they justified their rule by claiming the Mandate of Heaven (*tianming*) for themselves.[10]

Chinese dynasties rose and fell. With the collapse of the Han in 220 CE, three centuries of disunity followed, in which the empire broke apart into numerous competing kingdoms that occasionally fought violently with each other for domination of the central plain. Unification of what is now central China only occurred in 581 with the short-lived Sui dynasty (581–618) and the subsequent Tang dynasty (618–907). Indeed, even though there were enduring ideas, institutions, norms, and philosophies, these ideas changed and evolved over the centuries, of course. Zhao writes

This amalgam contributed to the resilience of China's imperial system. With such a structure in place, it was in the interests of any new ruler of China, whether indigenous or foreign, to seek the cooperation of the Confucian elite and to amend rather than overturn the Confucian-Legalist political arrangement. This is why, each time after conquering China, most nomadic rulers sooner or later adopted the Confucian-Legalist political arrangement and embraced Chinese culture.[11]

---

[9] Pines, *The Everlasting Empire*, 2.
[10] Joseph MacKay, "The Nomadic Other: Ontological Security and the Inner Asian Steppe in Historical East Asian International Politics," *Review of International Studies*, 42, no. 3 (2016), 474.
[11] Zhao, *The Confucian-Legalist State*, 14.

In fact, we should be cautious of implying too direct or linear a path toward modern China or toward a Confucian civilization. Cultural ideas influenced the various states that rose and fell over time, but modification, adaptation, and debate existed at every point. As Standen reminds us, "we should not ... foreclose the issue, by adopting terms and categories, like ethnicity, that imply the inevitability of the modern Chinese nation-state and posit a linear development toward it."[12] Indeed, some traits have historical roots, others do not, and all are constantly evolving depending on the circumstance, situation, institutional constraints, political and economic exigencies, and a host of other factors. From the perspective of someone living during the Three Kingdoms era (220–280 CE), for example, it would not at all have been clear that centralized rule would return in China. After all, four centuries of Han rule had crumbled and the Three Kingdoms were competing vigorously for domination.

Despite changes and reunification, the unmistakable pattern of East Asia has been the cultural, economic, and political centrality of China. For example, the term "Huangdi (皇帝)," or "emperor," was used from its invention by the Qin in 221 BCE until 1912 and the fall of the Qing dynasty. The basic form of the government that first emerged with the Qin endured for those two millennia, as well. As Edward Dreyer writes, "the autocratic, bureaucratic, centralized empire that Qin legalism had created remained the master institution of Chinese political life for the next 2,000 years, and its restoration was always the primary goal of Chinese political actors during periods of dynastic breakdown."[13]

When scholars study and theorize about hegemony in its various forms, it would seem plausible to begin with an examination of this East Asian international order, rather than the European one. After all, for all the utility in comparing Rome and the contemporaneous Han dynasty (206 BCE–220 CE), the most striking difference is that Rome never recovered after its fall, in contrast to China's remarkable ability to re-form after periods of chaos. As Wong notes, "After the fall of the Roman Empire, political authority remained fragmented for many centuries and was never again wielded on an imperial scale ... The

---

[12] Standen, *Unbounded Loyalty*, 30.
[13] Edward L. Dreyer, "Continuity and Change," in David A. Graff and Robin Higham (eds.), *A Military History of China* (Lexington: University Press of Kentucky, 2012), 23.

Chinese, however, sustained the vision and repeatedly recreated the reality of unified empire."[14]

Comparisons of Chinese hegemony with those that formed fleetingly in Europe in this regard are telling. To be sure, there is a longstanding theoretical tradition that attempts to explain the rise and fall of European hegemons.[15] But those hegemonies were either brief or associated with maritime powers, and sat uncomfortably within models that emphasized multipolarity and bipolarity. For example, scholars refer to a "Dutch hegemony" that might have lasted for a few decades in the early seventeenth century, but it was notoriously thin; a passing dominance in terms of trade.[16] The United Kingdom's hegemony lasted perhaps a century, but even then was nested within a wider continental system of great power rivalries.[17] The hegemony of the United States in the post-World War II period referred only to its relationship with the non-Communist world; the dominant character-ization of the Cold War era was bipolar, not unipolar. Belief in the emergence of a new unipolar order was relatively short-lived. None of Dutch, British, or US "hegemony" was anything like the centuries of Chinese hegemony, with its enduring civilizational influence across culture, religion, politics, society, and the economy.

3.2 Bellicism and State Formation in the Qin Dynasty

The empirical record of Phase I does not support the bellicist thesis. Although many ideas that eventually influenced state formation had their origins during the Warring States or Qin–Han era – such as Confucianism, Legalism, and the idea of a civil service – none were fully developed until centuries later, in Phase II. Furthermore, the Qin state emerged as a result of hegemony, not as a cause of conquest or war. State formation was a result of unification and the needs to administer a massive territory and to consolidate political rule beyond

---

[14] Wong, *China Transformed*, 73.

[15] George Modelski, *Long Cycles in World Politics* (London: Macmillan Press, 1987).

[16] E.g., P. J. Taylor, "Ten Years That Shook the World? The United Provinces as First Hegemonic State," *Sociological Perspectives*, 7, no. 1 (1994), 25–46.

[17] K. Edward Spiezio, "British Hegemony and Major Power War, 1815–1939: An Empirical Test of Gilpin's Model of Hegemonic Governance," *International Studies Quarterly*, 34, no. 2 (1990), 165–181.

the aristocracy in the state and royal court itself. Holcombe notes that "The First Emperor of Qin famously standardized the writing systems, legal codes, coins, and weights and measures of all the conquered kingdoms in an effort to promote a single unified imperial culture."[18] The Qin Emperor created forty-four administrative units and relocated hundreds of thousands of people to settle the northern frontier.

However, these main Qin innovations under the first emperor, Qin Shi Huangdi (r. 221–210 BCE), occurred *after* the Qin unification of China, not before. The main bureaucratic innovations at the time – better roads and canals, standardization of weights and measures, division of the country into thirty-six commanderies appointed from the capital, and nascent meritocratic appointments – all occurred after unification and were designed to help govern the vast new empire with greater efficiency, rather than to increase warfighting capacity. Furthermore, the mere fact that centuries of fighting preceded the Qin conquest of China does not mean that war was the cause of state formation. The real question is whether the Qin was the most innovative in building state structures, and whether those state structures were designed to help them with war.

It appears that this was not the case: The Qin bureaucratic innovations were the result of hegemony, not its cause. Zhao finds that "Qin's strong-state weak-aristocracy tradition ... must have expedited Legalist reform in Qin. But in comparing Qin with former superpower Wei, it is hard to determine based on the existing evidence whether Qin's Legalist reforms were in fact more successful than Wei's."[19] Zhao continues by arguing that the Qin reforms were not only rudimentary but also not necessarily the type of Confucian-Legal state that became the Chinese model. He writes that "Qin rulers became overconfident about the effectiveness of the organizational capacity and harsh ruling techniques they had acquired during the Age of Total War ... by the time of unification, Qin had already developed into a state that based its rule more on stringent control of society than on cooperation with the society."[20] Patricia Ebrey and Anne Walthall observe that

[18] Holcombe, *A History of East Asia*, 46.
[19] Zhao, *The Confucian-Legalist State*, 256.
[20] Zhao, *The Confucian-Legalist State*, 263.

Once Qin ruled all of China ... the First Emperor initiated a sweeping program of centralization that touched the lives of nearly everyone in China. To cripple the nobility ... to administer the territory that had been seized, he dispatched officials whom he controlled through a mass of regulations ... writing systems were standardized, as were weights, measures, coinage ... private possession of arms was outlawed in order to make it more difficult for subjects to rebel.[21]

Despite the many new ideas and institutions, the Qin dynasty fell after less than two decades, as palace infighting split the country apart. Upon the death of Qin Shi Huangdi, his sons fell into bitter squabbling over succession, with at least twelve family members killed or ordered to commit suicide. Within a few years, the court intrigue had ruptured the country and rebellions broke out across the country. Clearly, the nascent state formation and institutions that the founding emperor had initiated were not strong enough to survive or constrain the familial dynamics. The country immediately splintered into small fiefdoms – the Qin unification had not yet taken deep root. After five years of civil war, Liu Bang unified the country under his rule, proclaiming the Han dynasty. Wong notes that "the weakness of the Qin lay in its inability to create a stable set of relations among groups in Chinese society. This dynasty failed to develop bureaucratic capacities of government and lacked the political imagination to create an ideology to guide political practice, social beliefs, and personal expectations. The succeeding Han dynasty developed both."[22]

Significantly for the question of state formation, the far longer enduring Han dynasty (206 BCE–220 CE) also only began its bureaucratic innovations a century after its conquest of the Qin. As Kiser and Cai note, initially "two-thirds of Han territory was under the rule of semi-independent kings ... by 143 B.C., there were 40 commanderies and only 25 kingdoms, and soon after that Han emperors successfully expanded the bureaucratic system to all their territory."[23] Han bureaucratic innovations, like those of the Qin, were created to govern a vast territory, not to extract resources to wage war. Indeed, the scant proto-bureaucratic innovations that did arise in Phase I were nascent and superficial in scope, and even in China the full Chinese state is

[21] Ebrey and Walthall, *Pre-Modern East Asia*, 39.
[22] Wong, *China Transformed*, 76.
[23] Kiser and Cai, "War and Bureaucratization in Qin China," 531–532.

usually seen to have emerged in the seventh and eighth centuries CE, not 800 years earlier during the Qin. Zhao observes that "In the beginning of the Western Han dynasty, rule over all of China through a centralized bureaucracy was still a new model, whose advantages were not yet fully realized."[24]

A famous tale recounts the establishment of Confucianism as the imperial philosophy. The founders of the Han dynasty had been sol-diers: Aggressive and rough. As Holcombe recounts the story, "A scholar presented the first Han emperor with copies of the [Confucian] classics. Patting his mount, the emperor said that he had won his empire from horseback and had no need for books. The scholar's swift reply was, You may have conquered the empire on horseback, but can you rule it that way?"[25] The Han embrace of Confucianism was significant, but it was not the only philosophical or religious ideas that their rulers utilized. Many traditions influenced their rule, and Zhao notes that Confucianism "incorporated many religious elements common to ancient China, such as ancestor wor-ship, a concept of heaven as a conscious overseer of the affairs of the human realm, divination, predetermination, and yin–yang cosmology."[26]

Wong notes that "Taking moral instruction as a basic aspect of rule, the Chinese state aimed to shape the education of both elites and the common people ... Chinese state efforts find little parallel in Europe ... the Chinese effort to reach the minds and hearts of peasants contrasts strongly with European states, which left such matters to religious authorities."[27] Here again, the contrast with simple mechan-ical ideas about war leading to institutional innovation is clear: Ideas, culture, and philosophy had central roles in the creation and function-ing of the Chinese state. Its moral purpose was, to use Christian Reus-Smit's phrase, clear and central to its legitimacy.[28] According to Wong, "Chinese efforts at education and moral training ... represent efforts by a state to influence belief and behavior patterns of the general population well before such activities were imagined, let alone

[24] Zhao, *The Confucian-Legalist State*, 272.
[25] Holcombe, *A History of East Asia*, 53.
[26] Zhao, *The Confucian-Legalist State*, 15.   [27] Wong, *China Transformed*, 97.
[28] Christian Reus-Smit, *The Moral Purpose of the State: Culture, Social Identity, and Institutional Rationality in International Relations* (Princeton, NJ: Princeton University Press, 1999).

pursued, in Europe."[29] Moreover, "From a Chinese perspective, the lack of concern for education and moral indoctrination in Europe constitute a basic limitation on European rule."[30]

To educate the elites, the Han first established the imperial academy for the study of Confucian classics in 124 BCE. By the end of the Han dynasty, the academy had 30,000 students and over 1,850 classrooms. Systems of testing and regional recommendations of students created an institutionalized framework of higher learning, the first of its kind. However, the landed aristocracy still wielded the majority of power, and most appointments were made based on family and clan relationships, not an actual meritocratic examination. As Benjamin Elman points out, before the ninth century "the principal means of entry into the social and political elite had been through the mechanisms of official recommendations or kinship relations."[31] The Han dynasty, for example, used textual expertise in the classics as a prerequisite for an official appointment, but it was not nearly as institutionalized or as encompassing as it would be in later centuries. Elman observes that "in essence, this simple recruitment process was the precursor of the elaborate Confucian civil service examination system set up during the Tang and Song dynasties."[32] By the time of the Han, "military conflict had largely become the past and the regime's stability depended increasingly on cooperation from the bureaucracy and other elite sections of society."[33]

For the governing of the Han empire, nine ministries were established, covering rites, public works, and punishments. Officials were graded by rank and salary, and they were appointed by the central government. There were public granaries, public ritual halls, and limits on private landholding. Borders only truly become possible when there is more than one state. Li Feng notes the existence of clearly demarcated borders 2,000 years ago: "in China, the 'territorial states' had one more defining physical characteristic: the earth or rock walls that ran hundreds of miles on the borders of these states ... walls gradually extended over 300 km to form three edges of a square ... counties

---

[29] Wong, *China Transformed*, 97.   [30] Wong, *China Transformed*, 97.

[31] Benjamin Elman, "Political, Social, and Cultural Reproduction via Civil Service Examinations in Late Imperial China," *Journal of Asian Studies*, 50, no. 1 (1991), 9.

[32] Elman, "Political, Social, and Cultural Reproduction," 9.

[33] Zhao, *The Confucian-Legalist State*, 275.

(*xian*) were the building-blocks of the new territorial state."[34] As other states grew around China over the centuries, they also engaged in formal diplomacy to mark borders for purposes of trade, diplomacy, and border control.

In sum, the real state formation in China came after the fighting ended, not before. And state formation was not aimed at further conquest, but rather at justifying authority and ruling a vast nation. The ideas of legitimacy and moral purpose of the state were central to its functioning and practices. There was clearly evolution over the centuries in Chinese military and civilian technology, institutions, and ideas. But the institutions of the bureaucratic Chinese states, its focus on Confucian classical education, the role of scholar-officials to run a meritocratic bureaucracy, and the focus that endured for centuries all only began to emerge during and after the Han dynasty. We now turn to perhaps the key value that animated rule across East Asia: The Mandate of Heaven.

3.3 Hierarchy and the Mandate of Heaven

Just as important for state formation around the region were the ideas and philosophies that emerged there. Perhaps the most influential, enduring, and fundamental political philosophy that emerged in East Asia is the idea of the Mandate of Heaven. This idea, emerging in the broad milieu of ancient China, had a powerful effect across the entire region. Rulers in historical East Asia have been seen as the chief mediators between heaven and earth since at least the Zhou dynasty (1046 BCE–256 BCE) in ancient China.[35] Most visibly embodied in the concept of the Mandate of Heaven, the ruler's legitimacy and right to rule were based on his moral authority and the blessing of Heaven. Heaven would bless a just ruler and be displeased by a despotic ruler, and a central duty of the ruler was engaging in rituals and sacrifices as the legitimate intermediary between Heaven and Earth. The Mandate of Heaven was an overarching cosmological idea – preceding Confucianism, Buddhism, and Daoism – and presaged and influenced

[34] Li Feng, *Early China: A Social and Cultural History* (Cambridge: Cambridge University Press, 2013), 185–187.

[35] Dingxin Zhao, "The Mandate of Heaven and Performance Legitimation in Historical and Contemporary China," *American Behavioral Scientist*, 53, no. 3 (2009), 416–433.

these later religious traditions. So important was the ruler's cosmological role that the Board of Rites was one of only six governmental ministries in China, Korea, and Vietnam. As Ya-pei Kuo puts it, "Ritual in the world of imperial Chinese politics aimed much higher than the theatrical effect of power evocation. Chinese rituals initiated, animated, and constituted imperial power itself."[36]

The enduring social contract in East Asia was fundamentally different from that in Europe. Wong notes that

the ideology of rule was moral, and this necessarily carried commitments to shape the peasant's mental world and sustain his material well-being. The very familiarity of Chinese maxims for rule leads specialists to discount their significance ... but these commitments take on clearer importance when we realize their different in substance and intent from the kinds of ideological commitments developed by early modern European states.[37]

All societies must decide how to organize state and society and the social contract between ruler and ruled. Institutions reflect those ideas – no institution is content or context free: Rather, they are infused with deep meanings and intentions. In East Asia for over 2,500 years, the fundamental issue between ruler and ruled was the "responsibility of power": How to get the ruler to perform the duties he was expected to undertake on behalf of his people. Most commonly reflected in the Mandate of Heaven, across East Asia this social contract, and the institutions of the state, reflected basic values and ideas that predated even Confucius and Mencius. In contrast, from the time of the Romans and Greeks through the Magna Carta and to Hobbes and beyond, the fundamental concern in Europe was "abuse of power": How to limit the ruler's ability to take advantage of her people.[38] This different social contract led to very different types of state formation in the two regions, an important implication of our argument that we will revisit in the book's concluding chapter.

The substance of East Asia's social contract – the moral purpose of the state – was different, as well. Put differently, Rosenthal and Wong point out that East Asian leaders' primary focus was a strategy

---

[36] Ya-pei Kuo, "Redeploying Confucius: The Imperial State Dreams of the Nation, 1902–1911," in Mayfair Mei-hui Yang (ed.), *Chinese Religiosities: Afflictions of Modernity and State Formation* (Berkeley: University of California Press, 2008), 71.

[37] Wong, *China Transformed*, 93.   [38] Levi, *Of Rule and Revenue*.

of rule – not a strategy of conquest.[39] Sem Vermeersch notes that "according to the most ancient formulations of this doctrine, Heaven (Ch. *tian*) selects someone of outstanding virtue and ability and confers a mandate on him to rule 'all under Heaven.'"[40] As the center of human communication with the gods, the ruler was directly responsible for conducting numerous rites and sacrifices. Legitimacy – the Mandate of Heaven – was manifested in a stable political and social order, and instability challenged the ruler's authority. Rebellion, famine, or other calamities were seen as an indication that the ruler had lost the Mandate of Heaven and were "Heaven's way of removing the mantle of leadership from immoral rulers and bestowing it instead upon those who were virtuous enough to replace them."[41]

As the center of human communication with the gods, the ruler was directly responsible for conducting numerous rites and sacrifices. Sacrifices, rituals, and virtuous study and behavior by the ruler were more than Geertzian symbolism. Rather, it was the source of moral authority and the embodiment of both action and belief. Anthony Yu notes that

ancestor-making was much more than a ceremonious act dictated by the obligations of kinship. It was, rather, a ritual designed to recruit and invoke agencies of transcendence, wherein ancestors were to be transformed from a term of kinship to become symbols of divine power ... the significance of the ancestral shrine for imperial governance remained constant from pre-Qin times to the Qing.[42]

Thus, although China, Korea, Japan, and Vietnam are often called "Confucian," in fact the moral authority of the ruler derived from a much deeper, prior, cosmological belief. From the seventh century, Chinese homage to Confucius was ranked as only a middle sacrifice, for example. The "grand sacrifices" included Heaven, Earth, imperial ancestors, and the Spirits of Land-and-Grain. Confucius as a middle sacrifice coexisted with the Sun, the Moon, and the God of Agriculture.

---

[39] Rosenthal and Wong, *Before and beyond Divergence*, 12–17.
[40] Sem Vermeersch, *The Power of the Buddhas* (Cambridge, MA: Harvard University Asia Center, 2008), 9.
[41] Elizabeth Perry, "Chinese Conceptions of 'Rights': From Mencius to Mao – and Now," *Perspectives on Politics*, 6, no. 1 (2008), 39.
[42] Anthony C. Yu, *State and Religion in China* (Chicago: Open Court, 2005), 34–37.

Lower sacrifices included the God of War, the God of Literature, the
God of Fire, and the Dragon God, among many others.[43]

The Mandate of Heaven and the role of the ruler as the chief
mediator between Heaven and Earth became the key ruling idea across
the region. Even in Japan, although the emulation and copying of
Chinese institutions had begun to temporarily fade by the thirteenth
and fourteenth centuries, a main function of the Japanese emperor
remained performing legitimating rites that linked Heaven and Earth.
Prasenjit Duara notes that "Like China, Tokugawa Japan
(1600–1868) had a similar mold of state cult based on Confucian ideas
of Heaven; Shinto rites and control of Buddhist temple structures
shored up the authority of the shogunate."[44] The state's moral authority in historical East Asia was built upon religious ideas that were
overarching and interacted with many different religious traditions.
Ji-Young Lee observes that "warrior rulers of Muromachi Japan legitimized their positions by seeking and receiving investiture from the
Japanese emperor."[45] Elizabeth Berry agrees: "Yorimoto and his successors sought the sanction of the throne not only because it was an
eminent, adaptable, and politically useful institution, but also because
they shared with their contemporaries an unconscious world view
which admitted of a single locus of ultimate authority."[46]

The Mandate of Heaven was central to Korean kings, as well. Sun
Joo Kim writes about Korea that

In the history of East Asia, including Korea, numerous rebellions have
broken out under many different facades, but they have often been ideologically guarded by the Mencian notion of the mandate to rebel. Thus, monarchs
and their officials have always been apprehensive of the voice of the people
because popular revolts have been viewed as a public manifestation of the

[43] Kuo, "Redeploying Confucius: The Imperial State Dreams of the Nation,
1902–1911," 71.
[44] Prasenjit Duara, "Religion and Citizenship in China and the Diaspora," in
Mayfair Mei-hui Yang (ed.), *Chinese Religiosities: Afflictions of Modernity and
State Formation* (Berkeley: University of California Press, 2008), 47.
[45] Ji-Young Lee, *China's Hegemony: Four Hundred Years of East Asian
Domination* (New York: Columbia University Press, 2016), 121.
[46] Mary Elizabeth Berry, *Hideyoshi* (Cambridge, MA: Harvard University Press,
1982), 176.

existing regime's inability to rule well – and a sign of dynastic decline – in Confucian historiography.[47]

This enduring East Asian focus on "rule through virtue" or the "responsibility of power" would have such an affect for a number of reasons. Substantively, this political philosophy had elements that made it palatable to a wide variety of societies. Ideas were reinforced by institutions: By the thirteenth century, less mystical, more rationalist neo-Confucianism went hand in hand with Song-style imperial examinations. These examinations ensured that neo-Confucian ideals would permeate society far more than earlier philosophies had, and that they would ensure that the leadership of these countries were ideologues (or good at pretending to be). Neo-Confucianism was cosmic and metaphysical. By grounding its principles in something more than tradition, neo-Confucianism gave a hard-edged, black-and-white flavor to philosophical and political debate. Furthermore, unlike older variants of Confucianism or Buddhism, it explicitly tied the legitimacy of government to a hierarchical vision of global society centered on the Chinese empire. As Han writes, "the tradition of ethnic integration and the attitude of expanding cultural influence make China's relations with neighboring ethnic groups not lie in national conquest, but in tolerance, exchange, assimilation and integration. This feature is fundamentally different from Roman Empire's [strategic] thoughts."[48]

3.4 The Syncretic Nature of Confucianism, Buddhism, and Daoism

As briefly discussed in Chapter 2, the substances and nature of East Asian religious–political philosophies were different from those of European Christendom. This difference in substance and form was a key reason for the different paths and timing of state formation in the two regions. Selective emulation was possible and voluntary across East Asia because the fundamental religious philosophies were inclusive and syncretic, not exclusive and messianic. Rosenthal and Wong observe that "Chinese historians sometime express skepticism

---

[47] Sun Joo Kim, "Taxes, the Local Elite, and the Rural Populace in the Chinju Uprising of 1862," *Journal of Asian Studies*, 66, no. 4 (2007), 993.

[48] Sheng Han, *Dongya Shijie Xingcheng Shilun* (东亚世界形成史论), 1st ed. (Beijing: Zhongguo fang zheng chu ban she, 2015).

regarding the efficacy of Confucian ideology, but there can be little doubt that in contrast to European political ideologies, Confucian thought succeeded in providing simple and relatively persuasive rules for the behavior of peasants, elites, and the emperor."[49] In particular, the emphasis on the hierarchic nature of society, the syncretic nature of the philosophies, and the emphasis on the "responsibility of rule," or ruler's virtue, by those higher in the hierarchy were key elements of this philosophical approach. The inclusivist and syncretic nature meant that there was no messianic urge to interfere in other societies.

Confucianism, Buddhism, and Daoism are general terms to describe religious and philosophical traditions that varied widely across time and space and that encompassed numerous divisions. So loose were these traditions that Elman cautions that "it remains unclear whether the current terms we use in English, such as 'Confucianism' or 'Neo-Confucianism,' in imperial China, shogunal Japan, and royal Korea and Vietnam were entirely appropriate to generalize about scholarly and religious traditions in East Asia before 1900."[50]

The Western definition and image of what comprises a religion – formal, centralized, and institutionalized – arises from a different historical experience from East Asian religious traditions. East Asian religious traditions and political philosophies of all types conform more to the model of teacher–disciple, with numerous unconnected teachers providing various types of approach. They are thus difficult to classify. There was no centralized order in Confucianism, Buddhism, or Daoism. Rather, there were different schools with different approaches to religious, intellectual, philosophical, and social traditions. In each of these, there was a mix of philosophical, theological, artistic, and humanistic ideas, which used different texts and between which the boundaries were unclear. In this way, these "teachings" have more in common with tea ceremony, martial arts, calligraphy, and other humanistic pursuits than they do with the clearly demarcated Christian and Islamic religions.

This lack of a clear definition – by Western standards – has given rise to an enduring question about whether Confucianism, and even Buddhism and Daoism, can be considered "religions" as something equivalent to Christianity and Islam. Although it was a philosophical,

---

[49] Rosenthal and Wong, *Before and beyond Divergence*, 196–197.
[50] Elman, "Political, Social, and Cultural Reproduction," 524.

political, and intellectual tradition, Confucianism clearly contained a cosmology as well. Confucianism contained a distinction between supernatural and natural; moral values that endure across time and space; ancestor worship and burial rituals; and other cosmological concerns, and many of its historical adherents approached and practiced it accordingly.[51]

It is this looseness that defies easy categorization that lies at the heart of East Asian political and religious traditions. The three best-known traditions are Confucianism, Buddhism, and Daoism, which are known as "teachings" (*jiao*), rather than as discrete religions separate from other intellectual categories. Indeed, the non-rivalry of these traditions has been noted for some time. In the sixth century, scholar Li Shiqian made one of the earliest references to the three teachings (*sanjiao*), writing that "Buddhism is the sun, Daoism the moon, and Confucianism the five planets."[52] Eric Sharpe argues that "to talk of syncretism of religious thoughts or threads, and particularly in any discussion about the 'three religions of China,' any scholar has to admit that it was possible for a Chinese to belong to all three systems at the same time."[53] Yet even that description implies too clear a distinction between these religions, and privileges those three traditions over the vast array of folk religions, which often coexisted and comingled with each other. Stephen Teiser notes that "Common rituals as offering incense to the ancestors, conducting funerals, exorcising ghosts, and consulting fortunetellers; belief in the patterned interaction between light and dark forces or in the ruler's influence on the natural world; the preference for balancing tranquility and movement – all belong as much to none of the three traditions as they do to one or three."[54]

The substance of these religious and philosophical traditions mattered immensely in practical terms for behavior and institutions. Indeed, in premodern East Asia, China, Korea, Japan, and Vietnam rarely engaged in anything like the type of religious violence that

---

[51] Mario Poceski, *Introducing Chinese Religions* (New York: Routledge, 2009), 36–37.
[52] Stephen F. Teiser, *The Ghost Festival in Medieval China* (Princeton, NJ: Princeton University Press, 1996), 1.
[53] Eric J. Sharpe, *Comparative Religion* (London: Bristol Classical Press, 1994), 82.
[54] Teiser, *The Ghost Festival in Medieval China*, 19–20.

existed for centuries in historical Europe, despite having vibrant religious traditions, including numerous folk religions. In East Asia, the particular mix of actors, groups, and institutions combined with a particular substantive type of inclusivist religion that made religious interstate wars unlikely. Thus, even instrumentally, religion was not a major political cleavage within East Asia. There was plenty of war in East Asian history, to be sure, but it tended not to be religious in nature.[55] The dominant inclusivist and syncretic religions of historical East Asia – Confucianism, Buddhism, Daoism, and the numerous folk religions – did not easily lend themselves to appropriation by political leaders as a means of differentiating groups or justifying war.

If religiously motivated interstate war appears to be largely absent in historical East Asia, what about religious conflicts internal to countries, such as insurrections, pogroms, and rebellions? William Crowell distinguishes several different types of peasant rebellion in China: Uprisings resulting from natural disasters; protests against government exploitation; religious rebellions; separatist rebellions; ethnic disturbances; and ordinary banditry and piracy.[56] In most cases the classification is obvious, such as revolts by mine workers or peasants as a result of repressive local officials or a heavy tax burden. Previous research on war and violence in East Asia between 1368 and 1841 found 488 incidents of internal conflict in China. Among them, religion was mentioned in only twenty-four instances (5 percent), and of those, often there was almost no indication that religion was a central factor in the conflict. Korea did not have the same experience with local rebellion as China. There were only seven local rebellions during the Chosŏn dynasty (1392–1910), for example, none of which can be considered motivated by religion.[57]

Thus, while internal rebellions were somewhat common in China (and Japan and Vietnam) during the era under study, *religious* rebellion was not. Korea faced almost no insurgencies in the premodern era, while Japan and Vietnam occasionally faced rebellions based more on family or clan lines. A materialist approach explains many of the rebellions in historical East Asia; what it does not do is help explain why *religious* uprisings were rare while other rebellions were not. It is

[55] Kang, "Why Was There No Religious War in East Asian History?"
[56] William Crowell, "Social Unrest and Rebellion in Jiangnan during the Six Dynasties," *Modern China*, 9 (1983), 322.
[57] Kang, "Why Was There No Religious War in East Asian History?"

yet another contrast with the extraordinary violence of the European experience. Given the abundant religious wars, crusades, pogroms, and witch hunts that occurred in Europe throughout the centuries, the lack of religious wars in East Asian history is remarkable.

Although Confucianism eventually became the dominant philosophical and theological tradition of East Asia, it remained inclusivist and syncretic. Confucianism interacted with and borrowed from folk religions as well as Buddhism and Daoism. What Frederick Mote observes about China was applicable to all countries in the region: "one must not rush to assumptions about the implications of 'popular' in describing religion in later imperial times ... Many members of elite families, men and women, participated in the cultic and sectarian practices of 'popular religion.'"[58]

The substance of these foundational East Asian philosophies also affected the role of the military in society, leading especially to the general devaluation of military leaders in East Asian culture. As will be discussed in Chapter 4, the military was clearly subservient to the scholar-official: Mark Lewis notes that "the prince, whether as the moral exemplar of the Confucians or the distributor of rewards and punishments of the Legalists, could only rule if his commands were trustworthy, so the deceit and trickery that defined the Way of the commanders undercut the foundations of the Way of the ruler."[59] Nathan Rosenstein notes as well that both Legalist and Confucian schools insisted on the "unquestioned supremacy of a ruler who upheld the social order through proper laws or appropriate rituals."[60]

3.5 Multiple Traditions

Despite the obvious Chinese influence in all aspects of government and society, none of Korea, Japan, or Vietnam were miniature replicas of China: They employed Chinese language, cultural ideas, and political

[58] Frederick Mote, *Imperial China 900–1800* (Cambridge, MA: Harvard University Press, 1999), 527.

[59] Mark Edward Lewis, *Sanctioned Violence in Early China* (Albany: State University of New York Press, 1990), 125.

[60] Nathan Rosenstein, "War, State Formation, and the Evolution of Military Institutions in Ancient China and Rome," in Walter Scheidel (ed.), *Rome and China: Comparative Perspectives on Ancient World Empires* (Oxford: Oxford University Press, 2009), 41.

systems, yet retained elements of their own unique indigenous cultures, as well. This is best exemplified by their diglossic linguistic traditions: The Chinese language was used for writing in Korea, Vietnam, and Japan during the entire time under study, and up to 80 percent of Vietnamese vocabulary is of Chinese origin, with similar proportions in Korea and Japan. Yet these countries also retained their own indigenous languages and, in some cases, script.[61] Lina Zheng uses primary Japanese, Korean, and Chinese sources to lay out the history of Buyeo (k. Puyŏ, second century BC–494 AD).[62] Zheng points out that Buyeo, a kingdom located in modern day northeast China, was deeply imitative of Han practices, including Han dress, legal codes, and other cultural practices.

Confucianism and Buddhism were grafted onto quite different social and cultural patterns in these other countries. During the first millennium CE, a rough division had obtained, with Confucian ideas influencing governance and Buddhist ideas influencing social norms. Yet Confucianism slowly began to influence and transform both state *and* society – in what was largely a top-down process carried out by elites. This process accelerated in the fifteenth century with the neo-Confucian revolution in Korea and Vietnam. However, although Confucianism seeped deeply into the social fabric of society, it never fully eradicated Buddhism or indigenous social practices in any of the societies. This transformation was neither quick nor complete, and even today elements of indigenous culture and Buddhist ideas coexist with grafted-on Chinese ideas about family life and social structure, the proper role of societal actors, and their relationship to the state. It should be noted that this was also the case in China itself, and that all of these countries existed within a cultural context that had local and more general influences, and we should be wary about overemphasizing the distinctiveness of these places.

Although Korea was deeply influenced by Chinese culture and ideas, this Chinese influence overlaid an indigenous culture and society, and the two coexisted without truly synthesizing. Thus, although Koreans used Chinese characters for writing and borrowed a large portion of

---

[61] Young-mee Yu Cho, "Diglossia in Korean Language and Literature: A Historical Perspective," *East Asia: An International Quarterly*, 20, no. 1 (2002), 3–23.

[62] Lina Zheng, *Fuyu Li Shi Bian Nian* 夫余历史编年 (*The Chronicle of Buyeo History*), 1st ed. (Beijing: Ke xue chu ban she, 2016).

their vocabulary from China, indigenous Korean writing and vocabulary continue to exist today, and often there are two words for the same thing – one Chinese, one Korean. Similarly, culture and society borrowed many Chinese customs while retaining many uniquely Korean customs. As Martina Deuchler comments, "[Korean] Confucian scholar-officials emerged from the old aristocratic matrix and carried over some distinct elements of this heritage, notably an acute consciousness of status and descent."[63]

The creation of a Vietnamese state involved essentially the interweaving of Chinese ideas with indigenous Vietnamese ideas. As in Korea, a tension existed between, on the one hand, military and court men who viewed kinship, Buddhism, and aristocratic ties as important for Vietnamese order and, on the other, scholars who emphasized Confucianism, education, and impersonal state institutions as the bases of leadership. Numerous scholars have noted the flexible, syncretic nature of Vietnamese social and political institutions, and Mahayana Buddhism was the prevailing religion well into the Lê dynasty (1427–1789). Although the Trần (1225–1400) and Lê dynasties used strict patrilineage for royal succession, primogeniture did not become deeply rooted until the neo-Confucian reforms of the fifteenth century, for example.

However, Vietnam was more deeply influenced by China than the rest of Southeast Asia. As Lieberman concludes, "If Sinic influences varied by class and locale, in terms of social structure, administration, law, and religion, such influences increasingly did distinguish the eastern lowlands as a whole from the rest of Southeast Asia."[64] Lieberman notes that "[the] Chinese model probably appealed to the literati and to their royal patrons because it promised a variety of practical benefits: Chinese bureaucratic techniques offered to curb regionalism in an unfavorable geographic environment, [and] to strengthen central control over local units."[65]

In Japan, by the time of the Tokugawa shogunate (1600–1868), the civil service had become much smaller and a warrior caste had grown up. David Pollack notes that throughout language, culture, arts,

[63] Martina Deuchler, *The Confucian Transformation of Korea* (Cambridge, MA: Harvard University Press, 1992), 292.

[64] Lieberman, *Strange Parallels*, vol. 1, 341.

[65] Victor Lieberman, "Local Integration and Eurasian Analogies," *Modern Asian Studies*, 27, no. 3 (1993), 513.

government, and economics, China either as model or as context "exerted a powerful pressure on every act of culture."[66] He notes that even so quintessentially Japanese a product as the *Tale of Genji* – a Heian masterpiece – is "everywhere underlaid by a structure of Chinese archetype." During the Tokugawa era, there were Chinatowns with up to 5,000 Chinese residents, not only in Nagasaki but also in Edo, Kyoto, and other cities, where numerous artists, scholars, religious leaders, and other artisans lived. From the foundation of the Mampukuji temple in Uji (near Kyoto) in 1661, the abbots were Chinese from the Fujian "parent temple" until 1740, and after that Chinese abbots alternated with Japanese counterparts until 1800.[67]

Buddhism often interacted and merged with local folk religions in Korea, Vietnam, and Japan as well. Robert Buswell observes that Korean Buddhism was a "thoroughgoing amalgamation of the foreign religion and indigenous local cults."[68] It continued to coexist with Confucianism during the subsequent Chosŏn dynasty, and at times received explicit support of the royal court.[69] John Duncan's fascinating study of the higher civil service examination in Korea (*munkwa*) finds that between 1392 and 1800, although the majority of questions concerned practical matters such as politics, the economy, or borders, the examination also included questions about heterodoxy (Buddhism), prophecy and portents, and rituals.[70]

Similarly, Holcombe notes that "early Japanese Buddhism also retained aspects of local native culture … many local pre-Buddhist spirits (*kami*) were absorbed into Japanese Buddhism."[71] Perhaps the

---

[66] David Pollack, *The Fracture of Meaning: Japan's Synthesis of China from the Eighth through the Eighteenth Centuries* (Princeton, NJ: Princeton University Press, 1986), 7.

[67] Marius Jansen, *China in the Tokugawa World* (Cambridge, MA: Harvard University Press, 1992), 56.

[68] E. Robert Buswell, Jr., "The 'Short-cut' (徑截) Approach of K'an-hua (看話) Meditation: The Evolution of a Practical Subitism in Chinese Ch'an Buddhism," in Peter N. Gregory (ed.), *Sudden and Gradual: Approaches to Enlightenment in Chinese Thought, Studies in East Asian Buddhism 5* (Honolulu: University of Hawaii, 1987), 322.

[69] JaHyun Kim Haboush, *Culture & State in Late Chosŏn Korea* (Cambridge, MA: Harvard University Asia Center, 2002), 234.

[70] John Duncan, *The Origins of the Chosŏn Dynasty* (Seattle: University of Washington Press, 2000), 85.

[71] Holcombe, *A History of East Asia*, 78.

best-known folk religious tradition in East Asia is Japanese Shintoism, which is not a distinct religion but rather a general term that describes the wide variety of indigenous animistic and folk religions in Japan. Buddhism in Japan merged with and interacted with the various indigenous folk religions until distinctions between the two became difficult. As Theodore de Bary observes, Buddhist syncretism "readily combined with other beliefs, whether the Buddhism of other sects, Shinto, or even disparate teachings like yin–yang. And a place for some new god could always be found in its spacious pantheon."[72] Buddhist and Shinto shrines were simply merged together, and local Shinto gods were called the Japanese manifestation of Buddhist deities. Kate Nakai notes that "By the Tokugawa period, what was called Shinto – whether practice or theory – consisted largely of a mixture of elements drawn from esoteric Buddhism, Chinese cosmology, and Song metaphysics."[73]

In sum, East Asian political, philosophical, and religious traditions were far more syncretic and inclusivist in historical East Asia than they were in the Western experience. These East Asian traditions were neither centralized with an overarching institutional hierarchy and leadership, nor did they use a canonical set of texts. The teacher–disciple model manifested itself in numerous diverse temples with different teachings; temples themselves developed different martial arts, and even Japanese tea ceremony traditions and temples were closely interlinked. Religion was not a social marker, it did not distinguish or divide groups of peoples, and thus was rarely viewed as a way to organize political or social movements.

Multiple traditions have always existed in East Asia, with Buddhism, Confucianism, and indigenous ideas mixing, interacting, and evolving, but rarely seamlessly blending. We note this complexity of philosophical and religious traditions in East Asia – but at the same time, compared to Europe, there were clear regional differences, as well. There was far more violence associated with European religions. European philosophical traditions have also emphasized the "dangers of rule" rather than the "responsibility of rule" from the time of the

---

[72] William Theodore de Bary, *Confucian Tradition and Global Education* (New York: Columbia University Press, 2008), 709.
[73] Kate Nakai, "Chinese Ritual and Japanese Identity in Tokugawa Confucianism," in Elman et al. (eds.), *Rethinking Confucianism*, 281.

ancient Greeks. And these traditions have had a clear impact on the pace and type of, and justifications for, state formation in both regions.

3.6 Beyond Phase I: Examinations and Bureaucracies in the Sui–Tang Dynasties

The Han dynasty fell apart in 220 CE, but the ideas, institutions, and philosophies endured and evolved during the time China was divided, remaining influential throughout this era of divided China. There were almost three and a half centuries of division, in which various kings tried to unify China. Hegemony returned with the Sui unification of 581. It was during this era that the active emergence of Chinese state formation fully emerged. Two enduring institutional innovation of the Sui–Tang era stand out: the examination system and the Six Ministries.

3.6.1 The Examination System

Before the Tang, the landed aristocracy still held most power. The Tang dynasty (618–907 CE) made arguably the most direct advances in governance, introducing a key institutional experiment: A government run by talent, not heredity, with civil servants selected through a public competition assessing candidates' qualification, open (in theory) to all males, and held at regular, fixed intervals. This key institutional innovation built on the Han innovations of five centuries earlier. But, as Woodside describes the Tang civil service, these were "embryonic bureaucracies, based upon clear rules, whose personnel were obtained independently of hereditary social claims, through meritocratic civil service examinations."[74] These were officials selected in open examinations, particularly as a "countervailing force to the power of entrenched aristocrats."[75] As to bureaucracy, Woodside notes that "it was the Tang dynasty that made success or failure in the struggle for Chinese government positions theoretically dependent upon the scrutiny of candidates' talent, by means of public competitions held at fixed periods."[76]

---

[74] Woodside, *Lost Modernities*, 1.
[75] Elman, "Political, Social, and Cultural Reproduction," 9.
[76] Woodside, *Lost Modernities*, 1.

Under the Tang, the examination system became fully institutionalized. As it evolved over the centuries, certain features remained central
to the system. The highest degree, the *jinshi* (進士; k: *chinsa*; v: *tiến sĩ*; j:
shinshi; "presented scholar"), was awarded as the culmination of a
multi-stage process: Candidates who succeeded in local or prefectural
examinations were allowed to sit the provincial exam and then, if
successful, the metropolitan exam in the capital. Graduates of the first,
prefectural exam were offered a small government stipend as they
studied in preparation for the provincial exam. The highest was the
palace exam. *Jinshi* was awarded to those who passed the metropolitan
or palace exam. The number of *jinshi* candidates was low throughout
the Tang Dynasty: Of a total of 1,000–2,000 test takers, perhaps thirty
jinshi degrees would be awarded (1.5–3 percent). Holcombe observes
that "the *jinshi's* prestige was incomparable."[77] By the Song dynasty
(960–1279), the examinations produced 200 to 300 *jinshi* candidates
each year. Foreigners were allowed to take the exam and actually earn
office in China from the Tang dynasty.

By the Ming (1368–1644) and Qing (1644–1912) dynasties, the top
of the examination system was the Imperial College, which enrolled
those who earned the provincial degree (舉人, *juren*) and who were
studying for the metropolitan and court exams. As Duncan notes, "the
most important function of the Imperial College was to prepare students to sit for the *jinshi* examination."[78]

The government also attempted to coordinate this examination
system with an elementary school system across the country. In 624,
the Gaozu Emperor, founder of the Tang dynasty, ordered every
province and county to establish an elementary school. By the eighth
century, this resulted – on paper, at least – in over 19,000 official
schools. These were government-run and -financed schools, and
Charles Benn concludes that, by 754, the government was supporting
over 130,000 students throughout the country. Benn notes that "by
modern standards the number is small, but it is enormous for premodern societies."[79] The civil service examinations were so important
that, over the centuries, they engendered a "national school system

[77] Holcombe, *A History of East Asia*, 99.
[78] John Duncan, "Examinations and Orthodoxy in Chosŏn Dynasty Korea," in
Elman et al. (eds.), *Rethinking Confucianism*, 71.
[79] Charles Benn, *China's Golden Age: Everyday Life in the Tang Dynasty* (Oxford
University Press, 2002), 255.

down to the prefectural level ... these high-level public schools initially prepared candidates for the written tests devised by state-appointed examiners. Fully seven centuries before Europe, the imperial Chinese state committed itself financially to support an empire-wide school network."[80]

During the Qing, when the Qianlong Emperor realized that Mongol and Manchu nobles on his frontiers could not read court edicts, he "tried to restore communications with his Mongol nobles by ordering a 'back to basics' reform of examination-system writing."[81] There was even affirmative action – in 1777, the central government allowed border students a special amnesty of thirty years in which to learn the "Central Domain" speech tones necessary for poetry examinations.

The examination system was used for over fourteen centuries. By the late eighteenth century, China's population had grown to about 300 million. During the Qing dynasty, the more than 1,200 counties, divided into eighteen provinces, were governed through an imperial bureaucracy of only 3,000–4,000 ranked degree-holding officials.[82] The examination system was used until 1905, when it was finally abolished (temporarily) as the Qing government attempted to react to modernity. It then returned, in modern form, under the Communist Party.

3.6.2 *The Six Ministries*

The second enduring institutional innovation of the Sui–Tang era was the organization of the bureaucracy into six ministries. The seeds of the Chinese bureaucracy had been sown in the Qin–Han era of Phase I, but they only came to full fruition during Phase II, in forms that lasted into the twentieth century. The Sui dynasty first organized the government into Three Departments and Six Ministries (三省六部). The Three Departments were the top-level offices of the administration: The Secretariat, the Chancellery, and the Department of State Affairs. The Six Ministries (or "boards") were Personnel, Finance, Rites, War,

---

[80] Elman, "Political, Social, and Cultural Reproduction," 10.
[81] Woodside, *Lost Modernities*, 6.
[82] Department of Asian Art, "Scholar-Officials of China," in Heilbrunn Timeline of Art History, Metropolitan Museum of Art, New York (2004), www .metmuseum.org/toah/hd/schg/hd_schg.htm.

Punishments, and Public Works. In addition, there were six lower-level departments, and six courts below them.

Although the idea of a "separation of powers" among departments had existed for centuries, the Three Departments and Six Ministries were first organized in the Sui–Tang era. In 583 CE the Sui replaced the distinction between aristocrat and commoner with the distinction between officials and ordinary subjects. Von Glahn observes that, under the Sui, "The emperor strengthened the central government, establishing the Three Departments ... and the Six Ministries bureaucracy that would remain the standard structure of central government administration throughout later Chinese imperial history."[83]

By the Ming era, China was centrally organized into administrative districts down to the province level, with appointments made from the capital for most tax, commercial, and judicial posts. The Qing dynasty developed a centralized process by which the government reacted to food shortages anywhere within the country. Wong notes that these "[state-sponsored] granaries represented official commitments to material welfare beyond anything imaginable, let alone achieved, in Europe."[84] Remarkably, this institution survived for another 1,000 years.

3.7 Conclusion

The astounding achievements of the Qin and Han dynasties in Phase I as well as the Sui–Tang era during Phase II are justly celebrated. Yet, perhaps more important than Chinese state formation is how and why other countries in the region also developed states and a coherent sense of nation a millennium earlier than in Europe, as well as the powerful effects of China's hegemony on the rest of the region. Over the centuries, the states of East Asia attempted to implement consistent tax policy, land reform, and nascent welfare states for famine relief. Indeed, the four main political units in East Asia emerged centuries before the state system in Europe and over 1,000 years before Max Weber. This regional story of state formation is the heart of this book. We now turn to that story.

---

[83] von Glahn, *The Economic History of China*, 182.
[84] Wong, *China Transformed*, 98.

4 | *The Absence of Bellicist Pressures in State Formation, 400–800 CE*

War and preparations for war were not the cause of state formation in historical East Asia, particularly in Phase II. Nor was further war the effect of state formation. Rather, a relative *absence* of war was the result of a particular type of state formation within a particular regional civilization centered on China. Korea, Japan, and Vietnam all initially developed state formation in the absence of war and bellicist pressures. None of the three countries engaged in further war once they became fully fledged states. Although these three countries occasionally fought wars, there is very little evidence that links state formation to war or other forms of violence as either cause or effect.

The concern for relative rank order was the primary priority for all countries in their relations with each other in the region. In fact, the concept of a world composed entirely of equal, sovereign, independent states that viewed each other primarily through the lens of relative capabilities did not exist in historical East Asian international relations. Rather, when two states could negotiate a mutually accepted rank-order status, their relations were stable no matter what the distribution of material capabilities. If they could not, relations were unstable no matter what their relative power. The international order that developed in East Asia grew out of ideas, as discussed in Chapter 3, that were fundamentally different from those that endured across the centuries in Europe. Their relations with each other were the outward-facing manifestation of the same political and religious philosophies that animated their domestic affairs.

The ideas foundational to their domestic and international politics were different, the international order was different, and hence patterns of warfare in Europe and East Asia were systematically different.[1]

---

[1] David C. Kang, *East Asia before the West: Five Centuries of Trade and Tribute* (New York: Columbia University Press, 2010); and David C. Kang, Dat Nguyen, Ronan Tse-Min Fu, and Meredith Shaw, "War, Rebellion and Intervention

As opposed to the recurrent bellicosity of similarly sized states in multipolar Europe, East Asia was a hegemonic system dominated by China that also shared a particular set of norms and values. Chiu Yu Ko et. al. point out that "It is well established that interstate warfare, or military conflicts between sedentary societies, was more common in Europe, whereas military conflicts with nomads from the Eurasian steppe featured more prominently in China."[2]

Mark Dincecco and Yuhua Wang are representative of the scholarly consensus that "in centralized China ... the most significant recurrent foreign attack threat came from Steppe nomads ... external attack threats were unidirectional, reducing the emperor's vulnerability."[3] Rosenthal and Wong concur: "periodically, the people living beyond the Great Wall mobilized armies that could threaten major disruptions. These types of threats typically brought dynasties to their knees, but they occurred very infrequently and were separated by long periods of stable rule ... rates of conflict were radically different in China and Europe."[4] David Wright observes that "for two thousand years, the primary military and diplomatic preoccupation of the Chinese empire was the northern frontier."[5] Put differently, China's relations with the peoples of the Central Asian steppe to its north and western frontiers were characterized by skirmishing, whereas relations with the Sinicized states on its eastern and southern borders were characterized by stability.

It was not just China: Korea, Japan, and Vietnam also experienced patterns of war very different from those in Europe. Robert Kelly finds "a lengthy period of peace among Confucian states, plus strong evidence that this peace was based on their shared Confucianism."[6] Indeed, compared to European polities, China, Korea, Japan, and

Under Hierarchy: Vietnam–China Relations, 1365–1841," *Journal of Conflict Resolution*, 63, no. 4 (018).

[2] Chiu Yu Ko, Mark Koyama, and Tuan-Hwee Sng, "Unified China and Divided Europe," *International Economic Review*, 59, no. 1 (2018), 289.

[3] Mark Dincecco and Yuhua Wang, "Violence Conflict and Political Development over the Long Run: China versus Europe," *Annual Review of Political Science*, 21, no. 1 (2018), 342.

[4] Rosenthal and Wong, *Before and beyond Divergence*, 162–168.

[5] David C. Wright, "The Northern Frontier," in David A. Graff and Robin Higham (eds.), *A Military History of China* (Lexington: University Press of Kentucky, 2012), 57.

[6] Robert Kelly, "A 'Confucian Long Peace' in Pre-Western East Asia?" *European Journal of International Relations*, 18, no. 3 (2012), 422.

Vietnam were remarkably stable and long-enduring, both internally and externally. In the case of Korea, Mark Peterson observes that its history "is remarkably stable and peaceful," while Kirk Larsen notes that there were "critical moments in which the Chinese dynasty possessed both the capability and the momentum necessary to complete aggressive expansionistic designs [against Korea] but decided not to do so."[7]

This chapter assesses patterns of war and other violence in the international relations of historical East Asia, with a particular focus on the emergence of states in the fifth to eighth centuries CE. We show that war was neither cause nor effect of initial state formation in Korea, Japan, or Vietnam during this era, Phase II. We also discuss the tribute system of international order that developed and grew out of the Chinese civilizational influence as the outward-looking manifestation of state (and national) formation within a particular cultural, philosophical, and religious context.

4.1 The Korean War of Unification, 660–668 CE

Between the fifth and eighth centuries, there was only one interstate war involving China, Korea, and Japan: The Korean War of Unification of 660–668 CE. For centuries before and after the time period discussed here, the three countries did not compete with each other for territory, prestige, or authority. Most importantly, from the third to the fifth centuries, China was divided and posed no clear military threat to the Korean Peninsula or Japan. Thus, the centuries of initial state formation in both Korea and Japan occurred without any threat from China at all and without any war between these countries. Michael Seth points out that

Chinese culture was introduced to Korea at a time when China itself was politically weak and divided ... Chinese states were useful sources of cultural ideas and practices, but during this period of political disunity in China they were not in a position to threaten the existence of the Korean states. Nor was there any great empire with universalistic pretensions and the ability to

---

[7] Mark Peterson, "View of the Frog Out of the Well," *Korea Times*, July 8, 2018; and Kirk Larsen, "Roundtable Discussion of Yuan-kang Wang's *Harmony and War: Confucian Culture and Chinese Power Politics*," *International Security Studies Forum*, 4, no. 3 (2012), 4.

dazzle its neighbors with cultural brilliance or intimidate them with military might. As a result, the process of state building during the Three Kingdoms period was largely an indigenous development, and Chinese cultural borrowing was done on a purely voluntary basis.[8]

At the beginning of the seventh century, three kingdoms existed on the Korean Peninsula: Koguryŏ, Paekche, and Silla. All had origins in the first century BCE and had coexisted for seven centuries. Over an eight-year period beginning in 660, Silla allied with the Chinese Tang dynasty to crush Koguryŏ and Paekche, unifying the Korean Peninsula for the first time. This evolution of the East Asian world marked the emergence of political units in Korea and Japan that would endure until the modern era. Yet the Korean war was not a regional war; it was a Korean war. A century earlier, the Sui had made passing failed attempts at attacking Koguryŏ. Yet those ambitions ended quite quickly. Gaoxin Wang examines the classics of the "Twenty-Four Histories," concluding that across Chinese history, a recurring theme in analyses at the time was that "although there were some fluctuations of relations between the Chinese and other nations ... in general the aim has always adhered to the tradition of distinguishing the Chinese and other ethnic groups through etiquette and cultural practice."[9] Writing about failed Sui attempts to conquer Koguryŏ in the sixth century, Wang notes that "Even at that time of the Sui and Tang dynasties, scholars analyzed and lessons of dealing with other countries ... For example, in *Sui Shu, Memoir of Eastern Barbarian*, historical commentary argued that by the Sui use of force against Koguryŏ ... triggered hatred [from Koguryŏ], [and that] It is unheard of since ancient times that this behavior would not lead to a collapse of a country [the Sui]."[10] Neither China nor Japan had territorial ambitions on the peninsula. Indeed, the direction of attention was from the Korean kingdoms toward the Tang, not from a newly powerful Tang dynasty expanding its ambitions to the Korean Peninsula. As Nadia Kanagawa describes it, "Efforts to draw the Tang into the conflicts on the Korean peninsula began early – in 626 CE, both Paekche and Silla

---

[8] Michael Seth, *A Concise History of Korea* (Lanham: Rowman and Littlefield, 2016), 37.

[9] Gaoxin Wang, *Er Shi Si Shi De Min Zu Shi Zhuan Shu Yan Jiu* (*Studies on the Ethno-Historical Recounts in Twenty-Four Histories*), 1st ed. (Hefei Shi: Huang Shan shu she, 2016), 16.

[10] Wang, *Er Shi Si Shi De Min Zu Shi Zhuan Shu Yan Jiu*, 198–199.

sent envoys to the Tang complaining that Koguryŏ was preventing them from sending tribute and asking the Tang ruler to take action."[11] Christina Lai's detailed study of these wars further emphasizes that point: "the Sui and Tang only had limited ambitions in occupying Koguryo and only asked that tribute be paid ... China's troops withdrew numerous times after victories and did not seize full control of Koguryo's territory."[12] Han observes:

Silla's comprehensive implementation of the Tang's legal system had farreaching implications on East Asia ... The importance to East Asia is highlighted by the fact that Silla succeeded in receiving the comprehensive support of the Tang Dynasty, and cooperated with the Tang Dynasty to destroy Baekje and Goguryeo to unify the Korean Peninsula.[13]

In 660, Silla and the Tang formed an alliance, and Silla's envoy to the Tang, Kim Ch'unch'u, "obtained China's agreement that in the event the Silla–Tang army won the war against Koguryŏ, the territory south of Pyongyang would belong to Silla."[14] The Silla–Tang alliance first attacked Paekche, which, in turn, sought assistance from Yamato Japan. In 663, Japan sent a naval force to the Korean Peninsula in support of Paekche, which was wiped out by a Silla–Tang force. This battle was so peripheral to the overall war that most histories barely mention Japan's support of Paekche.[15] After that, Paekche was destroyed, ending Japanese participation in the war, its involvement on the peninsula, and its "influence on the continent for almost a millennium."[16] The Korean annals *Samguk sagi* (History of the Three

---

[11] Nadia Kanagawa, "East Asia's First World War, 643–668 CE," in Stephan Haggard and David C. Kang (eds.), *East Asia in the World: Twelve Events That Shaped the Modern International Order* (Cambridge: Cambridge University Press, 2020).

[12] Christina Lai, "Realism Revisited: China's Status-Driven Wars against Koguryo in the Sui and Tang Dynasties," *Asian Security* (published online 30 June 2020), 2, 15.

[13] Han, *Dongya Shijie Xingcheng Shilun*, 67–68.

[14] Peter Lee and Theodore de Bary, *Sources of Korean Tradition*, vol. 1, *From Early Times through the Sixteenth Century* (New York: Columbia University Press, 1997), 57.

[15] Ebrey and Walthall, *Pre-Modern East Asia*; Brett L. Walker, *A Concise History of Japan* (Cambridge: Cambridge University Press, 2015); Seth *A Concise History of Korea*; and Kyung Moon Hwang, *A History of Korea* (New York: Palgrave Macmillan, 2017) do not even mention Japan in their descriptions of the Silla unification of the peninsula.

[16] Holcombe, *A History of East Asia*, 111.

Kingdoms, written in 1145) recount that "Tang general Su Ting-fang said to [Silla general] Yusin, 'My command allows me to exercise authority as conditions dictate, so I will now present to you as maintenance lands all of Paekche's territory that has been acquired, this as reward for your merit. How would that be?'"[17]

In 668, the Silla–Tang alliance defeated Koguryŏ, the gates to the Koguryŏ capital having been opened from within by a traitor. By 676, all Tang forces had withdrawn from the peninsula, "and the Korean peninsula (up to a line somewhere north of modern Pyongyang) was unified."[18] As Kanagawa describes it

> The *Samguk sagi* records suggest that Silla leaders had long recognized that the Tang were both a potential threat and a potential ally ... by 679 CE the Tang had abandoned the peninsula, allowing Silla to consolidate its control over the territory. Over the course of the 680s, Tang–Silla relations would gradually improve, and Silla would once again send regular envoys bearing tribute to the Tang court and receiving investiture from the Tang ruler.[19]

There is almost nothing in the historical record to link state formation with this war. In particular, there are three bellicist hypotheses that do not find support in the historical record: The more advanced the state formation, the better the state performs in war; state formation as an effect of war; and state formation as a cause of war.

First, if the bellicist account applied in East Asia, it should have been the most state-like polity that defeated its rivals; and that state should have continued to pursue territorial expansion. Yet the victor – Silla – was considered the most backward of the Three Kingdoms and was the last to Sinicize because it was isolated and far away. Koguryŏ was the first to import Buddhism and Confucianism, and even Paekche was considered culturally and institutionally superior to Silla. As Seth points out, "it would be wrong to regard Silla as the most advanced of the [Korean] states ... Silla was very much a latecomer as an organized state, and compared to Paekche, Sillan culture was less refined and sophisticated."[20] Peter Lee and Theodore de Bary reflect

---

[17] *Samguk sagi*, 41:394, quoted in Lee and de Bary, *Sources of Korean Tradition*, 60.

[18] Holcombe, *A History of East Asia*, 111.

[19] Zhenping Wang, *Tang China in Multi-Polar Asia: A History of Diplomacy and War* (Honolulu: University of Hawai'i Press, 2013), 84. Wang notes that Silla sent twenty-five envoys to the Tang between 686 and 886 CE.

[20] Seth, *A Concise History of Korea*, 40.

a historiographic consensus that Silla "had the lowest standard of culture and was the last to develop as a state."[21] The signs of state formation that had slowly been adopted over the centuries were not reforms aimed at warfighting; they were aimed at governance and prestige.

The second causal mechanism in the bellicist thesis is state formation as effect: War and preparations for war result in state formation. But there is no evidence that Korean or Japanese state formation was undertaken as preparations for war or for war itself. The centuries in which these countries did not fight but instead engaged in emulation, learning, and state formation belie the idea that war was the cause and state formation the effect. As Seth points out, there was no interstate war over a span of nearly three centuries that spurred institutional development in Korea or Japan.[22]

The third bellicist causal mechanism is state formation as cause: The more state formation, the more war. According to this hypothesis, those countries that did develop state institutions were more powerful: The more "state-like" countries should have engaged in more war than the less state-like, and the former should have used their relative advantage in state-building capacity to expand. However, this also was not the case in the East Asian experience. Tang China refrained from annexation and Silla did not expand beyond the peninsula. Moreover, as shown in this chapter, Japan before and after the Korean War of Unification had quite clear boundaries that did not include continental expansion.

In addition to the three causal elements of the bellicist argument, there is a temporal assumption embedded in its logic: State-building and war should occur at or around the same time. However, the timing of the Korean War of Unification does not fit with the bellicist argument. This war occurred long after state consolidation began in East Asia, and it ended quickly with no further impact on state formation, even while state consolidation continued for centuries thereafter. There were no identifiable shifts in military technology that sparked the only war during these centuries. Therefore, it is only plausible to conclude that the war was incidental to state formation in Korea, either as cause or effect.

---

[21] Lee and de Bary, *Sources of Korean Tradition*, 34.
[22] Seth, *A Concise History of Korea*.

Moreover, Korea remained smaller than the domains of various Chinese dynasties throughout its history: Yet for the entire time, Korea managed to remain an independent state. Over more than 1,000 years of tribute relations, the larger power did not exploit the smaller power or attempt to renege on its commitments. Even the Mongol depredations in the thirteenth century did not extinguish Korea as a country: It was one of the few countries that managed to survive intact during the Mongol invasions. The rise of the powerful Ming dynasty in 1368 reinforced the Ming–Chosŏn tributary relations, as did the rise of the Qing in the seventeenth century.

4.2 The Absence of Japanese Territorial Ambitions

Japanese state formation was also not aimed at war. In the 400 years of slowly evolving Japanese state formation under consideration here, the Korean War of Unification was the only interstate war in which Japan was involved. Furthermore, it is still not clear why Japan participated in that war. Bruce Batten sums up the historiographic consensus when he concludes that "Why the Japanese should have thrown themselves with such vigor into a war that, if not quite an intramural Korean conflict, had at least no direct bearing on Japanese territory, is not easy to answer."[23]

Japan was not involved militarily on the continent for centuries before or after the 663 intervention. As with the Korean state-building experience, war did not lead to Japanese state formation either: For about a decade after the defeat in 663, Japan feared possible Silla or Tang reprisals. The Japanese built three fortresses and a series of signal fires for the possibility of an invasion. However, there was no imminent threat, and within a few decades such efforts were abandoned. Batten notes that "scattered references to construction or repair of fortifications continue until 701, when the final Takayasu Fortress was abolished."[24] By the end of the eighth century, the military had atrophied from disuse. Holcombe observes that "Japan no longer faced any serious foreign military threats, and the conscript army was allowed to lapse by as early as 792."[25] As Batten describes it, during

[23] Bruce Batten, "Foreign Threat and Domestic Reform: The Emergence of the Ritsuryō State," *Monumenta Nipponica*, 41, no. 2 (1986), 212.
[24] Batten, "Foreign Threat and Domestic Reform," 216.
[25] Holcombe, *A History of East Asia*, 119.

the Sui–Tang era of the sixth to tenth centuries, Japanese relations with China continued, but "there is no hint of military interaction ... Japanese contact with Tang was carried out almost exclusively by diplomatic channels, specifically via *kentoshi* or 'Japanese missions to Tang.'"[26] Berry further notes that "the ocean ... formed outer boundaries that were assailed regularly by piracy but rarely by invasion."[27]

Throughout centuries of state formation, Japan did not involve itself in war at the beginning or at the end of the time period studied here. Nor did more state formation lead to more war. As with the Korean peninsula, there was no interstate war in the fourth or fifth centuries that provoked Japanese state formation, nor were there more wars in the seventh and eighth centuries either. Japan's foreign borders had been largely fixed by this time, and they remained fixed for centuries into the future. Batten notes that "the most important section of the border was the Korea Strait, located between the island of Tsushima and the Korean peninsula ... aside from the late sixteenth century, during Hideyoshi's invasions ... the strait has always defined the western limit of Japanese territory."[28] In fact, after the defeat in 663, Japan had no military interaction with the peninsula, and "With the exception of Hideyoshi's invasions in the 1590s, Japan never crossed the East China Sea to encroach upon Korean ground (or vice versa)."[29] The historical Japanese state was involved in war so rarely that most scholarship on Japan treats premodern foreign relations as a subset of cultural history. There is, in fact, a historiographical consensus that Japanese leaders engaged in foreign relations with other Asian states mainly for economic or cultural exchange, not war and conquest. As Batten writes, "in order to gain access to luxury goods, ideas, and other aspects of 'advanced' culture ... this culminated in the Nara period with Japan's full integration into what Nishijima Sadao refers to as the 'east Asian world.'"[30]

Indeed, the entire Japanese historical experience in its foreign relations is a puzzle when viewed through a Eurocentric lens. Unlike England, Japan never played the role of an "offshore balancer"

[26] Bruce Batten, *To the Ends of Japan: Premodern Frontiers, Boundaries, and Interactions* (Honolulu: University of Hawai'i Press, 2003), 149.
[27] Mary Elizabeth Berry, "Was Early Modern Japan Culturally Integrated?" *Modern Asian Studies*, 31, no. 3 (1997), 553.
[28] Batten, *To the Ends of Japan*, 30.   [29] Batten, *To the Ends of Japan*, 236.
[30] Batten, *To the Ends of Japan*, 147.

intervening on the continent to restore a balance. Japan experienced centuries of stable relations with China, Korea, and the continent, interrupted only by the Mongol invasions (1274–1281) six centuries after the Korean War of Unification and the Japanese invasion of Korea three centuries after that (1592–1598). Put differently, from its emergence as a recognizable state in the seventh century until the nineteenth century – a period of over 1,200 years – Japan suffered only one invasion and initiated only one invasion. Abbey Steele et al. note that Tokugawa Japan (1600–1868) "was remarkably stable; Japan saw no foreign or domestic wars ... and even the threat of such conflicts, until the mid-nineteenth century."[31] In short, there is overwhelming historical evidence that clearly refutes any relationship between war and state formation in Japan as well as in Korea.

4.3 The Emergence of Vietnam

Vietnam is a particularly important and instructive case of emulation and the causes of state formation because twentieth-century nationalist narratives in Vietnam have largely obscured what actually happened ten centuries earlier. Vietnam came into existence not to fight China, but rather to coexist within the shadow of hegemony. There is an anachronistic twentieth-century nationalist myth of Vietnamese history that tends to be taken at face value by Western scholars and, indeed, most Vietnamese themselves: That, historically, Vietnam feared China and saw China as its main external threat. So deeply has this modern Vietnamese narrative of chronic war with China taken root that it is often repeated without reflection by observers and scholars of East Asian security and is used uncritically to argue that Vietnam fears China in the twenty-first century. It is widely accepted today that Vietnam's history has been one of constant struggle for autonomy against China. Yet this account is a recent, twentieth-century nationalist narrative. It originated during Vietnam's colonization by France and was aimed at uniting Vietnamese in struggles against imperial powers, including the United States. Liam Kelley observes that

---

[31] Abbey Steele, Christopher Paik, and Seiki Tanaka, "Constraining the Samurai: Rebellion and Taxation in Early Modern Japan," *International Studies Quarterly*, 61, no. 2 (2017), 352.

So thoroughly did the Western academy adopt the modern Vietnamese nationalist view of the past in the 1960s, 1970s and even 1980s that we have yet to fully disengage from this conceptual framework [with] emphasis on the historical importance of foreign intrusions, especially those of a supposedly expansionist China, as a major element.[32]

Reflecting this theme, Craig Lockard writes about "The long-term struggle for survival of the Vietnamese nation against tremendous odds (including conquest by foreigners and chronic internal discord)."[33] Michael Sullivan has said, "No country weighs on Vietnam like China, and it has been that way for centuries ... Vietnam's 2,000 year history with its northern neighbor is complex."[34] Vietnamese scholar Le Hong Hiep also notes that

Geopolitical conditions leave Vietnam with little choice in dealing with China. In fact, Vietnam is entrapped in a long-standing dilemma. In the past, it had to unflaggingly struggle for its own survival and national identity in the face of a more powerful and inherently expansionist China. As such, China was perceived as a permanent security threat that the country had to keep an eye on.[35]

Yet a close examination of Vietnamese history reveals that China was not necessarily the constant, looming threat that it has been made out to be. Indeed, much recent scholarship has emphasized the essential and enduring stability of the China–Vietnam relationship. Viewing the 1,000-year-old China–Vietnam border as simply the result of a military balance between the two sides is imposing a European lens on East Asian history. It obscures how tribute relations moderated risk and

[32] Liam Kelley, "Vietnam as a Domain of Manifest Civility (Văn Hiến Chi Bang)," *Journal of Southeast Asian Studies*, 34, no. 1 (2003), 63–64.
[33] Craig A. Lockard, "The Unexplained Miracle: Reflections on Vietnamese National Identity and Survival," *Journal of Asian and African Studies*, 29, no. 1–2 (1994), 10.
[34] Michael Sullivan, "Ask the Vietnamese about War, and They Think China, Not the U.S.," *National Public Radio*, May 1, 2015. Also see Jonathan London, "Vietnam Needs Bold Responses to Its China Dilemma," *cogitAsia, Center for Strategic and International Studies, CSIS Asia Program*, March 29, 2016; Simon Denyer, "China's Assertiveness Pushes Vietnam Toward an Old Foe, the United States," *Washington Post*, December 28, 2015; and Kyle Mizokami, "China's Scrappiest Enemy is a Familiar Foe," *The Week*, March 24, 2015.
[35] Le Hong Hiep, *Living Next to the Giant: The Political Economy of Vietnam's Relations with China under Doi Moi* (Singapore: ISEAS-Yusof Ishak Institute, 2016), 30.

stabilized the China–Vietnam relationship over the centuries, even as their relative capabilities shifted over time. Particularly important was the negotiated status within the tribute system that established Vietnamese regional independence while maintaining a check on Chinese incursions.

As the Tang dynasty (618–907) began to decay in the late ninth century, its imperial power diminished, especially in the outlying areas. Various Tang governors had ruled over the area of what is now Vietnam for centuries, as will be discussed in more detail in Chapter 7. With the slow collapse of the Tang, control in these outer areas gradually diminished and ultimately evaporated. As Taylor points out, by the late ninth century, "The Tang was now too weak to dominate Vietnam. Tang, in its weakness, gave the Vietnamese what in its strength it was too proud to grant. The Vietnamese now had the benefits of an imperial umbrella without the unhappiness of direct imperial rule."[36] Tang China disintegrated into warlord fiefdoms by the early tenth century.

Even as the Tang was collapsing, various Vietnamese warlords sought investiture by the Tang authorities. In 906, the Tang recognized Khúc Thừa Du as military governor of Đại La (later known as Hanoi), and his family ruled Vietnam until 930. Khúc is recognized as the ruler who marked the beginning of Vietnamese independence, even while "[his family] posed as loyal representatives of the Chinese imperial order." The time under the rule of the family "gave the Vietnamese a half-century of prosperity and tranquility ... yet beneath the surface, important changes were taking place."[37] With the final Tang collapse in 907, a number of competing dynasties sprang up in China, each claiming to be the legitimate imperial power. For the Vietnamese, this time of collapse in China was an opportunity and also a potential danger: As new groups came to power in the north, the leaders in the south needed to decide which group to declare allegiance to and be invested by. The "Sino-Vietnamese border became a bandit lair."[38] Known as the "Anarchy of the Twelve Warlords," the years 965–967 were chaotic, with various Vietnamese rulers attempting to unify the area under their rule. Over the better part of a decade, Đinh Bộ Lĩnh

[36] Keith Taylor, *The Birth of Vietnam* (Berkeley: University of California Press, 1983), 249.
[37] Taylor, *The Birth of Vietnam*, 263.   [38] Taylor, *The Birth of Vietnam*, 277.

defeated the other warlords sequentially, beginning by pacifying the Red River plain. As Taylor writes, "the anarchy that followed the death of Ngo Xuong Van in 963 gave him the opportunity to do so."[39]

After seven centuries of nominal Chinese control, in 967, Đinh Bộ Lĩnh became the first ruler of a truly independent Vietnamese state, Đai Cồ Việt.[40] Having defeated other warlords, and pacified and unified the region, Đinh began to focus on his relationship with the Song dynasty. By the 970s, the Song had pacified the area that had been held under the Southern Han and were now comfortably in charge of what is now central China. The first Vietnamese envoys approached the Song under the authority of Đinh Bộ Lĩnh as "Peaceful Sea Military Governor," who requested that the Song confirm the title. This was quickly granted, and the Song sent envoys to Vietnam who also conferred other titles on Đinh's family members. His son, Đinh Liễn, was invested as "Annam Protector General" and with the rank of a duke. In stepwise fashion, two years later Đinh Liễn sent envoys to the Song, requesting that they invest his father as "King of Giao Chi prefecture." This was a new, invented title, without precedent. As Taylor writes

Bo Linh's diplomatic status opened a new era in the long history of Sino-Vietnamese relations. Song was in effect recognizing the Vietnamese kingdom on two levels. One was the traditional relationship with Bo Linh's son ... on the other hand, Song recognized Bo Linh with an irregular title ... Thus, Bo Linh succeeded in translating a degree of distance into a diplomatic relationship with Song that lent weight to his claim of true independence. The title, "King of Giao-chi Prefecture" became the standard way for Song to recognize Vietnamese kings until the mid-twelfth century, when Song officially changed the name of Vietnam from Giao-chi Prefecture to An-nam Kingdom and began to recognize Vietnamese kings with the title "King of the An-nam Kingdom."[41]

This tributary relationship with China would continue essentially until the nineteenth century. This time was also the beginning of the political organization of what came later to be known as Vietnam. "In 973 and again in 975, Dinh Bo Linh sent envoys to establish and expand

[39] Taylor, *The Birth of Vietnam*, 278.
[40] Stanley Karnow, *Vietnam: A History* (New York: Penguin Books, 1997), 113.
[41] Taylor, *The Birth of Vietnam*, 286–287.

relations with the Song court."[42] The Song court in 986 recognized Lê Hoàn as the next ruler of Vietnam; throughout his reign, envoys regularly carried tribute to the Song court.[43]

Kelley notes that "It should be clear to the reader that the manner in which we view the world today – that is, as divided between equal nations, each of which takes pride in its own cultural uniqueness – is perhaps inappropriate for viewing the world of the East Asian past."[44] The actual emergence of Vietnam in the late tenth century was nothing like a glorious victory against a rapacious neighbor. In short, there is considerable scholarly evidence, and indeed what might approach a conventional wisdom, that Vietnam's chief security concerns did not include China. Yet this also flies directly in the face of the conventional nationalist Vietnamese narrative.[45] Kelley is worth quoting at length:

In 968 a man by the name of Dinh Bo Linh became the ruler of the area of the Red River delta. He did this not by fighting off the Chinese and declaring "independence." Instead, he allied himself with a Cantonese warlord and defeated other warlords in the region, some of whom were undoubtedly Han Chinese, but others who were likely Vietnamese or Tai-speaking peoples. Two years later, the Song Dynasty dispatched an envoy who granted Dinh Bo Linh the position of commandery prince (*quan vuong/junwang*), continuing a long-running practice of granting titles to powerful individuals in the region. What would be different this time, however, is that eventually this title would be elevated to the level of "king" (*quoc vuong/guowang*), and this kingdom would maintain its position of as a tributary state for centuries to come.[46]

From that time on, the Vietnamese court explicitly recognized its unequal status in its relations with China through a number of formal institutional mechanisms and norms. Explicit recognition of the

[42] Taylor, *A History of the Vietnamese*, 47.
[43] Taylor, *A History of the Vietnamese*, 49.
[44] Liam Kelley, *Beyond the Bronze Pillars: Envoy Poetry and the Sino-Vietnamese Relationship* (Honolulu: University of Hawaii Press, 2005), 28.
[45] Nationalist Vietnamese historians often point to these earlier struggles as extending the concept of "Vietnam" back long before there was any centralized political rule. Although the idea of Vietnamese resistance to foreign aggression has become the accepted nationalist history, it is fairly difficult to conceive of the peoples in 40 CE as "Vietnamese" in any way we use the term today.
[46] Liam Kelley, "Inequality in the Vietnamese Worldview and its Implications for Sino-Vietnamese Relations," Paper presented at the Roundtable on the Nature of Political and Spiritual Relations among Asian Leaders and Polities from the 14th to the 18th Centuries, University of British Columbia, Institute of Asian Research, Vancouver (April 19–21, 2010), 8.

hierarchy began with Đinh Bộ Lĩnh in 968 and continued essentially unquestioned until the arrival of the French in the nineteenth century. As discussed later in this chapter, investiture was an enduring diplomatic protocol in which one party would explicitly accept subordinate tributary status, thus recognizing the legitimate sovereignty of another political unit, and explicitly identifying the king in that subordinate tributary state as the legitimate ruler. Successive Vietnamese rulers received investiture, and envoys "regularly carried tribute to the Song court."[47]

Vietnamese rulers also paid very little military attention to their relations with China, which were conducted extensively through the institutions and principles of the tribute system. Kelley observes that "Vietnamese envoys passionately believed that they participated in what we would now call the Sinitic or East Asian cultural world, and that they accepted their kingdom's vassal status in that world."[48]

The historical record suggests that the rulers of the Đai Việt period were usually much more concerned with internal stability than they were with invasion from China. James Anderson observes about Vietnam that "By 1086 a clear border had been mapped out between the two states, the first such court-negotiated border in China's history ... The existence of a formal border between the two polities was successfully challenged only once in the next eight hundred years."[49] As would be expected in a relationship organized by hierarchy, the Vietnamese court even occasionally sought the Chinese court's cooperation in putting down rebellions, as will be covered in Chapter 7.

In sum, Vietnam – like Korea and Japan – did not emerge and begin its existence as a state as a means to pursue war against China. State formation was also not aimed at pursuing further competition with China or other states. Rather, Vietnam emerged and developed as a state within the cultural and institutional influence of Chinese civilization, and as a full and willing member of that political order and arrangement.

[47] Taylor, *A History of the Vietnamese*, 49.
[48] Kelley, *Beyond the Bronze Pillars*, 2.
[49] James A. Anderson, "Distinguishing between China and Vietnam: Three Relational Equilibriums in Sino-Vietnamese Relations," *Journal of East Asian Studies*, 13, no. 2 (2013), 271.

4.4 The Tribute System and State Formation

The spread of Chinese civilization carried with it a foundational philosophical and political order that was fundamentally different from that which developed in Europe. These different fundamental principles and institutions manifested in domestic politics, as the bulk of this book will show. Yet these ideas were also central in ordering the international relations of the four states with each other. The same foundational ideas that animated state formation, political, social and cultural life, and science within these countries were also the basis of their relations with each other. Over millennia, the ideas and principles became more regularized and institutionalized, and they are now described as the "tribute system" of international relations. Those principles and philosophies were discussed at length in Chapter 3; here we show how they affected relations between these states.

Given that the bellicist thesis emphasizes war as the key driver of state formation, we devote considerable space here to showing how the international relations of historical East Asia were different from those in historical Europe. This system had a different foundational order than in Europe, built on different ordering principles. Most centrally, East Asia was a hegemonic system in which status and hierarchy were the key factors, not a balance-of-power system in which relative power was the key concern.

East Asian countries have had an enduring and fundamental concern for status and hierarchy even during eras characterized by multipolarity, not hegemony. It is simply not possible to separate the relations of these states with each other from the political, philosophical, and religious ideas and institutions that formed the core of their domestic development. The tribute system and international order grew out of Confucian, Buddhist, and Daoist ideas, and the Mandate of Heaven that preceded them. It is the foreign manifestation of these domestic, Chinese ideas.

The concept of the tribute system, however, remains a somewhat controversial scholarly idea. Writing about "the concept of a 'tributary system'," historians such as Peter Perdue have argued that "well-informed historians have repeatedly denied that such a system ever existed," while James Millward writes that "some IR scholars and popular writers on international relations have revived the Fairbankian package, assuming the tributary system ... to have been real elements of Chinese history ... accepting its own (demonstrably false) historical assumptions."[50] Yuan-kang Wang argues that "the Northern Song dynasty decision to use force ... was consistent with structural realist expectations: Considerations of the balance of power – not cultural aversion to warfare – dominated the decisions to use force."[51] Similarly, Morris Rossabi argued a generation ago that "Chinese dynasties from the tenth to the thirteenth century adopted a realistic policy toward foreign states ... Diplomatic parity defined the relations between China and other states during these three centuries ... The tribute system did not, by itself, govern China's contacts with foreigners."[52] Millward has argued that Chinese history "looks a lot like power politics as usual."[53] This ostensibly "realistic" foreign policy of China is often misunderstood as confirming the universality of a "realist," or balance of power, theory that was inductively derived from the European historical experience.[54]

We challenge this reading of history. We show instead that the primary – and overwhelming – concern of all fours states was their rank-order status. The concept of a world composed entirely of equal, sovereign, independent states that viewed each other primarily through the lens of relative capabilities did not exist in historical East Asian international relations. Instead, the hierarchy of the rank order was expressed in the international relations of this period through the tribute system. The relations of two states that could negotiate a mutually accepted rank-order status were stable, no matter what the distribution of capabilities. If they failed, relations were unstable, no matter what their relative power. The theoretical alternative to the equality of balance of power theory is hierarchy, not a particular cultural or philosophical tradition from one part of the world. In fact, it is now widely accepted that long stretches of international order in

---

[50] Peter Perdue, "The Tenacious Tributary System," *Journal of Contemporary China*, 24, no. 96 (2015), 1002–1014; and Millward, "Qing and Twentieth-Century Chinese Diversity Regimes," 76–77.

[51] Yuan-Kang Wang, *Harmony and War: Confucian Culture and Chinese Power Politics* (New York: Columbia University Press, 2010), 74.

[52] Morris Rossabi (ed.), *China among Equals: The Middle Kingdom and Its Neighbors, 10th–14th Centuries* (Berkeley: University of California Press, 1983), 12.

[53] Millward, "Qing and Twentieth-Century Chinese Diversity Regimes," 78.

[54] Elizabeth Economy, "China: Harmony and War," *Council on Foreign Relations Blog*, February 11, 2011, https://www.cfr.org/blog/china-harmony-war.

East Asian history were characterized by hierarchy, not balance of power.[55] As Ji-Young Lee has written, "Chinese hegemonic authority was in large part a function of symbolic power contingent upon other East Asian actors' recognition of Chinese ways of defining socially acceptable behavior."[56] Seo-Hyun Park concludes that tribute relations "functioned as a well-institutionalized, if regionally confined, system of states."[57] Similarly, Yongjin Zhang and Barry Buzan write

> That there existed an indigenous social order in the history and politics of what we call East Asia today is beyond dispute, be it called the Chinese world order, the tributary system, Pax Sinica, the East Asian order, international society in East Asia or any other. Acknowledging this is to recognize that East Asian states and peoples had historically chosen and established complex institutions and practices informed by their history and culture.[58]

Empirically, it is clear that countries used relations based on institutional and normative models that emphasized hierarchy and difference, not equality and sameness. We provide detailed evidence in this book that the actual negotiations, diplomatic relations, and indeed even the words that actors used at the time all conclusively show that tribute relations as an international order existed in East Asia throughout the historical era. China, Korea, Japan, and Vietnam used these ideas in their foreign relations with each other and other actors throughout the region. Indeed, all countries in the region were willing to suffer significant material costs in order to pursue status and relative rank. Far from being superficial, a concern with relative status and hierarchic rank order was the primary consideration regionwide. As such, we further sharpen and move this debate forward by being precise about definitions, meanings, and historical evidence.

Scholars have not yet fully embraced the possibility that international relations across time and space is as likely to be hierarchic and based in hegemonies as it is multipolar and based on balance of

[55] Feng Zhang, *Chinese Hegemony: Grand Strategy and International Institutions in East Asian History* (Stanford, CA: Stanford University Press, 2015); and Seo-Hyun Park, *Sovereignty and Status in East Asian International Relations* (Cambridge: Cambridge University Press, 2017).
[56] Lee, *China's Hegemony*, 13.
[57] Park, *Sovereignty and Status in East Asian International Relations*, 54.
[58] Yongjin Zhang and Barry Buzan, "The Tributary System as International Society in Theory and Practice," *Chinese Journal of International Politics*, 5, no. 1 (2012), 10.

power. In this way, we also directly refute the conventional wisdom that this era in East Asian history was a balance-of-power system in which relative capabilities were the primary determinant of war and other violence. For example, Rossabi's important 1983 book is often cited as the definitive work on a particular era in East Asian history, and one that ostensibly established that the tribute system did not exist and that realist power considerations were instead the key factor in regional relations. Critiquing two of Fairbank's works, Rossabi argued that

The papers in this volume suggest that the so-called Chinese world order ... did not persist for the entire period from the second century B.C. to the Opium War. From the tenth to thirteenth centuries, China did not dogmatically enforce its system of foreign relations ... Diplomatic parity defined the relations between China and other states during these three centuries.[59]

As noted in Chapter 2, there was no constant, enduring "China" as a country and no international order that existed unchanging over 2,000 years. Indeed, Rossabi and others were perhaps criticizing an extreme view of Chinese foreign relations by potentially mischaracterizing Fairbank's 1968 edited volume, *The Chinese World Order*.[60] Indeed, for forty years or more, Rossabi, Millward, Perdue, Hui, and other scholars have been attacking a version of Chinese history that is so extreme that we have been unable to find any scholar who actually claims that China engaged in two millennia of identical, unchanging foreign policy. Fairbank himself criticized "hoary stereotypes of the Chinese tribute system," writing that "states and peoples were expected in theory to be properly tributary to the Son of Heaven in the Central Country, but the theory frequently was not observed in fact ... the Chinese culture-based theory of the Son of Heaven's supremacy had to come to terms with the geographic fact of nomadic Inner Asian fighting power."[61] Fairbank also pointed out that many of the chapters in *The Chinese World Order* "contrast the myth and reality in China's traditional attitude towards outsiders."[62] Puzzlingly, even these same scholars who criticize Fairbank also admit

[59] Rossabi (ed.), *China Among Equals*, 2–12.
[60] John K. Fairbank (ed.), *The Chinese World Order: Traditional China's Foreign Relations* (Cambridge, MA: Harvard University Press, 1968).
[61] Fairbank, *The Chinese World Order*, 1–3.
[62] Fairbank, *The Chinese World Order*, 14.

he did not argue that China conducted 2,000 years of identical foreign policy. Millward, for example, writes that "several chapters in *The Chinese World Order* volume discussed countries and frontiers where things worked quite differently than in the Fairbankian scheme."[63]

Intuitively, it would seem obvious that, over two millennia, different leaders facing different situations at different times might act differently, even if some of the ideas and principles that guided them were similar. For example, a more nuanced argument about historical East Asian international order shows that "tributary relations were the primary institution of the historical East Asian international order, yet ... this tributary order was incomplete and flexible ... tribute did not represent the whole range of hierarchical relationships in the region, nor did it characterize all of China's relations with its neighbors."[64]

In fact, criticisms of Fairbank aside, the substantive arguments of both Millward and Perdue complement the approach taken in this book. Millward emphasizes the cultural bases of legitimation. Despite his protestation that East Asian history "looks a lot like power politics as usual," the patterns he identifies actually show that "the Qing ruling elite functioned in multiple languages and cultural registers simultaneously, legitimizing their rule in different ways for the Manchus as well as the Chinese, Mongol, Turkic-Muslim and Tibetan domains."[65] Realists in the field of international relations would find Millward's argument about cultural legitimation to be epiphenomenal to the distribution of capabilities in the region. His reminder that there were multiple sources of legitimacy and authority beyond the umbrella term "Confucianism" is a useful step in the right direction and is consistent with the more nuanced argument about historical international relations and order in East Asia – and one that largely works with the research presented in this book.

Perdue, for his part, acknowledges the complexity of relationships but also points out that they were fundamentally about status and rank order, and that they depended on ideas about appropriateness, not the materialist logic of consequences or great power politics. For instance,

[63] Millward, "Qing and Twentieth-Century Chinese Diversity Regimes," 75.
[64] David C. Kang, "International Order in Historical East Asia: Tribute and Hierarchy beyond Sinocentrism and Eurocentrism," *International Organization*, 74, no. 1 (2020), 66–73.
[65] Millward, "Qing and Twentieth-Century Chinese Diversity Regimes," 78–79.

Perdue explicitly discusses how Chosŏn Korea (1392–1910) was reluctant to switch tribute relations from the Ming to the Manchus in the early seventeenth century, precisely because they "Regarded the Ming as the truly Confucian state and the Manchus as barbarian interlopers ... Koreans had sent tribute missions to China for hundreds of years, as they regarded themselves as integral parts of the neo-Confucian realm, and supporters of Ming." Emphasizing that the balance of power was not a key factor in Korea's foreign policy decision-making, Perdue continues to observe that "Prudential calculations supported a policy of 'serving the great [power]', but Koreans did not automatically submit to their giant northern neighbor [the Manchus]."[66]

Indeed, both Perdue and Millward provide clear evidence that status and hierarchy were the key causal factors in foreign relations, not the material balance of power. Discussing tribute relations, Millward writes: "[Fairbank] pointed out that the value of the 'gifts in return' granted by the emperor to 'tributaries' often exceeded the value of the 'tribute,' and thus amounted to a price paid by the Chinese court to maintain a lofty self-image ... presenters of *gong* [tribute, 貢] to Chinese courts endured the ritualized brown-nosing because they went away the richer for it."[67] These arguments are entirely complementary to the arguments made in this book. Countries were often willing to forego considerable material gains in the pursuit of relative status.

Both Millward and Perdue point out how deeply issues of status drove foreign policy decisions; and how small the role of the material balance of power was. Furthermore, they both show in detail how *gong*, or tribute, was conducted directly against the realist prediction of the large exploiting the small, and *not* like a bully taking lunch money. Rather, the larger power often provided incentives for the smaller power to submit to investiture willingly, something that would be impossible in a realist theoretical world dominated by relative power considerations. The smaller states that developed in emulation of China did not, in fact, fear for their survival from China. Instead, they crafted centuries of stable relations with China.

Yet almost all contemporary international relations theory predicts that the larger power will exploit the smaller power. The ostensible

---

[66] Perdue, "The Tenacious Tributary System," 1009.
[67] Millward, "Qing and Twentieth-Century Chinese Diversity Regimes," 75.

difficulty in crafting a credible commitment in bargaining theory, the causal dynamics of the security dilemma, and the balancing hypothesis itself all rely upon the possibility that tomorrow a stronger power may renege on any agreement it makes today. As Kenneth Schultz and Hein Goemans recently pointed out, almost all international relations literature contains these assumptions about constant exploitation:

a view of the world in which states have insatiable appetites for conquest, limited demands disguise unbounded ambitions, and any concession to an adversary only invites further aggression. This view is rooted in the belief, summarized by Holsti (1991, 14), that "whatever the window dressing, propaganda lines, and self-serving justifications for the use of force, the basic issue is always a power contest between two or more protagonists in which" – now quoting Aron (1966, 8) – "the stakes are the 'existence, the creation, and the elimination of states.'" This view is echoed in Mearsheimer's (2001, 2) argument that all states have a common aim: to maximize their power.[68]

But these are based on assumptions about the world, not an empirical description of the world. As Schultz and Goemans argue, "historically states bargain within far more limited confines defined by well-bounded claims ... the size of claims is weakly related to the relative power of disputants and unaffected by dramatic changes in power, and smaller claims are associated with a higher probability that the challenger will receive any concession."[69] Although they do not use the social scientific terminology used by international relations scholars, both Millward and Perdue also call for more clear scope and boundary conditions, and for making more specific claims about types of relation and types of state in certain times and places, rather than broad sweeping claims.

4.5 The Tributary Order of International Relations

The tribute system itself was an international order comprising both institutional and normative features. Built on a mix of legitimate authority and material power, the China-derived tribute system provided a normative and institutional social order that also contained

[68] Kenneth Schultz and Hein Goemans, "Aims, Claims, and the Bargaining Model of War," *International Theory*, 11, no. 3 (2019), 345.
[69] Schultz and Goemans, "Aims, Claims, and the Bargaining Model of War," 344.

credible commitments by China not to exploit secondary states that accepted its authority.[70] Among the institutions and norms were the exchange of missions, explicit hierarchic ranking of polities, and differential rights and trade privileges based on ranking. Anderson's research on China–Vietnam relations in the fifteenth century concludes that "tribute missions were important opportunities to negotiate the balance of status and authority existing between the Chinese and Vietnamese rulers," while Ji-Young Lee shows that the ritual of investiture communicated China's authority, including its potential for coercion on a regular basis, and importantly, in a symbolic manner that was acceptable to Korea's identity as a Confucian society.[71]

The core of the tribute system was a set of institutions and norms that regulated diplomatic and political contact, cultural and economic relations, and in particular explicitly stated a relationship between two political units. In contrast to the modern Westphalian ideal of equality among nation-states, the tribute system emphasized the "asymmetry and interdependence of the superior/inferior relationship," and inequality was the basis for all relations between two units.[72] The tribute system was formalized in two key institutions: Diplomatic recognition by the superior state, known as "investiture," and the sending of embassy envoys to the superior state. Tribute embassies served a number of purposes – they stabilized the political and diplomatic relationship between the two sides, provided information about important events and news, formalized rules for trade, and allowed intellectual and cultural exchange among scholars. Missions themselves, composed of scholar-officials, interpreters, physicians, alternates, messengers, and assistants, could comprise hundreds of people. Two examples will suffice: One from Korea and one from Vietnam.

4.5.1 Negotiating the Border around Mount Paektu, 1711–1713

Korean history is essentially a continuous set of tribute relationships with successive Chinese dynasties. As they rose and fell, Korea had to

---

[70] Kenneth Swope, *The Military Collapse of China's Ming Dynasty, 1618–44* (New York: Routledge, 2014).

[71] Anderson, "Distinguishing between China and Vietnam," 261; and Lee, *China's Hegemony*.

[72] James Louis Hevia, *Cherishing Men from Afar: Qing Guest Ritual and the Macartney Embassy of 1793* (Durham, NC: Duke University Press, 1995), 124.

renegotiate its tribute status with the new dynasty. Once that relationship had been established, relations were stable and there was no Chinese attempt to renegotiate that status or to exploit Korea. This section explores the negotiation between the Chinese Qing and the Korean Chosŏn of their border around the wilderness area of Mount Paektu (known as Changbaishan or Changbai Mountain in Chinese) in the early eighteenth century as an intriguing illumination of the institutions at work in the tribute system, and also to reveal how the actors viewed the system and their relations itself.

A key international institution is the negotiation and demarcation of a clear border.[73] Part of a legitimate hierarchy is a credible commitment on the part of the dominant state not to exploit the subordinate states. The tribute system provided a range of flexible institutional and discursive tools with which to resolve conflicts without recourse to war, and a good indicator of the stability in the system was that the borders between China, Korea, Japan, and Vietnam were relatively fixed and did not significantly change during the five centuries under review. As Simmons notes, "when they are mutually accepted, [borders] drastically reduce external challenges to a government's legitimate authority . . . and clarify and stabilize transnational actors' property rights."[74] Yet borders may represent more than a rationalist means for clarifying intentions: They also represent a willingness on both sides to view the border as legitimate and to view the political unit on the other side of the border as also legitimate.

By the tenth century, Korea and China had established the Yalu River as their border, and it was affirmation of this border and Korean acceptance of tributary status in the fourteenth century that precluded a war between the new Ming Chinese and Chosŏn Korean dynasties. In 1389, near the beginning of the Ming dynasty (1368–1644), the Ming notified the Koryŏ dynasty (918–1392) that it considered the

---

[73] Some have argued that demarcation of clear borders is purely a European innovation, although the East Asian experience of stable and clearly demarcated borders occurred much earlier than in Europe. See Jordan Branch, "Mapping the Sovereign State: Technology, Authority, and Systemic Change," *International Organization*, 65, no. 1 (2011), 1–36.

[74] Beth Simmons, "Rules over Real Estate: Trade, Territorial Conflict, and International Borders as Institutions," *Journal of Conflict Resolution*, 49, no. 6 (2005), 827; and Taylor Fravel, "Regime Insecurity and International Cooperation: Explaining China's Compromises on Territorial Disputes," *International Security*, 30, no. 2 (2005), 46–83.

area of northeastern Korea that had been under direct Mongol control (the Ssangsŏng Commandery) to be part of its territory. Koryŏ decided to fight the Ming over the demarcation of the border; this campaign, and General Yi Sŏng-gye's unwillingness to fight it (preferring negotiation), led to the fall of Koryŏ and, three years later, the creation of a new dynasty, Chosŏn, with Yi as its first king.[75] Yi immediately opened negotiations with China, and the Ming did indeed settle for Chosŏn's tributary status. Significantly, in exchange for entering into tribute status with China, Chosŏn Korea retained all territory previously held by Koryŏ. By the fifteenth century, Korean political control had expanded in the northeast along both the Yalu and Tumen rivers. Those two rivers have formed the border between China and Korea to the present day. What concerns us here is the status of the wild Mount Paektu area, which was negotiated in 1711–1713.[76] This Qing–Chosŏn border negotiation is a vivid example of the ways in which these historical institutions and authority interacted.

In the early eighteenth century, the Qing decided to clarify the border between the two countries in the mountainous terrain around Mount Paektu. The area was – and continues to be – wild and uninhabited, and there was considerable smuggling and migration through this uncontrolled area. When some Koreans crossed deep into Chinese territory and murdered ginseng farmers, stealing their crops, the Qing decided to demarcate the border and clarify the responsibilities on both sides. In the spring of 1711, Qing imperial envoy Mukedeng came to Korea and declared he would travel northwards to map and demarcate the border. The Koreans were not happy about this. Their main worry was that the Qing might soon lose power, and would then retreat northwards, perhaps even toward or into Korean territory; allowing the Qing to survey the frontier would allow them to learn much more about the terrain, roads, and Chosŏn defenses.

The Korean side spent months dissembling and delaying the actual trip up Mount Paektu, following what Andre Schmid calls a policy of

---

[75] Young-Soo Kim, *Kŏngukui chŏngch'i: yŏmal sŏncho, hyŏkmyŏnggwa munmyŏng jonhwa* [The Politics of Founding the Nation: Revolution and Transition of Civilization during the Late Koryŏ and Early Chosŏn] (Seoul: Yeehaksa, 2006).

[76] Gari Ledyard, "Cartography in Korea," in J. B. Harley and David Woodward (eds.), *Cartography in the Traditional East and Southeast Asian Societies* (Chicago: Chicago University Press, 1994), 290.

"unproductive cooperation."[77] The Korean side claimed that the passage to the mountains was too dangerous for the Qing imperial envoy to travel; they argued that the trip was not necessary; and made a number of excuses to avoid showing Mount Paektu to Mukedeng. Eventually, Chosŏn officials even considered writing to the Qing Board of Rites in hopes of having Mukedeng recalled. Schmid writes that when Mukedeng heard that after Chosŏn officials had stalled him for months, they were hoping to circumvent his trip by appealing to Qing officials,:

> At this point Mukedeng confronted Song [the Korean envoy]. "If your small country has no faith, then I have a secret edict to show." From a yellow box he pulled out a piece of paper that was clearly an imperial edict. No doubt pleased to finally confront his recalcitrant counterparts, Mukedeng challenged them to question his privileged position. "Fabricating an Imperial edict is a capital offense, so is there anything to doubt?" he asked. Clearly there was no doubt. Nor was there much that Song could do. In the face of a direct imperial command, the decision to circumvent Mukedeng by appealing to the emperor through the Board of Rites lost all legitimacy.[78]

Korean resistance vanished after Mukedeng revealed the imperial edict, and they grudgingly led Mukedeng near Mount Paektu. The key to this story is that a direct order from the Emperor clearly superseded any bureaucratic direction that might come from the Board of Rites – Mukedeng was sent by the Qing emperor himself, not by anonymous scholar-officials. This alone was sufficient to cause the Korean side to fall in line and to cooperate.

This first trip met numerous difficulties, many created by the Koreans, although Mukedeng did not report this to the Kangxi Emperor. Returning home with an initial report about the mountainous area, Mukedeng returned on a second mission in 1712, again with orders to delineate the borders on Mount Paektu, and this time the Qing Board of Rites informed the Chosŏn side that it was to help Mukedeng if he needed assistance, and specified the route he would take. Schmid notes that "as in the previous year, the Seoul court could

---

[77] Andre Schmid, "Tributary Relations and the Qing–Chosun Frontier on Mount Paektu," in Diana Lary (ed.), *The Chinese State at the Borders* (Vancouver: University of British Columbia Press, 2007), 134.

[78] Schmid, "Tributary Relations and the Qing–Chosun Frontier on Mount Paektu," 136.

not directly refuse this instruction."[79] During this second trip, Mukedeng did reach Mount Paektu. He accepted the Korean argument that all the lands south of the Yalu and Tumen rivers were Korean; he remained concerned only with the uninhabited area around Mount Paektu, and where it was difficult to distinguish the headwaters of the two rivers because so many streams intersected. After traveling up the mountain and surveying the lands, Mukedeng erected a stele (later found to be inaccurately placed!) that demarcated the specific border between the two sides.

The Chosŏn side saw this as a relatively successful outcome. Chŏng Yag-yong, a Korean scholar-official writing in the eighteenth century, noted that

the southern slopes of Mount Changbaek, where both the Tumen and Yalu rivers have their headwaters, lay within our territory, but the winding ridges and layers of peaks make the exact location of the border unclear. However, [Qing] Emperor Kang-hsi, ordered Area Commander Wu-la Mukedeng to delineate the border and erect a stone boundary marker. As a result, the border between those two rivers is clear as well.[80]

Significantly, the Chinese reopened the issue of the border in the late 1880s. In the course of these negotiations, the Koreans documented their case with records and maps from the 1711–1713 negotiations. Rather than risk losing, the Chinese abandoned the negotiation and never returned to the table, and the Korean status quo stood.[81]

There are two possible explanations for this case – an instrumental explanation and a substantive explanation. The critical element of the story was Mukedeng's revelation of the imperial edict that finally eliminated Korean stonewalling. An instrumental explanation would immediately investigate the actual threat or pressure implicit in the edict. After all, the edict was merely a piece of paper and, despite the symbolic importance of a Qing emperor's command, it is probable that the edict was backed up by some type of implicit or even explicit threat of punishment if it were disobeyed. Thus, an instrumental approach to

---

[79] Schmid, "Tributary Relations and the Qing–Chosun Frontier on Mount Paektu," 142.

[80] Peter H. Lee (ed.), *Sourcebook of Korean Civilization*, vol. 2, *From the Seventeenth Century to the Modern Period* (New York: Columbia University Press, 1996), 234.

[81] Gari Ledyard, Personal communication, October 30, 2007.

the tribute system would look for the material underpinnings behind it. There was no threat, however: Mukedeng did not threaten military force as a solution to the issue.

In contrast, a substantive approach to the institutions of the tribute system would examine four key factors that show the importance of principles and norms.

First, there was no implicit threat; the nature of the imperial edict was not "do this or else," but rather "this is the authoritative word." That is, there is no evidence at all that the Qing would have mobilized force, that there was a military mobilization prepared, or even that there would be economic consequences for Korea.

Second, both the Qing and the Chosŏn officials knew exactly what the imperial edict symbolized and meant. There was no doubt in anyone's mind of the importance and gravity of a directive straight from the Qing emperor. In this sense, the larger influence of Chinese civilization carried meanings that were formative – the rules and norms developed between the two sides were understood and accepted by both sides. Korean elites consciously emulated Chinese institutional and discursive practices in their domestic and international behavior. Korea and China shared values, understandings, and goals.

Third and even more importantly, in addition to understanding the meaning of the edict, both sides saw the edict as legitimate, and Korean resistance and attempts to stall or even recall Mukedeng evaporated. Furthermore, the Chosŏn officials accepted the Qing Board of Rites as the ultimate arbiter, and much of their diplomatic strategy involved potentially appealing to the Board to ask for a recall of the mission. To buttress their position, Chosŏn officials also considered using a Qing document that noted that the lands south of Mount Paektu were Korean, but decided against referencing this document because it was not supposed to be in the hands of Chosŏn officials.[82] There is no indication that the Chosŏn officials ever questioned these larger rules. It is clear that they were working within a larger normative and institutional environment that was fully accepted: We see no evidence that the Chosŏn officials were resentful of these rules, nor do we find evidence of them working to overturn these rules. Rather, their strategy

---

[82] Schmid, "Tributary Relations and the Qing–Chosun Frontier on Mount Paektu," 143.

of grudging cooperation occurred within this larger institutional and normative framework.

Fourth, within the larger framework of their relations, the Korean and Chinese side used the various institutions, rules, and norms of the tribute system not only for communication but also for negotiation and bargaining. That this negotiation, clearly against the Korean king's desires, could take place and could result in a stable resolution of the border and stability for over 200 years is not surprising. After all, in the contemporary world far more disputes are resolved through negotiations without any hint of military or economic consequences than are resolved through coercion of some type. Of course, there were issues and disagreements between the two countries: To expect otherwise is to set unrealistic expectations. The international system, and the rules and norms that defined that system, did not eliminate disputes, but rather the set of tools were developed to manage and resolve those disputes.

More broadly, crafting a set of norms and rules that are viewed as legitimate by secondary states is an essential task for the dominant state. This consensual view of hegemony focuses on why secondary states would defer to the hegemon rather than on the structural position of the hegemon itself. Hegemony is a form of power itself, and derives in part from the values or norms that a state projects, not merely from the state's military might and economic wealth.

There was a hierarchical relationship in place in the context of China and the East Asian states that was generated by a common culture defined by a common worldview. These Sinic states possessed a shared sense of legitimacy that presupposed, in the context of Confucianism, that relations operate within an accepted hierarchy. For these states, Chinese civilization provided a common intellectual, linguistic, and normative framework in which to interact and resolve differences.

The territorial dispute and location of the border could have been resolved through a military intervention. But the resolution was achieved using the principles and institutions of the tribute system to both negotiate a resolution and, more importantly, to establish diplomatic relations between two sides of unequal power. Gari Ledyard concludes that

Chinese "control" was hardly absolute. While the Koreans had to play the hand they were dealt, they repeatedly prevailed in diplomacy and argument ... and convinced China to retreat from an aggressive position. In other words, the tributary system did provide for effective communication, and Chinese and Korean officialdom spoke from a common Confucian vocabulary. In that front, the relationship was equal, if not at times actually in Korea's favor.[83]

Seonmin Kim's detailed study of China–Korea border management during the seventeenth to nineteenth centuries concludes that "it was not equal relations between the Qing and the Chosŏn that enabled them to achieve this feat; rather, it was the asymmetrical tributary relationship that led the two countries to pursue the same solution."[84]

We emphasize this point: Not only was Qing willing to suffer costs for status, but when relative status was agreed upon by both sides the superior side gave up considerable material benefits, consistent with Millward's earlier observation. This is exactly the opposite of what realists predict, and indeed the opposite of what most international relations theory would predict about Qing's capacity to make a credible commitment not to exploit Chosŏn. Realists clearly predict that a more powerful actor will exploit a weaker actor. That is the basis of balancing behavior and all the other dynamics in realist theory; indeed fear of future exploitation is the basis of the commitment problem in bargaining theory, and the fear that drives the security dilemma. But the opposite occurred in historical East Asia: The Qing–Chosŏn relationship was stable until the end of the Qing and Chosŏn in the early twentieth century – a period of over 200 years. Having stabilized their relationship through the tribute system, there is no evidence that Qing considered reneging or that Chosŏn officials feared new or further exploitation from its larger neighbor.

4.5.2 The Chinese Occupation of Vietnam, 1407–1427

The second example of the workings of the tribute system comes from China–Vietnam relations. As discussed earlier in this chapter, a local warlord in the Red River plain, Đinh Bộ Lĩnh, sent emissaries to the Song court in 973 and 975, quickly receiving investiture. As relations between China and this emerging country in the south were beginning,

---

[83] Gari Ledyard, Posting on *Korea Web*, March 21, 2006, http://koreaweb.ws/pipermail/koreanstudies_koreaweb.ws/2006-March/005455.html.

[84] Seonmin Kim, *Ginseng and Borderland Territorial Boundaries and Political Relations between Qing China and Chosŏn Korea, 1636–1912* (Oakland: University of California Press, 2017), 3.

the status of investiture rose. The subsequent Vietnamese ruler, Lê Hoàn (黎桓), avoided a war with the Song Chinese by accepting investiture from the Song emperor in 986, and in return he was granted an apanage of over 4,000 families.[85]

After the establishment of the short-lived Đinh dynasty in 968, and its formal investiture by the Song, over the next eight centuries there was only one Chinese attempt to conquer Vietnam, in 1407–1427. As with Qing–Chosŏn relations, China–Vietnam relations represent an extraordinarily long span of time over which a far larger power did not attempt to renege on its credible commitment not to exploit the smaller. Furthermore, that sole Chinese intervention came at the request of the properly invested Vietnamese leader, who was facing an internal rebellion. The two-decade-long Chinese occupation of Vietnam in the fifteenth century was thus an anomaly in China–Vietnam relations.[86]

It is important to explore this one break in the China–Vietnam relationship in more detail because it presents insights into how the two countries managed their relations. Although China had invested the Trần dynasty (1225–1400) as rulers of Vietnam, that dynasty began to lose control in the 1390s. In 1400, a rebel – Hồ Quý Ly – deposed the Trần ruler, declaring himself the founder of a new dynasty. The Trần royal family sent emissaries to appeal to the Chinese court for help in overthrowing the usurper, and China initially sent troops and an envoy merely to restore a Trần as king. The Chinese party was ambushed and wiped out just over the border. The Yongle Emperor was enraged by the ambush. He noted vehemently,

蕞爾小丑，罪惡滔天，猶敢潛伏奸謀，肆毒如此。朕推誠容納，乃為所欺，此如不誅，兵則何用？ (The guilt of those shameful little wretches reaches up to the sky. [The Annamese Court] have dared to ambush and be traitorous and vicious to this extent. I have seen sincere with them and they have deceived me. If we do not destroy and punish them what are our armies for?).[87]

---

[85] Ben Kiernan, *Viet Nam: A History from Earliest Times to the Present* (Oxford: Oxford University Press, 2017), 146.

[86] John K. Whitmore, "Chiao-Chih and Neo-Confucianism: The Ming Attempt to Transform Vietnam," *Ming Studies*, 1 (1977); and Hok-Iam Chan, "The Chien-wen, Yung-lo, Hung-hsi, and Husan-te reigns, 1399–1435," in Frederick Mote and Denis Twitchett (eds.), *The Cambridge History of China*, vol. 7, *The Ming Dynasty, 1368–1644, Part I* (Cambridge: Cambridge University Press, 1988).

[87] Jung-Pang Lo, "Intervention in Vietnam: A Case Study of the Foreign Policy of the Early Ming Government," *Tsing-hua Journal of Chinese Studies*, 8, no. 1–2 (1979), 173.

To avenge this humiliation, the Chinese sent a punitive force of 215,000 into Vietnam in 1407. This force easily overthrew the usurper.

But the Ming do not appear to have had any idea what to do with Vietnam once Hồ was overthrown. The Trần family was in disarray, so a return to the preceding dynasty seemed unlikely to succeed. Eventually, the Ming decided to reclaim the territory, although clearly that had not been the intention behind the original intervention. Taylor notes that

> Vietnamese historians have unanimously viewed the experiment in Ming rule as a tale of woe with no redeeming features ... However, this was not a story with a pre-ordained narrative. It was initiated and abandoned as a result of decisions made in the Ming court. ... Ming rule had a transforming effect on the development of Vietnamese culture and politics.[88]

Lê Lợi (黎利) – one of Vietnam's greatest heroes – fought an unsuccessful ten-year campaign against the Ming, until he was defeated in 1422 and sued for peace. A few years later, successive Ming emperors decided that holding Vietnam was an unnecessary distraction, preferring to return the relationship to a tributary one under a Vietnamese ruler.[89] Unfortunately, unraveling two decades of Ming bureaucratic administration was not so easily done, and the withdrawal took years, hastened along by the return of Lê Lợi. In 1427, Lê Lợi defeated 100,000 Ming forces at the Chi Lăng pass.[90] Lê Lợi immediately became a tributary of China to ensure peace, telling the Ming "I will be content with my rank of vassal and pay tribute, as has been the custom."[91] In a face-saving move, Ming Emperor Xuande (宣德) wrote that "I am specially sending envoys with a seal and am ordering that Lê Lợi temporarily take charge of the affairs of the country (*guo*) of Annam and govern the people of the country."[92] Taylor writes that "an important matter was to regularize the tributary relationship with Ming. In 1431, the Ming court recognized Lê Lợi as king. Thereafter, relations with Ming were amicable and uneventful."[93]

---

[88] Taylor, *A History of the Vietnamese*, 175.
[89] Taylor, *A History of the Vietnamese*, 183
[90] Khav Vien Nguyen, *Vietnam: A Long History* (Hanoi: The Gioi, 2004), 63.
[91] Kiernan, *Viet Nam*, 197.
[92] Martin Stuart-Fox, *A Short History of China and Southeast Asia: Tribute, Trade and Influence* (Crows Nest: Allen and Unwin, 2003), 90.
[93] Taylor, *A History of the Vietnamese*, 191.

Even if there was not chronic war or endemic conflict between China and Vietnam, if Vietnam were constantly concerned about Chinese military invasion, then there should be ample and extensive discussion in the Vietnamese annals about how to deal with China's military threat and possible military strategies and actions. Similarly, had China wanted to conquer Vietnam but simply lacked the power to do so, we should find Chinese court debates in the following centuries about whether to invade Vietnam, and arguments about the futility of doing so. Yet during both the Ming and Qing dynasties, the sporadic discussion in the Chinese court about Vietnam concerned "normal" events about an accepted political unit, not whether China could conquer Vietnam.

Records of the Vietnamese court's discussions about its relations with China are revealing for their emphasis on emulation, not competition. Evaluating how the subordinate unit – the Vietnamese – viewed their position in the world, and their identity requires exploring how they expressed themselves at that time. As the Vietnamese annals reveal, China was viewed as a source of inspiration or as a country to emulate. Far more than military domination, Vietnam records show an admiration of China.

There is, in fact, almost no record that Vietnam sent costly, repeated signals to China about its resolve and preparations to fight. Vietnam did not invest heavily in fortifications and preparations for conflict with China. Indeed, there exists almost no evidence that the China–Vietnam relationship had a military aspect. Womack notes that "China provided an agenda of 'best practices.' ... it should be emphasized that if China were still an active threat, then Vietnam's political task would have been military cohesion, and its intellectual task would have been one of differentiation from China [not emulation]."[94] Put differently, historical Vietnam assiduously engaged in state formation and in the consolidation of military cohesion because China was *not* perceived as an active and significant threat. Over eight centuries, stability was maintained through diplomatic rather than military means. The centuries of stability between China and Vietnam reflect the legitimacy of the system more than the military balance between the two states.

---

[94] Brantly Womack, *China and Vietnam: The Politics of Asymmetry* (Cambridge: Cambridge University Press, 2006), 132–133.

4.6 The Position of the Military in East Asian States

A key element of state formation and extraction is the ability to field a military. Military expenditure was not a major part of the state budget throughout the Korean Chosŏn era (1392–1910); and there is extensive evidence that for centuries earlier the Korean state had similarly low levels of militarization. This is partially due to conscription, of course. Rosenthal and Wong note that, "War created pressures on regimes of all types to raise taxes in Europe ... there was a millennium of different experiences in the extent of warfare that explains why, in general, taxes were lower in China than in Europe."[95] Phillip Hoffman and Jean-Laurent Rosenthal estimate that European military expenditure in the seventeenth century was a major portion of budgets, consuming anywhere from 70 percent to 90 percent of government revenues.[96] In contrast, the Chinese government often devoted no more than 50 percent of its budget to the military.[97] And in Korea, the share of government expenditure devoted to the military was often far less than even 50 percent of the budget for centuries at a time.

Yet the ability of these historical states to mobilize a military was far beyond the capacity of any European ruler until the eighteenth century. The Koryŏ-era Korean state (918–1392) maintained a standing military of 30,000, mostly stationed as guards in the capital. There were, however, a further 300,000 militia who could be "called up in emergencies to fight the enemy or were mobilized as labor for special projects."[98] And yet the military clearly did not consume a major portion of the state budget. As will be discussed in more detail in Chapter 5, the Chosŏn dynasty experienced an era of unprecedented peacefulness, which led to the gradual reduction of focus on the military over the centuries. Chosŏn Korea had been so peaceful for two centuries that on the eve of the only Japanese invasion of Korea during the entire historical era (Hideyoshi's incursion that resulted in

---

[95] Rosenthal and Wong, *Before and beyond Divergence*, 179.
[96] Phillip T. Hoffman and Jean-Laurent Rosenthal, "The Political Economy of Warfare and Taxation in Early Modern Europe: Historical Lessons for Economic Development," in J. Drobak and J. Nye (eds.), *The Frontiers of the New Institutional Economics* (San Diego: Academic Press, 1997), 31–55.
[97] Rosenthal and Wong, *Before and beyond Divergence*, 182.
[98] James Palais, "Land Tenure in Korea – 10th to 12th Centuries," *Journal of Korean Studies*, 4 (1982), 99.

the Imjin War of 1592–1598), Korea had fewer than 1,000 soldiers in its entire army.[99] Supporting such a small military clearly did not consume much of the state budget.

The Korean state had the capacity to mobilize extraordinary military forces when necessary. During the Imjin War, Korea mobilized up to 84,500 troops along with 22,200 guerilla soldiers.[100] The Japanese had invaded with a force of 281,840 troops, with the initial invading contingent consisting of 158,700 men.[101] By way of contrast, the Spanish Armada of 1588 consisted of 8,000 sailors and 18,000 soldiers. The historical East Asian states had the logistical and organizational capacity to mobilize and deploy at great distances and across water military power that was ten times greater than was conceivable in contemporaneous Europe.

After the Imjin War, rather than sustaining a large military to extract more resources for the state, Korea demobilized its military, and both deployments and expenditure dropped drastically. Eugene Park observes that "the late Chosŏn state maintained an army no bigger than what was dictated by internal security," estimating that the Korean military in the eighteenth century comprised only 10,000 "battle-worthy men."[102]

Rosenthal and Wong note that "Peaceful economies can provide more public goods than war-torn ones ... in China a combination of low taxes and provision of public goods defined good governance ... the long periods of quiet in the Chinese empire enabled rulers and subjects to rely heavily on such strategies."[103]

Korea was the same. The stabilization of the Korean border with Ming China in the fourteenth century, regularization of relations with the Jurchen tribes to its north, and the waning of piracy along its coasts led to a decline in military preparedness. Kenneth Lee writes that on the eve of the Japanese invasion of Korea in 1592, "After two hundred years of peace, Korean forces were untrained in warfare and were

---

[99] Eugene Park, "War and Peace in Historical Korea: Institutional and Ideological Dimensions," in Young-Key Kim-Renaud et al. (eds.), *The Military and South Korean Society* (Washington DC: Sigur Center Asia Papers, 2006).

[100] James Palais, *Confucian Statecraft and Korean Institutions* (Seattle: University of Washington Press, 1996), 82.

[101] Palais, *Confucian Statecraft and Korean Institutions*, 78.

[102] Park, "War and Peace in Historical Korea," 6.

[103] Rosenthal and Wong, *Before and beyond Divergence*, 189–190.

scattered all over the country in small local garrison troops. Koreans were totally unprepared on land."[104]

Furthermore, Korea faced almost no internal dissension over 500 years. As Sun Joo Kim points out: "When more than seventy large- and small-scale popular uprisings broke out one after the other across the Korean peninsula in 1862, the central court of Chosŏn (1392–1910) was caught in great alarm and fear because no such widespread revolts had taken place in the more than 450 years since the dynasty had been founded."[105] In short, no matter what measure is used, historical Korea and China faced far more benign environments than did their European peers.

Each of these states had a sizeable permanent military or a long military tradition. So, if they were not fighting each other, what were these armies doing? They were putting down rebellions, guarding the central government, and maintaining essential systems. In Korea, the units of the army that were the best trained and the most dependable were always in Seoul to protect the palace and the bureaucracy. Each province had at least two major towns with military garrisons and, in the important southern provinces, naval units. The military ran the land and sea transport for grain taxes and other government logistics, and also communication (including the fire towers for overnight links to the capital) and postal facilities, which were almost entirely for official use. Every male commoner was in the reserves up to the age of sixty, and his household had to pay the cloth tax that supported the military.[106] The military handled the routine duties quite well but sadly proved worthless against foreign invasions.

Japan was perhaps an exception. In the shogunal system, military resources were under the separate and individual control of many magnates – the *daimyō* – in addition to the shogun. Mobilizing them was a mere extension of politics (it could be easy, difficult, or risky, depending on the circumstances). But since the participation of the *daimyō* was essential, each of them had a political stake in success, and since this factor provided for a special bond between commander

---

[104] Kenneth Lee, *Korea and East Asia: Story of a Phoenix* (London: Praeger, 1997), 99.

[105] Kim, "Taxes, the Local Elite, and the Rural Populace in the Chinju Uprising of 1862," 993.

[106] Eugene Park, *Between Dreams and Reality: The Military Examination in Late Chosŏn Korea, 1600–1894* (Cambridge, MA: Harvard University Press, 2007).

and troops, military effectiveness could be enhanced. Heroism could be locally recognized, and the rewards would significantly improve one's life opportunities.[107]

4.7 Conclusion

The relative absence of bellicist pressures means that war was neither cause nor effect of state formation. Rather, it was incidental. There was fighting in East Asian history, to be sure. But the essential stability of China, Korea, Japan, and Vietnam over a long span of time is noteworthy. Not only that, but unique elements foundational to East Asian political thought were seminal not only in state formation: The same ideas formed the foundational principles of their relations and interactions with each other.

---

[107] Thanks to Gari Ledyard for these insights.

5 Phase II

State Formation in Korea and Japan, 400–800 CE

Describing and explaining state formation in Korea and Japan is fundamentally about understanding the transformative and enduring impact of Chinese civilization across the East Asian region and across thousands of years.[1] The best way to understand Chinese civilization and its neighbors is as core and periphery – a massive hegemon's influence. Importantly, this was not multipolarity – East Asian state formation was distinctive from the 1,000 "state-like political units" in fourteenth-century Europe and 500 similarly-sized units in sixteenth-century Europe that competed viciously for territory and survival.[2]

State formation was inseparable from, and formed a central element of, wider Sinicization. Sinic civilization was an enduringly powerful force, even as Chinese hegemony waxed and waned over the centuries. Even during times of political division on the Chinese plain, there were regionwide expectations of a return to central, unified rule, and the ideas and institutions that had developed in China remained highly influential across the region.

The impact of Sinic civilization is evident in the states of Korea, Japan, and Vietnam, which emerged over 1,000 years ago as centralized political units, territorial states with internal control that conducted formal, legal international relations with each other, and for whom international recognition as a legitimate nation was an important component of their existence. As John Wills notes, "Chinese hopes that their 'civilizing influence' might spread to foreign peoples ... bore fruit among peoples of the most varied cultural and geographic backgrounds ... these included Korea; Japan and the Ryukyu islands,

---

[1] Parts of this chapter draw from Chin-Hao Huang and David C. Kang, "State Formation in Korea and Japan, 400–800 CE: Emulation and Learning, Not Bellicist Competition," *International Organization*, 76, no. 1 (2022), 1–31.

[2] Tilly, *The Formation of National States in Western Europe*, 15–76.

and the area that become modern Vietnam."[3] This creation of distinct
and enduring political identities was a central aspect to the stability of
the system. Indeed, the states of China, Korea, Japan, and Vietnam are
still recognizable today as roughly the same political units. These states
constituted the inner core of the Chinese-dominated regional system
where Chinese cultural, economic, and political influence was direct
and pervasive.

As Berry points out about early modern Japan, "this is nationalism:
a demonstrable relationship between centralized territorial governance
and collective identity."[4] Similarly, Kären Wigen notes,

Compared to most countries in the late twentieth century ... China, Korea,
and Japan are among the most venerable nations in the world; although their
boundaries have shifted over time, and the style of their imagining has been
continually debated, the notion of nationhood has resonated long and deeply
with the majority of each country's inhabitants ... this sense of region is
quite different from what might be encountered elsewhere in Eurasia or
Africa, where national space is often complicated ... by cross-cutting affili-
ations from a colonial or pre-colonial past.[5]

Korean, Vietnamese, and even Japanese elites consciously copied
Chinese institutional and discursive practices. State formation and
civilization were deeply intertwined in East Asia, the nature of their
relationship reflected in the formal, hierarchic, and institutionalized
manner in which they developed.

In the fifth century, the three Korean kingdoms, Silla, Paekche, and
Koguryŏ, were slowly evolving into states. We focus on Silla (57 BCE–
918 CE), since it unified the peninsula in 668, but all three Korean
states emulated and learned from China extensively and intensively.
The largest and most advanced was Koguryŏ. Weidong Jiang shows
that Koguryŏ had tributary relations with different dynasties of China
that can be traced back to the late Han Dynasty. Jiang writes that
Koguryŏ's "bureaucratic system can be traced back to the influence of
Buyeo's 'Jia' bureaucratic system, as well as the influence of the Han
county-level bureaucracy. Later, the system evolved into a central

[3] John E. Wills Jr., "South and Southeast Asia, Near East, Japan, and Korea," in
Maurizio Scapari (ed.), *The Chinese Civilization from Its Origins to
Contemporary Times*, vol. II (Turin: Grandi Opere Einaudi, in press).
[4] Berry, "Was Early Modern Japan Culturally Integrated?", 559.
[5] Kären Wigen, "Culture, Power, and Place: The New Landscapes of East Asian
Regionalism," *American Historical Review*, 104, no. 4 (1999), 1187.

bureaucratic system."[6] It was the first to import Buddhism and Confucianism: Koguryŏ founded Taehak in 372, an official Confucian academy and the first known center for study of Confucianism in the peninsula. In 373, Koguryŏ promulgated its first Chinese-style law codes.[7]

Paekche was also culturally more advanced than Silla, importing Buddhism and Confucianism at least a century before Silla did. Zhibin Zhao uses Chinese, Korean, and Japanese-language classics to lay out a comprehensive history of Paekche. Zhao concludes that Paekche had a long history of intensive interactions with China from the Han to Tang dynasty and that they actively learned from the Chinese. He notes that emissaries from Paekche "frequently came to pay tribute to Chinese kingdoms as far back as the sixth year of the Tai Kong period [286 BC]."[8] Zhao also points out that there is written evidence that as far back as the Han dynasty, in strengthening the court against the aristocracy, Paekche had "sent envoys to pay tribute to Chang'an [the Han capital] in order to gain recognition from the central heartland dynasty, and to better learn the centralized monarchical system."[9]

Historians call the new, centralized order built in Japan during the fifth to eighth century the *ritsuryo* state, because it was based on Chinese-style penal (*ritsu*) and administrative (*ryo*) codes. Masayoshi Sugimoto and David Swain characterize Japanese borrowing of culture and technology from China in two historical waves: "Chinese Wave I" began circa 600 CE and lasted until 894. They write:

Only twice in Japanese history has it been national policy to undertake an overall transformation of the entire social system according to an imported foreign model ... The first began with the Taika Reforms of AD 646 and continued through the Nara and early Heian eras (seventh–ninth centuries inclusive) when Japan sought to adopt the Chinese model of Tang society. Japan had been assimilating more elementary material forms of continental culture for several centuries, but the Taika transformation was the first effort

[6] Weidong Jiang, *Gao Ju Li Li Shi Bian Nian (The Chronicle of Goguryeo History)*, 1st ed. (Beijing: Ke xue chu ban she, 2016), 505.
[7] Holcombe, *A History of East Asia*, 82.
[8] Zhibin Zhao, *Baiji Li Shi Bian Nian (The Chronicle of Paekche History)*, 1st ed. (Beijing: Ke xue chu ban she, 2016), 14.
[9] Zhao, *Baiji Li Shi Bian Nian*, p. 15.

consciously based on systematic, large-scale importation of high culture directly from China.[10]

The influence of Sinic civilization in Japan was comprehensive, including language, education, writing, poetry, art, mathematics, science, religion, philosophy, social and family structure, political and administrative institutions and ideas, and more. The government-related strands are almost impossible to understand outside this larger civilizational context.

As Shosuke Murai describes it, "Needless to say, China was located at the center of this regional world-system; Japan and surrounding areas, [which] were located on its periphery, can be thought of as forming, or aspiring [to form], a subsystem with a certain degree of autonomy from China."[11] In the first centuries CE, the three Korean kingdoms were still essentially confederations of tribal chieftains, and in Japan the Yamato state was just emerging from Yayoi and Wa chiefdoms. Holcombe observes, it was "roughly in the third century CE when a coherent East Asian cultural region that included China, Japan, and Korea first emerged."[12] As Batten describes it, "Japan, like other regions of East Asia, can be regarded in many periods as a periphery of China. Not only were the two countries part of the same political/military network, but power relations took an unequal, hierarchical form, with China playing the role of core and Japan playing that of periphery."[13]

The peripheral states had their own unique cultures and social organizations. Although Chinese civilization was foundational in Korea and Japan, their societies retained key elements of indigenous cultures. China clearly was not engaged in diffusion by coercion – there was no Chinese pressure on its neighbors to adopt Chinese ideas or institutions. Even some of the most influential ideas – such as Buddhism – were not Chinese inventions but came to Korea and Japan through China. This allowed the surrounding peoples and polities to contest, modify, and adapt Chinese and other imported ideas to their own ends. Some societies closely copied a range of Chinese

---

[10] Masayoshi Sugimoto and David L. Swain, *Science and Culture in Traditional Japan* (Rutland: Charles E. Tuttle Company, 1989), 1.

[11] Murai 1997, 16–17, quoted in Batten, *To the Ends of Japan*, 142.

[12] Holcombe, *A History of East Asia*, 5.

[13] Batten, *To the Ends of Japan*, 228. Woodside, *Lost Modernities*, 25, agrees, calling it an "imperial center."

Table 5.1. *Timeline of Sinicization in historical East Asia, 400–800 CE*

Year	Korea	Japan
413–502		Thirteen tribute missions from Japan to various Chinese dynasties
508	Silla adopts Chinese-style titles	
514	Silla adopts Buddhism	
520	Silla adopts Chinese-style bureaucratic government, administrative law, legal codes, and seventeen official titles	
552		Buddhism introduced to Japan from Korea
570	National conscript military introduced	
604		"Seventeen Injunctions" promulgated, based on Chinese rituals and regulations
607–894		At least twenty Japanese embassies sent to China
620		Yamato adopts Chinese calendar
645		*Taika* Reforms based on Chinese administrative and legal codes
649	Silla adopts Chinese calendar	

practices, which were deemed highly prestigious. Others experimented with just some Chinese ideas, while some societies – such as the diverse semi-nomadic peoples of the northern and western frontiers – resisted almost all cultural and political ideas, but still interacted with China, occasionally using Chinese practices and ideas in their foreign relations.

Table 5.1 summarizes key events in the importation, emulation, and learning of Chinese ideas and institutions into and within Korea and Japan between 400 and 800 CE. State formation – such as taxes,

Table 5.1. (*cont.*)

Year	Korea	Japan
661	Korean capital of Kyongju remodeled to imitate Tang capital Chang'an	
663	Silla–Tang alliance defeats Paekche–Yamato forces in the only war involving any two of China, Korea, and Japan in over twelve centuries.	
668	Silla–Tang defeat Koguryŏ, leaving Silla as sole Korean kingdom	
670		Introduction of national tax, division of country into provinces, census decreed every six years
671		National Confucian Academy founded; attempt to create civil service exams
681	Division of country into nine provinces	
682	Royal Confucian Academy founded	
685		Centralized conscript military introduced
694		Japanese capital at Fujiwara-kyō built as a copy of Tang capital Chang'an
702		*Taiho* Code uses Tang model for administration and law
788	Civil service examination created	

meritocratic bureaucracies, and the military – was a key element of broader Sinicization and is inseparable from that larger Chinese civilizational influence. What is most obvious is the slow, gradual, and uneven transformation of these countries. As discussed in this chapter, Chinese civilization, Buddhism, and Confucianism were used for legitimacy and prestige within a domestic context, yet those elements of state formation were only effective within a larger intellectual, philo-sophical, and religious environment in which those ideas were not only valued and desired but were considered almost "inevitable."

Key events in the Sinicization of Korea and Japan began with the importation of Buddhism into Korea in the early fourth century, and the numerous Japanese tribute missions that traveled to China during the fifth century – most importantly, these both brought with them Chinese language and writing systems. Over the next century, the Korean kingdom of Silla adopted Buddhism and by the sixth century had begun to use Chinese-style titles and administrative codes for its government. In the sixth century, monks and kings from the Korean kingdom of Paekche introduced Buddhism to Japan, where it quickly became influential. In the seventh century, both Korea and Japan began to use the Chinese calendar and timekeeping to provide far more precise organization of state activities; and both increasingly used Chinese-style administrative and legal codes and engaged in national taxation. Both created national conscript armies, founded national Confucian academies to train bureaucrats, and implemented civil ser-vice examinations to select officials on the basis of merit, not heredity. The key institutional innovation in East Asia was the emergence of the world's first civil services. The transformation over these few centuries was remarkable: By the end of the eighth century, both Korea and Japan were recognizably Sinicized across government, religion, phil-osophy, and society.

5.1 Korean and Japanese Emulation during Phase II

By the eighth century, both Korea and Japan were centralized, bureau-cratically administered states defined over territory with a monopoly of violence within their borders. They arrived at this primarily through a process of emulation, but learning and competition were also factors. Recall that emulation reflects a similar process to learning but focuses more on how actors aspire to and copy from others that they respect or admire. Put simply, emulation reflects aspirations while learning is rooted primarily in cost–benefit calculations. As discussed in Chapter 2, we use three main ways to further distinguish between emulation and learning: Whether the overall scale of borrowing was total or selective; whether justification was based on the logic of consequences or of appropriateness; and, for each individual issue, whether there was mimicry or modification. In theory, emulation, learning, and competition could all coexist as causal factors, and indeed, we can find traces of each mechanism of diffusion in historical East Asia. But emulation seems to be the main determinant involved at the time as shown by the empirical evidence on state-building in historical East Asia outlined next.

5.1.1 The Overall Extent of Sinicization in Korea and Japan

The overall scale of borrowing can provide clues to distinguish emulation from learning. If the extent of copying is total, it implies more emulation than if only selective ideas are copied. In Korea and Japan, the extent of borrowing was essentially total and comprehensive.

Key elements of the state-building were Buddhism, Confucianism, and the Chinese language and writing system, which fundamentally transformed religion, philosophy, government, society, and political life in both Korea and Japan. Batten sums it up: "China, Korea, and Japan all share a common cultural heritage centered on Buddhism, Confucianism, and the use of the Chinese writing system."[14] Martin Lewis and Kären Wigen emphasize that the "distinctive" Chinese writing system "became the crucial vehicle for spreading Chinese notions of philosophy, cosmology, and statecraft to the neighboring peoples of Korea, Japan, and Vietnam."[15]

There was clearly a degree of learning, in that the body of Chinese knowledge in sciences, mathematics, architecture, and calendar was developed far beyond anything in Korea and Japan. Chinese learning was so advanced that being conversant with it was prestigious and impressive to Korean and Japanese elites. However, much of it was true emulation, as the following examples show.

During the fourth to sixth centuries, the "Korean states regularly sent tribute missions to the states in China ... in exchange, Korean rulers received symbols that strengthened their own legitimacy and a variety of cultural commodities: Ritual goods, books, Buddhist scriptures, and rare luxury products."[16] By 503, the Silla dynasty had adopted Chinese titles such as "king" and abandoned native Korean

---

[14] Batten, *To the Ends of Japan*, 66.
[15] Martin W. Lewis and Kären E. Wigen, *The Myth of Continents: A Critique of Metageography* (Berkeley: University of California Press, 1997), 144.
[16] Seth, *A Concise History of Korea*, 45.

titles. Ebrey and Walthall note that "Silla kings took steps to institu-tionalize their governments ... they made Buddhism the state-sponsored religion, and collected taxes on agriculture."[17] They also note that "The newly created board of academicians had specialists in medicine, law, mathematics, astronomy, and water clocks."[18] All of this was indicative of emulation and nearly wholesale adoption from China.

Japan in this first wave of Chinese influence was comprehensively importing Tang-style institutions, language and writing systems, and education, including Confucianism, Buddhism, Daoism, geomancy and divination, law, literature, history, mathematics, calendrics, and medicine, not to mention art and architecture. Indeed, all three Japanese writing systems – *hiragana*, *katakana*, and *kanji* – were derived from Chinese characters. As de Bary et al. put it,

The Yamato court adopted many features of the superior Chinese civilization ... included a reorganization of court ranks and etiquette in accordance with Chinese models, the adoption of the Chinese calendar, the opening of formal diplomatic relations with China, the creation of a system of highways, the erection of many Buddhist temples, and the compilation of official chronicles.[19]

By the time of the classical Japanese state (710–1185), rank and title "derived from courtly practice," and space was "ordered by classical system of provinces, districts, and highways."[20] Even though the phys-ical presence of China and Chinese were rare, Berry points out, "in one sense, China saturated Japan: its written language, polity, religions, material and high culture inflected all aspects of the classical Japanese state."[21]

Pointing out that the Chinese influence in early Japan is "quite conspicuous," de Bary et al. note that, in place of the old political clan organization, the Yamato court intended "systematic territorial admin-istration of the Chinese [model,] executing a uniform law."[22] But a

---

[17] Ebrey and Walthall, *Pre-Modern East Asia*, 104.
[18] Ebrey and Walthall, *Pre-Modern East Asia*, 106.
[19] William Theodore De Bary, Donald Keene, George Tanabe, and Paul Valery, *Sources of Japanese Tradition: From Earliest Times to 1600* (New York: Columbia University Press, 2002), 40–41.
[20] Berry, "Was Early Modern Japan Culturally Integrated?," 553.
[21] Berry, "Was Early Modern Japan Culturally Integrated?," 554.
[22] De Bary et al., *Sources of Japanese Tradition*, 63.

vast symmetric bureaucracy based on Tang China required sweeping changes that cascaded through different aspects of society – such as the economy, trade, taxation, and land rights and policies – that were all linked to state capacity and governance. According to de Bary et al., "Implicit in the erection of this state machinery was the need for economic changes ... this was a vast system of coordinated knowledge and belief of which the Chinese imperial structure was indeed the most imposing terrestrial symbol but that stretched out into realms of thought and action both transcending and penetrating the immediate political order."[23] For example, "the Tang tax system was indispensable to the functioning of the Tang-type administration. The Tang tax system, moreover, presupposed a system of land nationalization and redistribution."[24]

In the seventh and eighth centuries, Sinicization became more institutionalized in Japan, particularly through a series of major governmental reforms: The *Taika* Reforms of 645, the *Taiho* Code of 702, and the *Yoro* Code compiled in 718 and subsequently promulgated in 757. Sugimoto and Swain note that all three reforms "had [their] roots in China's Han dynasty."[25] *Taika* Reforms literally means "Great Change." This was a sweeping set of reforms aimed at deepening and widening the Tang-style institutions across the Japanese state. More broadly, Sugimoto and Swain observe that "the pervasive influence of Tang culture in Chinese Wave I [(*c.* 600–894)] is uniquely exemplified in the collection of handicraft specimens ... from Emperor Shomu (724–749) ... the items cover a wide range: Furniture, stationery, games, liturgical implements, musical instruments, armor and weapons, ceramics, wood and metal work, weaving, dyeing and embroidery, and so on."[26]

In sum, "This was an era when Korea and Japan turned to China as a model for everything from architecture to ceramics, music, and medicine."[27] The scale of borrowing in both Korea and Japan was so comprehensive as to imply emulation based on an aspiration to be like China, rather than a deliberate selective learning where individual traits were consciously selected and copied.

---

[23] De Bary et al., *Sources of Japanese Tradition*, 64.
[24] De Bary et al., *Sources of Japanese Tradition*, 64.
[25] Sugimoto and Swain, *Science and Culture in Traditional Japan*, 12.
[26] Sugimoto and Swain, *Science and Culture in Traditional Japan*, 27.
[27] Ebrey and Walthall, *Pre-Modern East Asia*, 93.

5.1.2 Confucianism as a Governance Model

The evidence for emulation is reinforced by examining the justifications made at the time. Overwhelmingly, the motivations were based on a logic of appropriateness, not consequences. An example of the influence of Chinese civilization on Korea comes from King Chinhŭng of Silla (r. 540–576). In 568, he installed a monument at Maun Pass, and the inscription is replete with Confucian ideas. Ideas such as the Way (or "*dao*") are woven into the justification for the King's reign. The inscription reads in part: "Emperors and kings established their reign titles, cultivated themselves to the utmost, and brought peace to their subjects ... I was fearful of going against the Way of Heaven ... The people now say 'the transforming process of the Way extends outward and its favor pervades everywhere.'"[28]

In Japan, the fifth and sixth centuries saw the gradual importation and implementation of Chinese ideas. For example, Prince Shōtoku (573–621) wrote a seventeen-article constitution in 602, suffused with Chinese ideas on appropriate social and political structures. Article I reflects the Confucian ideal that social harmony is a paramount goal: "Harmony is to be valued." Article III embodies the Confucian ideal of government: "The lord is Heaven; the vassal, Earth. Heaven overspreads, Earth upbears. When this is so, the four seasons follow their due course, and the powers of Nature develop their efficiency." Article IV refers to the Confucian emphasis on the responsibility of the ruler to embody virtue and moral rule for his subjects: "If the superiors do not behave with decorum, the inferiors are disorderly." Article VII draws on the Confucian ideal of a "wise man" or "Sage" who is fundamental to harmony: "when wise men are entrusted with office, the sound of praise arises. If unprincipled men hold office, disasters and tumults multiply." Finally, Articles XII and XVI are explicit expansions of the central authority of the court to tax and govern the entire country. Article XII reads: "Let not the provincial authorities or the local nobles levy exaction on the people. In a country there are not two lords; the people have not two masters. The sovereign is the master of the people

---

[28] King Chinhung's Monument at Maun Pass, from *Samguk Yusa* Appendix 14, from Lee and de Bary, *Sources of Korean Tradition*, 19.

of the whole country," while Article XVI reads: "Let the people be employed in forced labor at seasonable times."[29]

In 712, the authors of the oldest surviving Japanese history, *Kojiki* (Record of Ancient Matters), explicitly based their writing, their phrases, and their ideas on the social norms represented in Chinese models. *Kojiki* was composed using Chinese characters and is replete with Chinese ideas, writing style, references, and imagery.[30] The aspiration to emulate and conform to a more sophisticated style and complex form of writing in Chinese was clear. Its introduction states that "in high antiquity [of early Japan], both speech and thought were so simple that it would be difficult to arrange phrases and compose periods in the characters" – that is, Chinese ideographic writing.[31] Another early history, the *Nihon Shoki* (Chronicles of Japan) of 720, was based on Chinese histories, aimed at legitimizing and cementing political power. De Bary et al. have a detailed exegesis of the *Nihon Shoki* and the *Kojiki*, showing that they are suffused with Chinese thought, forms, and expressions in phrase after phrase, and how writing and ideas are copied verbatim from Chinese models. Both histories begin with invocations of Chinese Confucian ideology as represented in the principle of yin–yang. For instance, the *Kojiki* begins, "Heaven and Earth first parted, and the Three Deities performed the commencement of creation; the yin and the yang then developed," while the *Nihon Shoki* begins, "Of old, Heaven and Earth were not yet separated, and the yin and the yang not yet divided."[32] The *Nihon Shoki* declares "let the swords and armor, with the bows and arrows of the provinces and districts, be deposited together ... let all the weapons be mustered together ... let the officials who are sent there prepare registers of the population and also take into account the acreage of cultivated land."[33]

The appeals to Confucianism continued: In 757, for example, Empress Koken (r. 749–758) proclaimed, "To secure the rulers and

[29] "The 17-article Constitution of Prince Shotoku," in *Nihongi* II, 128–133, from de Bary et al., *Sources of Japanese Tradition*, 53–54.
[30] Holcombe, *A History of East Asia*, 21.
[31] De Bary et al., *Sources of Japanese Tradition*, 73–75.
[32] *Kojiki*, 4, and *Nihongi* I, 1–2, in de Bary et al., *Sources of Japanese Tradition*, 67.
[33] "Inauguration of the Great Reform Era," in *Nihongi* II, 200–226, from de Bary et al., *Sources of Japanese Tradition*, 78.

govern the people, nothing is better than the Confucian rites."[34] The justifications and debates in the historical record in both Korea and Japan lead to the clear conclusion that elites in both these countries desired and aspired to conform to Chinese traits simply because they were seen as more appropriate – that is, for reasons of emulation, rather than learning.

5.1.3 Systematic Mimicry in State-Building

When external ideas conflicted with internal or local identities, it was generally internal identities that changed. This applied systematically across the various aspects of state-building in Korea and Japan, from administration, taxation, and the civil service, via education and deep into culture and society: Architecture, writing, and even clothing style.

Under King Pŏphŭng (r. 514–540), Silla adopted Buddhism, and his reign also saw the first promulgation of Chinese-style bureaucratic government and administrative law. Issued in 520, the new laws included a seventeen-grade official rank system, and names and titles, based on Chinese models.[35] In 517, Pŏphŭng established a Ministry of War, which was part of the process of centralizing the military under court control.[36] Within a few decades, by the 570s, Silla was "replacing military lords with commissioners dispatched from the capital."[37]

King Sinmun (r. 681–692) reorganized the entire country into nine prefectures and five subsidiary capitals. Sinmun also further reformed the national military, creating a system of nine banners and ten garrisons deployed across the country. Taxation became national and uniform. Woodside notes that "tax rates could be treated by the mandarinates as contingent categories, subject to change from above, in societies that, unlike much of Europe before 1789, did not have provinces, nobles, or clergy with ... tax immunities."[38] Duncan explains the significance behind these reforms on state administration in that "The model Silla used was the Chinese prefecture–county

[34] Holcombe, *A History of East Asia*, 117.
[35] Seth, *A Concise History of Korea*, 40.
[36] "Popkon Declares Buddhism the National Faith," in *Haedong kosung chon*, 1A:1018c–1019b, from Lee and de Bary, *Sources of Korean Tradition*, 41.
[37] Ebrey and Walthall, *Pre-Modern East Asia*, 104.
[38] Woodside, *Lost Modernities*, 60.

system, which featured a regular hierarchy of administration ... in the mid-eighth century ... King Kyongdok (r. 742–765) carried out a major reorganization of local administration, apparently to make the Silla system conform more closely to the Chinese model."[39]

In Japan, the *Taika* Reforms of 645 greatly strengthened the state against nobles and the people themselves. The court appointed provincial governors and abolished previous land ownership. It started a population census, a centralized tax system, a legal code, and a civil service examination, all based on Tang models. The reforms instituted the use of Chinese-style era names. In 685, the court created a conscript army based on Chinese models.[40] As De Bary et al. describe it, "By their assertion of the imperial right to universal labor and military service, reformers went far toward achieving for the ruling house the control over all the elements of power characteristic of the greatest Chinese dynasties."[41]

The *Taiho* Code of 702 was a further centralization of state authority based on Chinese models. The Nara state (710–784) "received its clearest expression in a series of Chinese-style penal and administrative law codes."[42] Almost half of the drafters of the *Taiho* Code came from immigrant families that had come from China or Korea, and others had participated in Japanese embassies to the continent. These legal and administrative codes remained the basic law of Japan for over eleven centuries, being used into the Meiji Restoration of 1868.

Central to the *Taiho* Code were Chinese geomancy and ideas about political philosophy. So influential were Chinese ideas that a Department of Yin–Yang had been established in 675 to guide the government, and details of the department are provided in the *Taiho* Code. Yin–yang – as emblematic of the philosophies of Daoism, Confucianism, and Buddhism as well as the ideas of feng shui – affected everyday life as well as consequential decisions about statecraft.

Regarding national taxation in Japan, de Bary et al. note that

it was recognized from the first that the Tang tax system was indispensable to the functioning of the Tang-type administration. The Tang system,

---

[39] Duncan, *The Origins of the Chosŏn Dynasty*, 30.
[40] Ebrey and Walthall, *Pre-Modern East Asia*, 120.
[41] De Bary et al., *Sources of Japanese Tradition*, 64.
[42] Holcombe, *A History of East Asia*, 117.

moreover, presupposed a system of land nationalization and redistribution ... so meticulously was the Chinese example followed that land and tax registers for those period ... are almost identical in form and terminology to contemporary Chinese registers.[43]

Batten notes that "Large-scale conversion of domains began only in the late 660s ... it seems fair to conclude that the confiscation of some groups and private landholdings was actually planned and executed in 644–646."[44] The *Yoro* Code, which was modeled after the Tang civil and penal codes and promulgated in 757, furthered strengthened the national tax system. "Archeological research strongly supports the view that the Nara-period tax system functioned not only on paper but also in practice."[45]

Fundamental to running a Chinese-style government were scholar-officials who were educated along Chinese lines. In 682, Silla established a National Academy (also known as the Royal Confucian Academy), where a small number of young Koreans were instructed in a Chinese-style curriculum that included the Confucian Classics and Chinese (not Korean) history and literature. Belonging to the Board of Rites, the academy was called Taehakkam.[46] In 788, Silla inaugurated its first Chinese-style civil service examinations, graduating students into three ranks.

Along similar lines, Japan established a Confucian Academy at Nara, most likely in 671, with instruction in the Confucian classics, calligraphy, law, mathematics, and Chinese language. A network of schools extending to every province was ordered to be opened. In addition, as Sugimoto and Swain note, "three different kinds of institutes were founded in the *ritsuryo* system to propagate and utilize learning and science ... a university, an institution of divination, and an institute of medicine ... these institutes were all patterned after Tang models."[47]

Beyond mimicry in state administration, the physical construct of the capital cities in both Korea and Japan were also exact copies of the Chinese capital. Ebrey and Walthall note that "the Silla capital at

[43] De Bary et al., *Sources of Japanese Tradition*, 64.
[44] Batten, "Foreign Threat and Domestic Reform," 204–206.
[45] Batten, *To the Ends of Japan*, 165.
[46] *Samguk sagi*, 38: 366, from Lee and de Bary, *Sources of Korean Tradition*, 65.
[47] Sugimoto and Swain, *Science and Culture in Traditional Japan*, 32.

Kyongju was laid out in checkerboard fashion like the Tang capital at Chang'an."[48] Duncan points out that "The model Silla used was the Chinese prefecture–county system, which featured a regular hierarchy of administration ... in the mid-eighth century ... King Kyongdok (r. 742–765) carried out a major reorganization of local administration, apparently to make the Silla system conform more closely to the Chinese model."[49] In Japan, both Kyoto and Nara were also built to directly copy Chang'an, following yin–yang theories. The modeling of Nara after the Chinese capital was more than simply copying of a nice design. Chang'an – and Nara – were designed to be a "spatial dramatization of the *ritsuryo* geomantic order, court power, and theocratic authority."[50] The central boulevard of Nara "divided the city into symmetrical halves just as the Chinese-style bureaucratic structure balanced the minister of the left with the minister of the right ... in line with Chinese models."[51]

Similarly, Kyoto's layout was not accidental but methodically modeled after and planned with Chinese architectural ideas in mind. The palace, situated in the north in accordance with yin–yang, was surrounded by ninefold walls. The emperor was served by a bureaucracy organized into nine departments of state, with eight ranks of officials. A Buddhist monastery was built to protect the capital from baleful influences from the northeast, the unlucky quarter.[52] Kyoto itself was chosen because it had an auspicious number of mountains and rivers, based on feng shui.

Further evidence of emulation in Korea's and Japan's state-building could be seen in their culture, language, and clothing. The importation of Chinese writing and literary forms was so dominant that only fifty poems written in vernacular Korean survive from the entire period prior to the fifteenth century, "compared to thousands of Korean documents written in Chinese" from the same time.[53] Holcombe notes that "Chinese script, and even Chinese language itself, long remained the most prestigious vehicle for serious writing in Japan ... the intellectual primacy of Chinese writing in Japan would not be fatally

---

[48] Ebrey and Walthall, *Pre-Modern East Asia*, 106.
[49] Duncan, *The Origins of the Chosŏn Dynasty*, 30.
[50] Walker, *A Concise History of Japan*, 30.
[51] Ebrey and Walthall, *Pre-Modern East Asia*, 121.
[52] De Bary et al., *Sources of Japanese Tradition*, 70.
[53] Holcombe, *A History of East Asia*, 22.

challenged until modern times."[54] As Sugimoto and Swain point out, "the cultural gap that had to be bridged to introduce new knowledge from China for the reshaping of Japan was overwhelming. The Japanese had not even developed their own system of writing, yet they wanted to import the highest levels of Chinese learning and science, along with Sinicized Buddhist teaching."[55] De Bary et al. observe that "Outright imitations of Chinese thought and literature can be found in the *Kaifuso*, a collection of poetry written in Chinese dating from 751 CE."[56]

Even clothing in both Korea and Japan was copied identically from the Chinese. In 604, the Japanese Yamato court instituted cap-ranks in twelve grades – a direct copy of Chinese customs and specifically identical to the Sui dynasty, which distinguish rank by the form and materials of the official cap. Purple was for officials of the fifth rank and upward, with other colors for the lower ranks. Princes and ministers wore the highest rank.[57]

In Korea in the seventh century, a Buddhist monk, Chajang, spent seven years studying in China. Upon his return to Korea, he persuaded Queen Chindŏk (r. 647–654) to change court dress to Chinese style. The *Samguk yusa* (Tales of the Three Kingdoms, written in the thirteenth century) records that "In the third year [649], the caps and gowns of the Chinese court were first worn. The following year [650], the court adopted the Chinese calendar and for the first time used the Tang reign title of Yung-hui."[58]

Although it may seem that choice of clothing was tangential or unimportant to those who emphasize the bellicist thesis, choice and color of clothing was a central element of state formation. Remco Breuker studies the symbolism in Korean rituals that is represented through clothing and concludes that the choice of clothing is not just a matter of pragmatism or opportunism.[59] Breuker explains clothing's significance, where

---

[54] Holcombe, *A History of East Asia*, 22.
[55] Sugimoto and Swain, *Science and Culture in Traditional Japan*, 29.
[56] De Bary et al., *Sources of Japanese Tradition*, 68.
[57] De Bary et al., *Sources of Japanese Tradition*, 48.
[58] *Samgunk Yusa*, 4:191–194, from Lee and de Bary, *Sources of Korean Tradition*, 48.
[59] Remco Breuker, "Koryŏ as an Independent Realm: The Emperor's Clothes?," *Korean Studies*, 27 (2003).

In traditional East Asia, only the Son of Heaven was entitled to wear imperial yellow ... the [Koryŏ] Ministry of Rites, responding to an inquiry by the monarch if it would be possible for him to wear colors other than yellow and red, compiled the relevant passages of Chinese works and reported its answer back to the monarch ... the emperor's clothes hold valuable clues as to how [Koryŏ] rulers perceived themselves, not only in terms of fashion, but, more importantly, in terms of status, position, culture, and ontology ... the clothes of the [Koryŏ] ruler were intimately tied to his ritual functions. His clothes not only denoted his status as a ruler, but also his position in the human link between Heaven and the people.[60]

The choice of court dress, and even colors for ranks of the civil service, is state formation at its most elemental level but also importantly obvious: A pure mimicry of the Chinese model. These conscious choices and deliberate practices in state formation were part and parcel of wider emulation.

Holcombe further emphasizes the transformation of Japanese society along Chinese lines:

The Japanese imperial bureaucracy that was structured by these codes included a state council, eight ministries, forty-six bureaus. A comprehensive administrative hierarchy of provinces, districts, and villages was established throughout the empire. Household registration began in 670 as the basis for government-directed farmland allocation, tax collection, and military conscription. A new census was intended to be conducted every six years, and rice paddies were reallocated after each census, roughly along the lines of the Equal Fields system still in effect in China.[61]

Sugawara Michizane (845–903) wrote a poem, "Ten quatrains on *jinshi*" in the *Nihon Shoki* (volume 17). He was awarded the title roughly equivalent to "doctorate of literature" (文章博士), achieved fifth rank in the court's Ministry of Personnel, and served on an embassy to Tang China. In the eighth century, Sugawara Atsushige wrote a poem when he passed the exam: "Recalling the hard days of preparing for the exam, I feel the present happiness is greater than any other happiness; having passed the imperial exam, I feel my present standpoint is higher than any others."[62] There were debates about merit and fairness, just as there were across the region. In 827, a court

[60] Breuker, 52–53.   [61] Holcombe, *A History of East Asia*, 117.
[62] Haifeng Liu, "Influence of China's Imperial Examinations on Japan, Korea, and Vietnam," *Frontiers in the History of China*, 2, no. 4 (2007), 494.

official wrote a memorial to the throne, stating that "The university is a place of learning and the home of intellectuals who are not all born with noble blood. Moreover, in order to select talents for the court government, capacity of the candidates should be valued above all."[63]

Other aspects of Japanese society reflected further influence of Chinese civilization. With regard to medicinal development, Sugimoto and Swain report that "The first compilation of Chinese medical sources by a Japanese appeared in the ninth century ... the Japanese appropriation of Chinese medicine was designed to include all levels of medical theory and practice."[64] Even Shinto was not a purely Japanese religion. As de Bary et al. point out, "Strictly speaking, Shinto is not a purely indigenous religion, for it shares continental features and absorbed foreign elements from its earliest times."[65]

The scale of the Japanese emulation of China, and the scale of the state bureaucracy that Japan developed, dwarfed anything conceivable in contemporaneous Europe. "During the greater part of Chinese Wave I [(*c.* 600–894)] ... most important of these was the cultivation of a corps of trained personnel to staff the administrative organs through an official network of academic institutions for teaching and utilizing Chinese-style sciences and learning."[66] Batten observes that "Japan in the eighth century was already a state society with relatively efficient, centralized mechanisms for gathering information, formulating political decisions, and carrying them out."[67] As noted in Chapter 1, more than 7,000 men staffed the Japanese bureaucracy by the eighth century.[68] This dwarfs the level of development achieved in Europe 500 years later: Even by the thirteenth century, the Curia contained only 1,000 officials and could not compare to what had been achieved a half millennium earlier in East Asia.

In short, the overall scale of borrowing – as demonstrated by the breadth and depth of the previous examples – the justifications given for borrowing, and the level of mimicry lead us to conclude that borrowing was more emulation than learning in both Korea and

---

[63] Liu, "Influence of China's Imperial Examinations on Japan, Korea, and Vietnam," 495.

[64] Sugimoto and Swain, *Science and Culture in Traditional Japan*, 88.

[65] De Bary et al., *Sources of Japanese Tradition*, 17.

[66] Sugimoto and Swain, *Science and Culture in Traditional Japan*, 13.

[67] Batten, *To the Ends of Japan*, 242.

[68] Ebrey and Walthall, *Pre-Modern East Asia*, 121.

Japan. Both were undergoing profound social identity change – across the country, within elites, and even in family organization and practices down to the individual level. While retaining elements of their indigenous cultures, both began to overwhelmingly see themselves as members of a regional Sinic civilization in which China sat at the core. However, our conclusions go beyond characterizing the difference as a simple emulation–learning dichotomy. Adjudicating which motivation drove the diffusion process for state formation cannot be resolved easily, not least in an "either/or" approach. The evidence shows instead that these diffusion mechanisms occurred at different times and contexts, and that emulation – premised on the fundamental acceptance of Sinic influence – played a more significant role in Korea's and Japan's early state formation than hitherto appreciated. This conclusion is not a hunch but instead derives directly from the historical empirical evidence.

5.2 Domestic Politics: Prestige and Legitimacy against a Noble Class

To further the probative argument for emulation, we consider the central role of domestic politics in state formation. Specifically, why did Korean and Japanese elites borrow Chinese ideas so willingly in their state-building activities?

Simply put, Korean and Japanese elites borrowed Chinese ideas for both reasons of domestic legitimacy and prestige. The court needed to justify its assumption of power at the expense of the provinces and their nobles. One of the defining features of East Asian societies that was different from Europe was the general eradication, or weakness, of the noble class. Ji-Young Lee notes that "there were at least three political groups to consider in Korea and Japan: rulers (kings or shoguns in Korea or Japan, respectively), political opponents and supporters of rulers (ministers, cousins of kings, royal family members), and subjects."[69] Domestic political rivalries and internal security concerns motivated state centralization, and, in turn, the strategic adoption of institutions that would elevate their status and influence. This process is an extension of our argument centered on

[69] Lee, *China's Hegemony*, 70.

domestic legitimation; we briefly outline in this section how it worked in Korea and Japan.

The intra-polity competition between the court and the nobility did occur, of course. As a core dynamic of this rivalry, the court strategically imported Sinic norms and cultural practices primarily as an instrument to tame the nobility and thus consolidate its power. Obviously, the cultural norms and practices that elites imported were not merely resources used to boost legitimacy, but were deeply constitutive, and reconstitutive, of both court and noble identities over the longer term. Domestic political competition could only occur within the larger acceptance of, and value for, Sinic civilization. Acharya argues that diffusion is more likely when the new idea works within an accepted identity, while Goddard observes that "whether an actor's claim is legitimate depends on whether it resonates with existing social and cultural networks."[70]

Over the centuries, China, Korea, and Japan to varying degrees eliminated or reduced the influence of their noble classes. In China, the Sui dynasty (581–618 CE) replaced the distinction between aristocrat and commoner with the distinction between officials and ordinary subjects. In Korea and Japan, while the nobility survived up until the twentieth century, the aspirations of nobles and their use of power were channeled through the institutions of the state, not against it. Thus, nobles in Korea competed for scholar-official positions in the state itself; and passing the civil service exam and becoming a government official became one of the most prestigious achievements one could aspire to in historical East Asia. "The Chinese bureaucratic model, with its ideal of possible upward mobility based on demonstrated merit (and service to the throne) rather than hereditary, may have been useful in supporting the interests of the Korean kings."[71]

Status as a tributary of China was a powerful indicator of authority. As Ji-Young Lee and Zhang point out, the authority of investiture – the Chinese court's bestowing of reign titles on Korean and Japanese rulers – only mattered to other domestic actors who already viewed Chinese civilization as legitimate.[72] Holcombe observes that "The

---

[70] Acharya, "How Ideas Spread," 248; and Goddard, *Indivisible Territory and the Politics of Legitimacy*, 24.
[71] Holcombe, *A History of East Asia*, 113.
[72] Lee, *China's Hegemony*; and Zhang, *Chinese Hegemony*.

delegation of status from a Chinese sovereign gave Korean kings some leverage against the otherwise powerful Korean aristocracy."[73] Adopting Chinese statecraft thus enabled the Korean and Japanese rulers to "strengthen their own positions vis-à-vis the deeply entrenched nobility."[74] Moreover, beyond weakening the deeply entrenched nobility in society, Seth notes that "Chinese models ... appealed to the elites as forms of cultural enrichment."[75] Indeed, Holcombe observes that, "newly emergent East Asian rulers in Manchuria, Korea, and Japan all, at various times, tried to buttress their positions against possible rivals by offering tribute to Chinese dynasties and being invested in return with prestigious Chinese titles."[76]

To consolidate power, kings often adopted foreign religion and introduced it to further delimit the noble's influence. In Korea, Kyung Moon Hwang notes that "political rulers found Buddhism, in particular the Buddhist clergy, a useful ally in further consolidating their dominion and in strengthening their aura of authority."[77] Similarly, Ebrey and Walthall observe that

> Between 592 and 756, the Yamato kings and queens transformed themselves into Chinese-style monarchs ... they saw the need to overcome violent factional and succession disputes that weakened ties between center and periphery ... they reorganized the court by instituting a ladder of twelve official ranks bestowed on individuals to correspond to Sui practice ... in the Seventeen Injunctions promulgated in 604, Prince Shotoku announced a new ideology of rule based on Confucian and Buddhist thought ... drawing on Chinese rituals and regulations.[78]

De Bary et al. also note that Japan attempted to

> enhance its power and prestige in the eyes of foreigners and domestic rivals alike by adopting many features of the superior Chinese civilization and especially its political institutions. The measures included a reorganization of court ranks and etiquette in accordance with Chinese models, the

---

[73] Holcombe, *A History of East Asia*, 113.
[74] Ebrey and Walthall, *Pre-Modern East Asia*, 107.
[75] Seth, *A Concise History of Korea*, 36.
[76] Holcombe, *A History of East Asia*, 87.   [77] Hwang, *A History of Korea*, 13.
[78] Ebrey and Walthall, *Pre-Modern East Asia*, 118–119.

adoption of the Chinese calendar, the opening of diplomatic relations with China, the creation of a system of highways, the erection of many Buddhist temples, and the compilation of official chronicles.[79]

Ebrey and Walthall observe that "The Yamato court attracted followers through its access to Chinese elite culture, including a written language, Daoism, Confucianism, the literary arts, sculpture (particularly Buddhist icons), painting, and music ... Pilgrims to China brought back masses of Buddhist sutras and Chinese books."[80] They also note that "In addition to religion and political ideology, contact with the continent brought a written language with which to transcribe the poetry and history that had previously been transmitted orally. It brought music, dance, and new standards of civilized behavior. The ruling class that enjoyed these advantages taxed the farmers."[81] De Bary et al. reflect the historiographic consensus when they write that "As the Yamato people consolidated their position in central Japan and their rulers attempted to win undisputed supremacy over other clans of the confederacy, it was to the Chinese example that they turned more and more for political guidance and cultural direction."[82]

The promulgation of administrative statues and law codes had long-lasting effects. "Even chieftains who still lived in the provinces competed for official appointments and titles. County, district, and provincial offices and temples spread across the landscape."[83] Batten notes that "most of Japan's formal contacts with China, at least, were initiated by Japanese rulers in search of specific goals such as political legitimacy, security, or access to luxury goods."

5.3 Conclusion

From religion to the daily practices at the individual level, the historical evidence shows that the polities in Korea and Japan overwhelmingly saw themselves as members of a regional Sinic civilization in which

---

[79] De Bary et al., *Sources of Japanese Tradition*, 40–41.
[80] Ebrey and Walthall, *Pre-Modern East Asia*, 125.
[81] Ebrey and Walthall, *Pre-Modern East Asia*, 127.
[82] De Bary et al., *Sources of Japanese Tradition*, 63.
[83] Ebrey and Walthall, *Pre-Modern East Asia*, 121.

China sat at the core. Both countries were undergoing profound social identity change as states, elites, and family organization. But the overall scale of borrowing, the justifications given for borrowing, and the level of mimicry lead us to conclude that borrowing was more emulation than learning in historical East Asia.

6 | Korea and Japan over the Centuries

Korea and Japan were states by any definition: Centralized, bureau-cratically administered, and defined over territory. Chinese civilization as expressed through institutions lasted for many centuries in both Korea and Japan, and its norms and ideas were pervasive in Korean and Japanese society and culture. Although we have focused here on the initial formation of states in both countries, the resulting state institutions lasted an exceedingly long time: With modifications and changes, they survived up to the nineteenth century. Furthermore, a glance at their histories shows that many of the bellicist arguments about contracts and institutions also did not apply in East Asia. Neither country used public finance or debt to fund operations – they worked solely from tax revenues. They developed major institutions to provide public goods. And they did not devolve into rent-seeking or corruption on nearly the scale that the European rulers did.

After the initial state formation in both Korea and Japan, successive dynasties continued, deepened, and imported even more Chinese elements – the Chosŏn dynasty (1392–1910) in particular being seen as deeply influenced by neo-Confucianism.[1] Korea used the civil service examination system based on Confucian classics to staff the government with scholar-officials until 1896; and it used the lunar calendar until 1896. In Japan, the *ritsuryo* system survived for centuries. Five hundred years later, by the time of the Ashikaga (or Muromachi) Shogunate (1338–1573), the system had begun to break down. The tremendously long time frame – centuries of emulation – is significant. Yet the process of state formation is not linear, and there were reversions and evolution, as some ideas were kept and others discarded. Sinic civilization remained influential up until the twentieth century,

---

[1] Duncan, *The Origins of the Chosŏn Dynasty*.

even while some elements were modified and others were abandoned.[2]

This chapter surveys Korea and Japan in the successive centuries after they emerged as states, showing how deep and enduring were the ideas, institutions, and norms. There was change, evolution, and sometimes decay, of course. Yet Korea and Japan – like China – retained key features of their states for a remarkably long time.

6.1 The Enduring Korean State: The Koryŏ and Chosŏn Dynasties

Over fourteen centuries, Korea had only three dynasties: Silla (668–918), Koryŏ (918–1392), and Chosŏn (1392–1910). As he founded the Koryŏ dynasty, Wang Kŏn injoined:

We in the east have long admired the Tang style. Our literary matters, ritual, and music all follow their institutions. Yet, in strange regions and different lands, peoples' nature are each different. We need not improperly be made the same … Khitan is a nation of savage beasts, and its language and customs are also different. Its dress and institutions should never be copied.[3]

Significantly, even though the Mongols subjugated Koryŏ in 1259 and ruled through intermarriage for more than a century, Deuchler notes that "the almost one hundred years of Mongol domination of Korean affairs … seem to have left but a light imprint. The Mongols were admired for their military organization and prowess; but apart from some fancy fashions, they seem to have furnished little of substance for imitation."[4] In the words of Lee and de Bary,

Chinese culture also contributed to Koryŏ's development. As Koryŏ early kings searched for an effective system of government, they naturally turned to China's rich and varied experience and borrowed liberally from Chinese political thought and institutions, eventually affording Koryŏ a sophisticated system of administration. Koreans also adopted the Chinese system of official recruitment, which relied in good part on a state examination on skill in literary Chinese and Confucian classics.[5]

---

[2] Park, *Sovereignty and Status in East Asian International Relations*; and Jansen, *China in the Tokugawa World*.
[3] *Koryŏ sa*, 2:14b–17a, from Lee and de Bary, *Sources of Korean Tradition*, 155.
[4] Deuchler, *The Confucian Transformation of Korea*, 83
[5] Lee and de Bary, *Sources of Korean Tradition*, 140.

The late Koryŏ dynasty era in Korea was turbulent: The Mongols had attacked and subjugated the dynasty in the thirteenth century; extensive *wakō* pirates attacked and plundered along the southern coast 378 times between 1375 and 1388; Jurchens continually raided Koryŏ's northern border; and, most importantly, a resurgent and militarily powerful Ming China in the fourteenth century was potentially a major threat to the survival of the Koryŏ dynasty.[6] One obvious response to these security threats could have been a full militarization of the new Chosŏn dynasty and a resort to force. Yet the opposite occurred – Confucian scholars became increasingly influential, and the military was increasingly marginalized, as the new dynasty sought to establish domestic order and international stability.

The founders of the new dynasty were not outsiders rebelling against an established order – in fact, they came from the educated elite – and their dissatisfaction was driven by a desire to intensify neo-Confucian practices, not overturn them. Deuchler notes that "To the social architects of early Chosŏn, the adoption of ancient Chinese institutions was not an arbitrary measure to restore law and order, but the revitalization of a link with the past in which Korea itself had a prominent part."[7] Indeed, Chosŏn founder Yi Sŏng-gye looked to Ming China for legitimacy with his own aristocracy, who were skeptical of Yi's humble origins, and in the Chosŏn Founding Edict, he explicitly used the Chinese calendar, and the initial memorials also made explicit reference to Chinese dynasties of the past.[8] For example, in his "Admonition to the New King," the Inspector-General wrote:

The reason for the falls of Kings Chieh and Chou is that they lost virtue and ruled by force ... King Yu of Hsia demonstrated his virtue by building his palace low ... Emperor Wen of Han displayed his exemplary attitude by being thrifty ... how much less should the sovereign be careless in his expenditure in Korea, whose land is squeezed between the mountains and the sea and whose population and taxes are not numerous![9]

---

[6] Kenneth Robinson, "Policies of Practicality: The Chosun Court's Regulation of Contact with the Japanese and Jurchens, 1392–1580," Ph.D. dissertation, University of Hawai'i (1997), 1.

[7] Deuchler, *The Confucian Transformation of Korea*, 107.

[8] Ki-Baik Lee, *A New History of Korea* (Cambridge, MA: Harvard University Press, 1984), 189.

[9] *T'aejo Sillok*, "Admonition to the New King," 1:40a–42b, quoted in Peter Lee (ed.), *Sourcebook of Korean Civilization*, vol. 1, *From Early Times to the Sixteenth Century* (New York: Columbia University Press, 1993), 483–485.

Duncan's magisterial study of the founding of the Chosŏn dynasty has
pointed out the way in which *yangban* (landed elite) families interacted
with and promoted reforms to the government. Practical measures
such as the Rank Land Law (Kwajŏnbŏp), which reformed land ownership, "harked back to Chinese antiquity," and these new officials
selectively chose ideas and practices from various Chinese dynasties.
Duncan notes that "proposals were based on the reformers' understandings of historical Chinese and Korean systems," including the Qin
(221–206 BCE), Han (206 BCE–220 CE), and Tang (618–907 CE), as
well as from the preceding Koryŏ dynasty.[10]

Korean government and scholarly writings are replete with references to Chinese dynasties, Confucian thought, and the writings of
numerous Chinese scholars, historical as well as contemporary. In this
way, the role of China as civilization and model was thorough. For
example, in a 1786 memorial for Korean King Chŏngjo (1776–1800),
Pak Chega, a noted official, wrote:

Our country served the Ming as a tributary subject for more than two
hundred years ... even though the Qing have now ruled the world for more
than one hundred years, the descendants of the Chinese and their etiquette
still prevail ... thus, it is quite incorrect to rashly call these people [Manchu]
"barbarians." ... as an august country of one thousand chariots ... if we
want to revere China, there is no greater reverence than to put the Chinese
ways into practice.[11]

With the establishment of the Chosŏn dynasty and the intensification
of neo-Confucian practices, "scholar-officials ... became directly
involved in policymaking at all levels."[12] Deuchler notes that

The assessment of Korea's chances in an open conflict with the Ming had led
him [Chosŏn founder Yi Sŏng-gye] and his advisors to realize that the
country's economic situation would not sustain prolonged military
action ... rather than subject Korea to a military venture with uncertain
outcome, he started his offensive at the home front. Foremost on his agenda
was a reordering of economic resources.[13]

[10] Duncan, *The Origins of the Chosŏn Dynasty*, 208.
[11] Pak Chega, "On Revering China," in Lee (ed.), *Sourcebook of Korean
Civilization*, vol. 2, 87. A Ming tributary country is allowed "one thousand
chariots."
[12] Deuchler, *The Confucian Transformation of Korea*, 292.
[13] Deuchler, *The Confucian Transformation of Korea*, 91.

In some ways, Korea became more Confucian than China itself. Korea had almost ten times as many Confucian academies (*sŏwŏn*) as China on a per capita basis.[14] Korea also used a bureaucratic system borrowed from the Chinese model that emphasized the study of Chinese texts. Similarly, its civil service examination system (*munkwa*) emphasized knowledge of Confucian classics; it was in use from the Silla dynasty in the eighth century but only became fully incorporated into public life under the Chosŏn dynasty.[15] Passing the civil service exam was the only way to join the bureaucracy, which came to be seen as the highest position a person could attain. In an attempt at transparency and meritocracy, by the beginning of the Chosŏn dynasty, an extensive system had developed to protect the candidates. Candidates' names were concealed from the examiners before the test and, after completion, tests were re-copied into other handwriting before examiners saw them in order to assure anonymity. The exams were collected by different officers than those who recorded and read them, and were also read by more than one examiner to ensure fairness in grading.[16]

Based mainly on the study of Confucian classics, only sons from *yangban* families were eligible to take the test. Although meritocracy was the principle, the ways in which the exam system operated during Chosŏn benefited capital-based elites. Korea was more restrictive in this regard than China: All "good" status people were in theory eligible to take the exam in Chosŏn; those of "base" status, including serfs (*nobi*, more than 30 percent of the population up to the 18th century), were excluded. The exam system was controversial for as long as it existed. As one critic wrote in 1775,

Why do we use the civil service examination to identify potential civil servants, anyway? These days those examinations test candidates on their ability to write according to the currently accepted essay format. ... People study the essay format from childhood and finally pass the examination when they are old and gray. The examination system thus selects men who are useless, and it does so on the basis of useless writing.[17]

---

[14] Woodside, *Lost Modernities*, 23.

[15] David C. Kang, *Crony Capitalism: Corruption and Development in South Korea and the Philippines* (Cambridge: Cambridge University Press, 2002), 78–81.

[16] Woodside, *Lost Modernities*, 2.

[17] Pak Chega, "A Reexamination of the Civil Service Examination System," in Lee (ed.), *Sourcebook of Korean Civilization*, vol. 2, 26–28.

Chosŏn dynasty court dress was identical with the court dress of Ming dynasty officials, with the exception that the dress and emblems of a Korean rank were those of the Chinese rank two grades lower (in the nine-rank scheme). That is, the court dress of a Chosŏn official of Rank I (the highest rank) was identical to that of a Rank III official at the Ming court.[18] Korea patterned itself closely after the Chinese administrative model, and established Six Ministries (k: Yukcho) that covered Personnel, Taxation, Rites, Military Affairs, Punishments, and Public Works.[19]

The State Council (Ŭijŏngbu) was the highest organ, comprising three high state councilors, and served as the advisory council to the king and the administrative body that directed the Six Ministries.[20] The country was divided into eight provinces: Kyŏnggi, Chungchŏng, Kyŏngsang, Chŏlla, Hwanghae, Kangwŏn, Hamgyŏng, and Pyŏngan: Essentially the same provincial division that exists today. Within those provinces were various types of counties. County magistrates were not allowed to serve in the counties in which they resided, to keep their loyalties to the crown rather than the people they governed.[21]

Yet, in the twenty or more centuries before 1900, China simply did not dominate Korea: Korea was de facto independent and its Sinicization was most pronounced when Korean neo-Confucians quite self-consciously imposed that as an ideology on Korea, apart from whatever the Chinese might have wanted. Korea was clearly an independent state, conducting its own internal domestic politics and independent foreign policy. Chosŏn King Sejong (r. 1418–1450) believed that local society should not be completely overwhelmed by Chinese rites, arguing "How can we be bound by what the people of the past did?"[22] The Korean embassies to Japan referred to the Tokugawa shogun as *Ilbon kukwang* ("king of Japan"), while the Korean king was known as *Hankuk kukwang* ("king of Korea").[23]

The division of Korea into administrative districts took place in mid-Koryŏ dynasty, in the early eleventh century. It had been preceded by provincial-level divisions (*chu* and *mok*) dating back to Unified Silla, in

[18] Ledyard, Posting on *Korea Web*.
[19] Deuchler, *The Confucian Transformation of Korea*.
[20] Lee, *A New History of Korea*, 175.   [21] Lee, *A New History of Korea*, 176.
[22] Deuchler, *The Confucian Transformation of Korea*, 123.
[23] Key-Hiuk Kim, *The Last Phase of the East Asian World Order* (Berkeley: University of California Press, 1980), 16.

the late seventh century. Those administrative divisions are essentially the same today. Legal and judicial systems were also centrally administered: The proper channels for lodging complaints in Chosŏn Korea would proceed from the district government, via the provincial government and on to the central court, and only then to the king, while there were ways to appeal directly to the king "by beating a gong."[24] James Palais notes that, in 1392, "central control over every local district was expanded by replacing all local magnates with members of the capital bureaucracy."[25]

6.2 Japan: Tokugawa Shogunate, 1600–1868

As we saw in Chapter 5, the initial period of Japanese state formation in the fifth to eighth centuries saw close emulation of Chinese ideas: It was foundational for Japanese state formation, society, and culture. China has always loomed large for Japan. Pollack observes that, "until modern times the Chinese rarely troubled themselves about Japan; the Japanese, however, were preoccupied with China from the beginning of their recorded history until the opening of the West in the last century."[26] Donald Keene writes that "The central factor of Japanese literature – if not the entire traditional culture – was the love for and the rejection of Chinese influence."[27] Pollack further notes that "for the Japanese, what was 'Japanese' had always to be considered in relation to what was thought to be 'Chinese'."[28] Indeed, China loomed large as myth and reality in Japanese history.

Yet Chinese ideas never took as deep root in Japan as they did in Korea or Vietnam. They began to fail in the eleventh century in the smaller, more backward environment of Japan.[29] The Chinese influence waned for a few centuries, and in particular during the *sengoku* (warring states) era (1467–1568).

---

[24] Kim, "Taxes, the Local Elite, and the Rural Populace," 1002.
[25] Palais, *Confucian Statecraft and Korean Institutions*, 28.
[26] Pollack, *The Fracture of Meaning*, 3.
[27] Donald Keene, "Literature," in Arthur E. Tiedemann (ed.), *An Introduction to Japanese Civilization* (New York: Columbia University Press, 1974), 383.
[28] Pollack, *The Fracture of Meaning*, 3.
[29] William Farris, *Sacred Texts and Buried Treasures: Issues in the Historical Archaeology of Ancient Japan* (Honolulu: University of Hawai'i Press, 1998).

The Ashikaga shoguns of the fourteenth century encouraged the growth of the capital, Kyoto, and ties with China through diplomacy, commerce, Zen monasteries, and culture. The Bakufu – the government system of the shogunate – also developed a civil service and employed bureaucrats, although not on the scale of China and Korea. The Ashikaga Bakufu used these bureaucrats – known as *bugyōnin* – to administrate public finance, tax collection, adjudicate lawsuits brought to the Bakufu, and process land claims and other shogunal decrees.[30] Although those at the lowest rungs of society were often subject to personalistic rule by local magistrates, "if you were a civil, military, or ecclesiastical landlord, or a steward of such a person, then the system looked reliable, even modern ... 'law' was a salient feature of the Japanese medieval era: groups had rights and litigation was not yet suppressed, legal experts flourished both in the bakufu and the imperial system."[31] However, in comparison to the centralized control achieved by Korea, China, and Vietnam, Japan was clearly less statist in its organization. Indeed, as Kenneth Robinson records, "Koryŏ and Chosŏn court officials were acutely aware that the shogun and the Muromachi bakufu could neither prevent piracy nor regulate trade, much less govern areas far from Kyoto."[32]

The domestic process of expanding centralized political control occurred in Japan just as it did in other countries in the region. And, like all countries, Japan saw a waxing and waning of state power over the centuries, with competing centripetal and centrifugal forces. Martin Collcutt notes that "for much of the Muromachi [Ashikaga] period the Kanto and large tracts of Tohoku and Kyushu were outside the pale of Bakufu authority."[33] Yet the shogunate did gain financial control over the central provinces. John Whitney Hall notes that, although the centralized bureaucratic structures of the previous governments had weakened, they were also not replaced by fully

---

[30] Kenneth Grossberg, "Bakufu *Bugyōnin*: The Size of the Lower Bureaucracy in Muromachi Japan," *The Journal of Asian Studies*, 35, no. 4 (1976), 651–654.

[31] Carl Steenstrup, "The Middle Ages Survey'd," *Monumenta Nipponica*, 46, no. 2 (1991), 239.

[32] Robinson, "Policies of Practicality," 3.

[33] Martin Collcutt, "Kings of Japan? The Political Authority of the Ashikaga Shoguns," *Monumenta Nipponica*, 37, no. 4 (1982), 523–529.

patrimonial delegation of lord to vassal.[34] Instead, as Jeffrey Mass argues, family organization was the key building block of Japanese society, "providing the basic framework through which authority was exercised."[35] But we should note that the form of Japanese state organization, although sharing some similarities with feudal Europe, was unique, and any comparison with Europe is misleading. Politically, the state was strong and stable, and exerted central control across much of what is known as modern Japan.

Although central control broke down during the *sengoku* era, "the idea of 'Japan' as a single country remained strong."[36] Tellingly, at no time did any of the *daimyō* attempt to create an independent state. Indeed, they all remained explicitly committed to the emperor as ruler of Japan – the only question being who would be the most powerful actor, not who would reign. When one of them won a war, he became "shogun," not emperor.

Toyotomi Hideyoshi – a prominent *daimyō* of the late sixteenth century – conducted a national land survey and implemented a national system of taxation. The Tokugawa Bakufu (1600–1868) continued the centralizing trend. Although there remained important exceptions to centralized power, the Tokugawa Bakufu had complete authority in foreign affairs and military matters, control of the currency and the national highway system, and complete control over the religious life of Japan. Land registers and maps, and a national census, were implemented continuously from 1716 onward.[37] Products could be marketed nationally because of a national currency.

Indeed, the Chinese example as a normative precedent remained very important even in the Tokugawa era. Japan and China continued to trade, with up to ninety Chinese ships visiting Japan each year during the seventeenth and eighteenth centuries, and Japan imported

---

[34] John Whitney Hall, "The Muromachi Bakufu," in Kozo Yamamura (ed.), *The Cambridge History of Japan* (Cambridge: Cambridge University Press, 1990), 175–230.

[35] Jeffrey Mass, "The Early Bakufu and Feudalism," in Jeffrey Mass (ed.), *Court and Bakufu in Japan: Essays in Kamakura History* (New Haven, CT: Yale University Press, 1982), 262.

[36] Batten, *To the Ends of Japan*, 42.

[37] Ronald Toby, "Rescuing the Nation from History: The State of the State in Early Modern Japan," *Monumenta Nipponica*, 56, no. 2 (Summer 2001), 202.

over 1,000 Chinese books each year.[38] When Tokugawa shoguns were looking for legal and institutional models for how to structure their own government and society, "they were usually Chinese in origin," such as the Six Maxims first issued by the Ming founder, the Hongwu Emperor, in 1398, as well as Qing and even Tang and Song legal and administrative codes.[39] Indeed, the *Tokugawa jikki* (the official annals of the Tokugawa era) contains numerous references to Japanese legal scholars consulting with Chinese and Korean scholars as they attempted to interpret various Chinese laws and precedents and modify them for Tokugawa use.

By the time of Tokugawa Japan, "educational institutions at every level across the nation followed a similar curriculum of Japanese and Chinese texts ... the *Tangshixuan* collection of Chinese poetry was a required text, where it was regarded as a canonical work."[40] Chinese literature was in such demand that, between 1727 and 1814, one publisher – Suwaraya Shinbei – put out twenty-seven editions of the *Tangshixuan*.[41] Perhaps most interesting was a Tokugawa report from the 1730s, edited by Hayashi Shunsai, that compiled Chinese reports submitted by the captains of Chinese trading vessels that docked at Nagasaki. A source of information to the Japanese leadership about events in China, it was titled *Ka'i hentai*, or "The Transformation from Chinese to Barbarian": The Japanese were trying to find out what was going on in China as it changed from "Chinese" (華, *hua*) to "barbarian" (夷, *yi*). The book title comes from the conquest of China by the Qing, hence barbaric rulers. Implicit of course is both an acceptance and idea of what constituted rightful rule of China and a cultural distinction between China and other peoples.[42]

After Hideyoshi prohibited private warfare in 1588, the *daimyō* had no realistic recourse to military action in order to enlarge their lands: Economic advancement was the only avenue, and, as Batten notes, "rapid growth of state power was reflected in a recentralization of

[38] Oba Osamu, *Books and Boats: Sino-Japanese Relations in the Seventeenth and Eighteenth Centuries* (Translated by Joshua Fogel) (Portland, ME: MerwinAsia, 2012).
[39] Jansen, *China in the Tokugawa World*, 65–228.
[40] Toby, "Rescuing the Nation from History," 228.
[41] Toby, "Rescuing the Nation from History," 228.
[42] Gang Zhao, "Shaping the Asian Trade Network: The Conception and Implementation of the Chinese Open Trade Policy, 1684–1840," Ph.D. dissertation, Johns Hopkins University (2006), 225.

authority."[43] The period 1570–1630 was a "great transformation," according to Anthony Reid, and the "decisive turning point in the start of Japan's 'modernity.' Unification, urbanization, the creation of distribution and marketing networks, and the commercialization of attitudes were all a part of this Japanese leap."[44] Indeed, upon Tokugawa authority, the *daimyō* were regularly moved around the country, and spent half of each year in residence in Edo. The *daimyō* complied with Tokugawa dictates to conduct annual censuses. When the Bakufu changed the national maps to representations based on provinces and districts, rather than the *daimyō* domains, even the larger domains of Satsuma and Tosa were subject to these regulations – and they complied.[45]

6.3 Public Goods and Public Finance

In addition to having detailed surveys and comprehensive tax systems, the Chinese, Korean, Japanese, and later Vietnamese states were able to provide extensive public goods unimaginable in Europe before the nineteenth century. China and Korea were able to provide public lands, forest control, granaries for famine, and water works and water control by the eighth century, followed later by Vietnam. As far back as 1023, the Korean Koryŏ dynasty levied a surtax on land for support of the "righteous granaries" (의창, *ŭich'ang*, 義倉), which were to provide relief for peasants in time of famine. Chosŏn's founder, Yi Sŏng-gye, introduced land reform in 1390, as well as village granaries to guard against famine. The grain loan system (환곡, *hwan'gok*, 還穀) dated to the beginning of the dynasty and was intended to provide relief to people during spring grain shortage.[46]

The Chinese Qing dynasty (1644–1912) developed a centralized process by which the government reacted to food shortages anywhere within the country. R. Bin Wong notes that these "[state-sponsored] granaries represented official commitments to material welfare beyond

---

[43] Batten, *To the Ends of Japan*, 44.
[44] Anthony Reid, "An 'Age of Commerce' in Southeast Asian History," *Modern Asian Studies*, 24, no. 1 (1990), 10.
[45] Toby, "Rescuing the Nation from History," 208.
[46] Kim, "Taxes, the Local Elite, and the Rural Populace," 1001.

anything imaginable, let alone achieved, in Europe."[47] Rosenthal and Wong observe,

Chinese rulers viewed public goods as an important element in maintaining social order and control ... this criteria for political success made more sense in a large polity where external enemies were few relative to the domestic challenges of sustaining social order ... European rulers had to face the fiscal consequences of war. The costs of competition with other states occupied a proportionally larger amount of government finances than domestic rule.[48]

The historical East Asian states also operated without public debt or creating central banking institutions. This is a critical contrast with Europe and bears important implications for the role of the state in society in East Asia, a point which we will elaborate further toward the end of the book. It is related to the existence of a multistate system in Europe and international bankers that could bankroll both sides of the same war.[49] No such thing existed in East Asia. Debt markets were unheard of until the arrival of the West in the nineteenth century. There were small-scale moneylenders in Korea, who generally loaned small sums to peasants in the spring, being repaid ten months later, after the fall harvest. The government was concerned with attempting to regulate their activities but never developed a central bank or took on public debt.[50] This is in contrast to Europe, where interest rates were high during the Middle Ages, but over time credit markets grew and interest rates fell. Rosenthal and Wong note that "European empires were founded and survived on oceans of finance, but the Chinese empire was largely debt free until the intrusion of Europeans into its internal affairs."[51] Furthermore, they conclude that "before the 1840s one would be hard pressed to find much evidence of public credit in China. Neither the emperor's central treasury nor local administrations had much recourse to credit markets."[52] The same was true for Korea, Vietnam, and Japan: There was no public debt. The government paid for its operations from sufficient tax revenues.

---

[47] Wong, *China Transformed*, 98.
[48] Rosenthal and Wong, *Before and beyond Divergence*, 174.
[49] Geoffrey Parker, *The Grand Strategy of Phillip II* (New Haven, CT: Yale University Press, 2000) discusses Italian bankers and their relationship to the Dutch as well as the Spanish who were trying to defeat them.
[50] Palais, *Confucian Statecraft and Korean Institutions*, 924.
[51] Rosenthal and Wong, *Before and beyond Divergence*, 162.
[52] Rosenthal and Wong, *Before and beyond Divergence*, 155.

Practical fiscal reform measures, such as the provision of public goods through the Rank Land Law, drew on ideas from Chinese antiquity. The typical tax rate, dating back to Mencius in China, was 10 percent of the harvest. The early Tang consolidated the "two tax" reform of 780 CE, which replaced the "equal fields" system that had been implemented 300 years earlier. Woodside concludes that "By the eighth century, Chinese elites possessed what they thought was an untrammeled capacity to impose massive consolidating tax reforms from the top down."[53]

6.4 Taxes and Debt

By the eighth century, China had developed tax capacity far beyond anything European sovereigns could contemplate until perhaps the eighteenth century. Chinese taxation was also light compared to Europe. According to Rosenthal and Wong, "During the eighteenth century officials collected routine taxes amount roughly to some 5% to 10% of agricultural output, but the Chinese state managed to help maintain waterways, manage water-control works for irrigation, and build massive granary reserves and other projects that helps promote material security and economic growth."[54]

Taxation in Korea followed the same model. By the Silla dynasty of Korea (668–918 CE), Korea had imported Tang-era taxation forms. The early Koryŏ state (918–1392) asserted control over all salt production, as well as mining. The Koryŏ-era Korean state had control down to the household level, although effectively only about one-third of the 350–400 counties were governed by centrally appointed magistrates. There was also a general 10 percent tax on all crops during this time.[55]

The Korean Chosŏn dynasty (1392–1910) implemented taxation in three forms: land tax, corvée or military service, and local tribute tax. Land tax was still set at 10 percent of estimated harvest based on assessments of fertility of land (with six different grades). Corvée was assessed as deemed necessary, usually in the farming slack season, while military service was based on the principle of universal

---

[53] Woodside, *Lost Modernities*, 62.
[54] Rosenthal and Wong, *Before and beyond Divergence*, 175.
[55] Palais, "Land Tenure in Korea," 137.

compulsory service in which active service rotated among groups of three households.[56] By mid-Chosŏn, the land tax remained the same. As for military service, there was rotating universal compulsory service, although some commoners paid two bolts of cloth instead or installed a replacement soldier to serve on his behalf. A limited number of soldiers staffed newly created standing armies such as the Military Training Agency (Hullyŏn Dogam) and others. In the case of local tribute, the state decided to apply a 10 percent surtax to the land tax (so the effective land tax became 11 percent) and use the surtax to purchase goods.

In order to tax effectively, the state needs detailed information on economic activity and land ownership. These cadastral surveys were remarkably detailed. Writing about the tenth century, Palais notes that "in early Koryŏ when the state had better control over land, the total amount of registered arable land had to be in the range of 1 to 1.2 million (*kyŏl*)."[57] With the founding of the Chosŏn dynasty in 1392, the new government engaged in a comprehensive cadastral survey of all the land in the kingdom.[58] Palais notes that the survey revealed a total of 798,127 *kyŏl* of land, of which 623,097 was arable.[59] For example, Sun Joo Kim refers to a survey from 1720 that was detailed down to the level of sub-district and included measures of landholdings from *nobi* (serfs) to *yangban* (elites).[60] The king also utilized an ethics inspector (*amhaeng ŏsa*), who was sent to find corruption and make sure that the local magistrates were carrying out their responsibilities.

6.5 Conclusion

Korea and Japan – although experiencing changes and setbacks – were far more institutionalized, regularized, and bureaucratized by the nineteenth century than they had been in the seventh century. This should

---

[56] The 한국민족대백과웹전 section on 조선 전기의 조세제도 [출처: 한국민족문화대백과웹전(조세(租稅))]" ("Early Choson Tax System," *Encyclopedia of Korean Culture* (Academy of Korean Studies, 1980) (http://encykorea.aks.ac.kr/Contents/SearchNavi?keyword=%EC%A1%B0%EC%84%B8%20&ridx=3&tot=97)

[57] Palais, "Land Tenure in Korea," 103.

[58] Palais, *Confucian Statecraft and Korean Institutions*, 48.

[59] A *kyŏl* was roughly five acres of land. Palais, *Confucian Statecraft and Korean Institutions*, 106.

[60] Kim, "Taxes, the Local Elite, and the Rural Populace," 995.

come as no surprise – the level of progress and growth in society, politics, and science and arts over the centuries was as dramatic as it had been in Europe over that same time span. We should beware of viewing these countries as simply stagnant or cyclical: There was far more institutionalization and coherence by the end of the premodern era than there had been 1,000 years earlier. But our basic point is reinforced by this long history: These were recognizably states that were fully functional; and they rarely fought with each other over the centuries. Rather, the East Asian civilizational sphere was one of emulation, not necessarily of bellicism.

7 | *Vietnam Emerges*
Tenth to Fourteenth Centuries

As a country, and as a state administrative bureaucracy, Vietnam engaged in as much emulation of China as did Korea and Japan. The overall scale and intensity – and, indeed, even the way in which using Chinese ideas was simply taken for granted – make it clear that this was emulation. As was discussed in Chapter 4, competition played almost no role in Vietnam's emergence as a state in the tenth and eleventh centuries, nor was it the main driver for subsequent Vietnamese state formation throughout the centuries. Rather, Vietnamese elites existed within the same civilizational world as did Korean, Japanese, and even Chinese elites. Vietnamese elites did not question this civilization, nor could they imagine any other. Indeed, much of the emulation and borrowing appears to be unconscious or taken for granted. Rather than a deliberate choice, using Chinese civilization was the only possible option. Alternatives were not considered, since they did not exist, and nor did the elites conceptualize a different set of principles, values, rituals, or cultural practices.

At the same time, we should also not overemphasize the depth of Sinic penetration. Vietnam, although clearly modeling itself on many civilizational influences that originated in China, retained a number of indigenous ideas as well. Daoism and Buddhism were more influential in the Vietnamese court than in other Sinic countries throughout premodern times, polygamy was the norm (unlike in China), and, although the king was seen as the mediator between Heaven and Earth as in the Sinic civilizational philosophies, that mediation also included many indigenous religious elements.

Vietnam had both similarities and differences with Korea and Japan. Vietnam was in some ways more Buddhist, and certainly influenced more directly by India and its Southeast Asian neighbors, than were Korea and Japan, for whom Buddhist influences were almost completely mediated by China. Vietnam also experienced more war than Korea or Japan, and expanded far more over its history – almost doubling its size through expansion southwards. The Vietnamese state also faced considerably more internal dissent than Korea and Japan. Yet the similarities are also too pronounced to ignore: Vietnam was as Confucian and Sinic as Korea and Japan, if not more, and was far more influenced by China than any other country in Southeast Asia. Early state formation in Vietnam was also far more institutionalized than what was possible in Europe at the time. Vietnam only looks weakly institutionalized compared to its mighty Asian neighbors. But, compared to anything in Europe, the exertion of state control in Vietnam was far more regularized, institutionalized, and consistent.

If war made states adopt similar institutional forms, then Vietnam would likely have looked more like the religiously based "mandala" states of Southeast Asia, not the Confucian states of East Asia. After all, Vietnam fought more consistently with kingdoms to its south and west than it did with China to its north. Yet, Vietnam was clearly a full member of the Sinic world. Indeed, Buddhism and Confucianism arrived in Vietnam earlier than it arrived in Korea and Japan, even though state formation began much later in Vietnam. Lieberman's long survey of Southeast Asia concludes that "Interaction with China was probably more important in shaping Vietnamese self-identity than warfare with Chams, Khmers, or Thais."[1]

7.1 Sinic Influence in the Founding of Vietnam as a State

The extent to which borrowing took place provides important indicators for emulation. If the extent of copying is total and comprehensive, it implies more emulation than if only select ideas and norms are copied. Similar to Korea and Japan, the overall scale of borrowing was extensive in China's southern borders. The founding of Vietnam as a state drew heavily on China's cultural and religious influence, as well as on accepting and adopting Confucian principles for governance and bureaucratic administration.

The Chinese Han empire extended its rule into northern Vietnam in the second century BCE, eventually incorporating it into China as the province Giao Chi. For the next ten centuries, Chinese control over what is now northern Vietnam was direct, although its implementation waxed and waned depending on the fortunes of dynasties within China

---

[1] Lieberman, "Local Integration and Eurasian Analogies," 539.

itself. Buddhism arrived directly from India as early as the first century CE.

Over the centuries, the Chinese introduced administrative districts and built roads, ports, canals, dikes, and dams extending the empire's reach to Vietnam. Chinese immigrants also introduced Chinese-style schools, marriage rites and social customs, agriculture, and law. The influence of Confucianism and Chinese civilization was pervasive, affecting Vietnamese life down to the village level, in family organization, patrilineal inheritance, and even everyday traditional clothing. As in the rest of East Asia, Buddhism and Confucianism intermingled easily. At times, Buddhism and Buddhist monks had more influence at the court; at other times, Confucianism and the literati did. But it was not necessarily seen as a debate or struggle between two sides. The Vietnamese people retained their indigenous language for unofficial uses, and for indigenous social and religious customs.

With the slow collapse of the Tang dynasty (618–907) in the ninth century, almost a millennium of Chinese rule came to an end. Yet Sinic influence remained strong, even as the Vietnamese were finding their own national identity. For example, Gao Pian, the Tang general who led armies into Annam in the 860s, was remembered as a key figure by generations of Vietnamese. He was central in choosing Đại La (later known as Thăng Long, and eventually Hanoi) as the site of the capital city for Vietnam. He supervised food shipments to the region during a famine, built and extended dikes and canals, and built roads and bridges. As one of the last Tang officials in Vietnam, he "earned a good reputation among the Vietnamese, and his efforts to rebuild the war-torn land were praised by later Vietnamese historians."[2] Indeed, Taylor notes, in the early eleventh century, a "ruler from the Red River plain explicitly cited [Gao's] legacy for inspirational authority after wresting power from a regime based in the southern [Chinese] provinces."[3]

As with the Korean and Japanese states, during the scattered early attempts at creating a Vietnamese state, rulers used many Chinese practices simply because it was the civilizational universe in which they existed. John Whitmore records that, as the "strong northern hold

---

[2] Taylor, *The Birth of Vietnam*, 250.
[3] Taylor, *A History of the Vietnamese*, 44.

dissipated by the tenth century, regional powers began to emerge."[4] Ngô Quyền, for example, was the warlord who defeated a Southern Han (917–971) attempt to reassert control over Vietnam in 938 CE, as almost 1,000 years of formal Chinese control of northern Vietnam faded away. A district in the city of Haiphong is named after him. Yet, according to Lien and Sharrock, the government that Ngô created "followed the Chinese system with a court, formal rites, and mandarins."[5] Ngô died six years later, throwing the realm back into chaos as numerous warlords sought dominance, in an era called the "Anarchy of the Twelve Warlords." Yet even here, Vietnamese centralization of authority was not a cause or effect of war; indeed, emergence as a state had more to do with domestic ideas about how best to govern.

As Whitmore puts it, "out of this regional *mélange* emerged the realm of the Dai Viet in the century after 960."[6] After considerable fighting, Đinh Bộ Lĩnh emerged victorious and consolidated his rule in 968, enabling him to create a government that could rule the newly unified territory. Đinh organized a "rudimentary government," giving close advisers various titles, many derived from Chinese practice. For example, Lê Hoàn was named General of the Ten Circuits, a reference to the division of Tang China into ten circuits (*dao*). A Buddhist priest, Ngô Chân Lưu, was named Buddhist Unifier, a title dating from the Northern Wei dynasty in the fifth century, while also giving him the title Great Teacher, a Tang title given to "profound and virtuous priests."[7] Đinh's younger brother was given the title Commandant of the Spare Horses, an early Han title.

As elements of a state began to coalesce, the preoccupations of the rulers of what was to become Vietnam were similar to those of Chinese emperors – reliance on controlling spirits and mediating between gods and humans.[8] This "rule by virtue" was not only symbolic; it was one of the main duties of a king. As one of his main purposes as ruler of the realm, Đinh Bộ Lĩnh paid great attention to being the intermediary

[4] John K. Whitmore, "The Rise of the Coast: Trade, State, and Culture in Early Dai Viet," *Journal of Southeast Asian Studies*, 37, no. 1 (2006), 105.
[5] Vu Hong Lien and Peter Sharrock, *Descending Dragon, Rising Tiger: A History of Vietnam* (London: Reaktion Books, 2014), 56.
[6] Whitmore, "The Rise of the Coast," 106.
[7] Taylor, *A History of the Vietnamese*, 283.
[8] See, for example, Valerie Hansen, *Changing Gods in Medieval China, 1126–1276* (Princeton, NJ: Princeton University Press, 1990).

between Heaven and Earth. Styling himself as Đinh Tiên Hoàng Đế (the First August Emperor Đinh), he established shrines to the Gods of the Earth and Agriculture, a practice that dates from ancient Chinese times referring to the Coiled Dragon and the Grain Sovereign. Recent archeological findings reveal that Đinh's "first Viet imperial palaces were built in brick and wood and highly decorated with Chinese and Viet auspicious symbols such as phoenix hens and ducks."[9]

Eager to maintain close ties with Vietnam's northern neighbor shortly after taking power, Đinh sent his eldest son as the inaugural and formal emissary to pay tribute and seek validation and recognition from the Song Chinese Emperor Taizu. Đinh's relations with the Song dynasty reflected the tributary ties of other states in China's orbit. Đinh saw Vietnam as a formal tributary of China, and Taizu, in turn, recognized Vietnam as one of its protectorates and vowed to defend it from foreign enemies. Confucian norms, practices, and rituals that undergirded the tributary relations further cemented diplomatic ties between the two sides. For Đinh, establishing the tributary relationship early on helped strengthen his position within the country. China's recognition verified Đinh's political legitimacy and confirmed his authority as the unifier of Đại Việt. Unlike previous rulers, who were only accorded with a title equivalent to military governor, the Chinese courts conferred upon Đinh the title of king of Giao Chi, or of Vietnam. In bestowing this unprecedented and much-coveted title, Đinh strengthened his position and leveraged it against political rivals. Paying tribute to Chinese dynasties and receiving investiture in return not only gave Vietnamese rulers the status to rule; it further legitimized the importance and centrality of Chinese civilization and cultural influence.

Vietnam's state formation was gradual and slow but also continual over the centuries. The succeeding Lý dynasty (1009–1225) originated with strong indigenous roots but emulated Chinese practices over time. The Lý dynasty revealed how Buddhism played an important role in Vietnam's emulation of Chinese state practices. Buddhist monks, for instance, served an influential role in government. The literati had not yet developed into a powerful Confucian bureaucracy; instead, during the initial period of the Lý dynasty, they were servants of the king,

---

[9] Lien and Sharrock, *Descending Dragon, Rising Tiger*, 58.

while the ruling class remained a feudal, landed nobility.[10] The Lý kings consistently relied on political advisers who were also religious figures. Classic texts on Mahayana Buddhism from China were introduced to Vietnam for widespread dissemination, often with the support of Lý kings. Some 1,000 Buddhist temples were said to exist in Vietnam during the early Lý decades of the eleventh century. Vietnamese kings also became devout followers of Buddhism; for example, in 1020, Lý Thái Tổ (born Lý Công Uẩn) ordered the construction of an administrative palace, to be separate from the ceremonial palace. In 1042 the court introduced a new legal code, influenced by the Tang model, and replete with Confucian overtones.[11] Taylor notes that "literary Chinese was ... the language of education, scholarship, literature, and government in both China and Vietnam until the turn of the twentieth century."[12] Likewise, Woodside notes that Chinese culture and influence were markedly present in everyday life in Vietnam in the eleventh century.[13]

Vietnamese historian Phan Huy Chú dates the national Vietnamese tax system from 1013, barely a few decades after the creation of the nascent Vietnamese state. Lý Thái Tổ published what could be deemed a progressive scheme for taxation: Land was clearly divided between public and private; and during the Lý–Trần period (approximately 1000–1400 CE), the "upper class" paid almost twice as much taxes as did the "lower class."[14] Shiro Momoki notes that the Lý dynasty "enforced stable local rule during the period of the Tang–Song transition [utilizing] the Chinese-modeled hierarchy of local administrative units."[15] In Vietnam, the distinction between public and private concerned taxation, not ownership per se: Ideologically, all lands belonged to the kingdom and the state. But most lands were owned by private individuals (regardless of their status) and they paid land taxes to the state. Such practices were similar to Koryŏ-era Korea (918–1392), which also emulated the Chinese model and where commoners' land

---

[10] Womack, *China and Vietnam*, 122.   [11] Kiernan, *Viet Nam*, 155.
[12] Taylor, *A History of the Vietnamese*, 4.
[13] Alexander Woodside, "Vietnamese History: Confucianism, Colonialism, and the Struggle for Independence," *Vietnam Forum*, 11 (1988), 21–48.
[14] Taylor, *A History of the Vietnamese*, 62.
[15] Shiro Momoki, "Local Rule of Dai Viet under the Ly Dynasty: Evolution of a Charter Polity after the Tang–Song Transition in East Asia," *Asian Review of World History*, 1, no. 1 (2013), 47.

(for which farmers had to pay rent to the state) formed a part of public land along with plots under the direct control of the state or administrative offices.[16]

It is also notable that Vietnam had developed the state capacity to conduct a nationwide cadastral survey as early as the eleventh century.[17] These surveys reveal a significant level of development and sophistication far beyond what was possible in contemporaneous Europe or Central and South America. In European history, cadastral surveys of land ownership and productivity were relatively rare and recent. Roger Kain and Elizabeth Baigent point out that it was not until 1530 and then 1628 that Sweden initiated the first European comprehensive cartographic cadaster.[18] Eight countries did not perform a cadastral survey until the 1800s, including the United Kingdom.[19] State capacity developed even later in Central and South America. As recently as 1851 and 1852, the Brazilian government attempted a census, but never succeeded. As Centeno comments, "Despite the obvious benefits of a land tax, the sheer task of a cadastral survey would have also been beyond the capacity of the Brazilian state."[20] Yet land reform, as well as creation of local granaries for famine, were part of a nascent Vietnamese national welfare strategy by the fourteenth century.[21]

7.2 The Examination System

One of the defining features of Vietnamese emulation in its state formation was the introduction and adoption of the civil service

---

[16] Shiro Momoki, "Land Categories and Taxation Systems in Đại Việt (11th–14th Centuries)," *The Newsletter* (International Institute for Asian Studies), 79 (2019), 34.

[17] Momoki, "Land Categories and Taxation Systems in Đại Việt," 33.

[18] Roger J. P. Kain and Elizabeth Baigent, *The Cadastral Map in the Service of the State: A History of Property Mapping* (Chicago: University of Chicago Press, 1992), 47–67.

[19] Michelle D'Arcy and Marina Nistotskaya, "The Early Modern Origins of Contemporary European Tax Outcomes," *European Journal of Political Research*, 57 (2018), 53.

[20] Miguel Centeno, "Blood and Debt: War and Taxation in Nineteenth-Century Latin America," *American Journal of Sociology*, 102, no. 6 (1997), 1590.

[21] John K. Whitmore, *Vietnam, Ho Quy Ly, and the Ming (1371–1421)* (New Haven, CT: Yale University Press, 1985); and O. W. Wolters, *Two Essays on Dai-Viet in the Fourteenth Century* (New Haven, CT: Yale University South Asia Studies, 1988).

examination system. By the eleventh century, the Vietnamese civil service examinations – along with the role of scholar-officials and the use of classic Chinese texts – had become consequential in the governing of the country and the formation of the state. The scholar-officials were "professional elites ... whose hierarchies were created by public competition as much as by social class."[22] In 1075, the Vietnamese ruler Lý Nhân Tông ordered three levels of examination, "to select senior graduates familiar with the classics and broader learning."[23] The exams for civil servants were largely based on China's syllabus and focused on key aspects of Chinese history, literature, and classical studies, all meant to train a new crop of officials and administrators to concentrate the power of the central court, and to introduce a tax and legal code modeled after the northern neighbor.[24] The top scorers over the centuries have become national heroes, and many are remembered today. For instance, the title of *trạng nguyên* (top scorer, c: *zhuangyuan*, 狀元) was first awarded to Lê Văn Thịnh (1038–1096) for ranking first in that first exam. Lê had a storied career, and eventually rose to the position of chancellor and negotiated the border with the Song in 1084. The term *trạng nguyên* is still used today to describe the best performer in a competition.

In 1070, the Temple of Literature (Văn Miếu, 文廟) was built as a dedication to Confucius. It also housed the first national university, the Quốc Tử Giám (國子監), which opened in 1075. A subsequent examination in 1077 tested officials on "letters and laws."[25] By 1086, again in direct borrowing from Chinese practice, the government held a literary exam to select a *hàn lâm học sĩ* (academician). In Tang and Song governments, "such men were assigned to what was called the Hanlin Academy where erudite men were called upon for various tasks."[26] Often considered the most elite group of scholars, they managed the courts and were responsible for interpreting the Chinese classics for the kings.

The process of institutionalizing the civil service examination was a gradual one in Vietnam. Throughout the Lý dynasty, there were only four imperial exams, and the process of institutionalizing the examination system to recruit a civil service was halting. The subsequent Trần

[22] Woodside, *Lost Modernities*, 18.   [23] Kiernan, *Viet Nam*, 160.
[24] Truong Buu Laam, *New Lamps for Old: The Transformation of the Vietnamese Administrative Elite* (Singapore: Institute of Southeast Asian Studies, 1982).
[25] Kiernan, *Viet Nam*, 160.   [26] Taylor, *A History of the Vietnamese*, 87.

dynasty (1225–1400) more fully instituted the exams as a means to identify, train, and cultivate local talent as elite scholars to help manage state affairs. In 1232, local, provincial, and court exams were organized, with *trạng nguyên* awarded to the top scorer in the highest exam. Subsequent exams starting from 1247 were divided into three first-class grades along the Chinese model. By 1460, the degree of *tiến sĩ* (doctorate) was awarded to those who passed the highest exams. Three-stage regional examinations were held on successive weeks of the seventh lunar month, there were word limits (for example, 300 words for policy questions at the regional level), and winners were publicly announced in order of excellence.

By the fifteenth century, the number of candidates for each exam "never fell below 3,200," and the years 1450–1500 produced 501 *tiến sĩ*.[27] Although the exams emphasized Chinese and Confucian classics, in Vietnam the exams also included questions about Buddhism and Daoism. As in China, Korea, and Japan, the examinations included measures such as prohibitions against examiners meeting with each other privately, and special care was taken to ensure that families of candidates – fathers, sons, and uncles, for example – did not collude while taking the test. By the fifteenth century, up to 30,000 Vietnamese took the regional examinations. The civil service examination system came into its most complete form and use during the early years of the Later Lê dynasty (1427–1527). By then, 70,000 men were eligible for the first level of examination.[28] Yet the exam was exceedingly difficult: Between 1426 and 1643, only 1,694 scholars passed the examination, an average of eight per year.[29] These literati formed the core of Vietnam's turn toward neo-Confucianism. These scholars, such as Đào Công Soạn, Nguyễn Cư Đạo, and Nguyễn Bá Ký, were key figures in guiding the fifteenth-century Vietnamese state to incorporate and further embed Chinese ideas, cultural practices, and governance models to help strengthen the writ of the Vietnamese state. They created a bureaucracy with "modern examinations every three years, bureaucratic administration, and the moral Neo-Confucian orthodoxy."[30]

---

[27] Kiernan, *Viet Nam*, 205.
[28] John K. Whitmore, "Literati Culture and Integration in Dai Viet, *c.* 1430–*c.* 1840," *Modern Asian Studies*, 31, no. 3 (1997), 675.
[29] John K. Whitmore, "Vietnamese Embassies and Literati Contacts," Paper presented at the annual meetings of the Association of Asian Studies (2001), 5.
[30] Whitmore, "Vietnamese Embassies and Literati Contacts," 6.

The bureaucratic examination system was used for over 800 years. When the French arrived in the nineteenth century, success in the civil service examination still required use of Chinese characters and knowledge of Confucianism. The exams survived until 1915, when they were suspended by the French, thus making Vietnam the last country to hold Confucian civil service exams.

7.3 Sinic Intensification and Neo-Confucianism: Thirteenth to Nineteenth Centuries

By the thirteenth century, the turn toward nearly wholesale implementation of Confucianism in Vietnam's bureaucratic organization was intensifying. Building upon the cadastral surveys that had begun two centuries earlier, the Trần dynasty (1225–1400) set up Chinese-style population registers for each village, "the better to improve tax collections, the military draft, and river diking."[31] The Trần also founded the National College (Quốc Học Viện or Quốc Tử Viện), where scholars focused on the classical Chinese texts.[32] During the Lê dynasty (1427–1789), Vietnamese political structure more clearly modeled its political organization along Confucian lines. This era is often called the "neo-Confucian revolution," because the Chinese influence became much more thoroughly integrated into Vietnamese political and cultural life. Lieberman notes that

Although Confucian influence in Vietnam fluctuated after *c.* 1460 and although in practice patron–client ties remained crucial to the operation of the state, Chinese bureaucratic norms, first institutionalized during the so-called Neo-Confucian revolution of the 15th century, tended to encourage in that country a more impersonal, territorially uniform, and locally interventionist system than was found in Indianized polities to the west.[33]

The Trần dynasty also saw the writing of the first dynastic history – in 1272, Lê Văn Hưu completed his *Đại Việt Sử Ký* (Historical Annals of the Great Viet Kingdom) – like Korea, this was an attempt to separate Vietnam from China and create legitimate political space for Vietnam in Chinese eyes. The idea of "civilization" has been a key motivating factor across East Asia. Kelley, who prefers the term

[31] Lieberman, *Strange Parallels: Integration on the Mainland*, vol. 1, 360.
[32] Whitmore, "The Rise of the Coast," 117.
[33] Lieberman, "Local Integration and Eurasian Analogies," 484.

"manifest civility" to distinguish the older Chinese concept of civilization from the modern Western concept of civilization, writes:

To state that a kingdom was such a domain [of manifest civility] indicated
that it belonged to a category where it shared certain governmental, ritual,
educational, literary, intellectual, and social practices with other members of
this category, the proof of which could be found in the existence of a body of
"institutional records" that recorded such practices, as well as the presence
of "wise men" who maintained these records. Furthermore ... there was a
discernible inequality in this respect, especially between Vietnam and
China.[34]

Between 1663 and 1695, Confucian scholars compiled a history of the
Lê dynasty that, although not an official dynastic history (which were
normally written to legitimize a regime), did emphasize the dominant
position of the bureaucracy in the state.[35]

Indeed, the centralization of the state's authority and turn toward
Confucianism continued apace throughout this period. After a two-
decade Ming Chinese interregnum, state-building continued when Lê
Lợi founded the Lê dynasty in 1427 and began a series of neo-
Confucian reforms, including a new law code that regulated land sales,
debt interest, and relief for peasants.[36] Of particular note was the
protection of peasant rights to communal land, the only land subject
to taxation at the time. Although the Ming occupation was relatively
short, it had a lasting effect on Vietnam, hastening the centralization
and organization of the state. Whitmore notes that "while the
Vietnamese violently rejected Ming political control, [the] literati
equated Ming models with modernity."[37] When Lê Lợi asked his
ministers why the Chinese had failed in their occupation of Vietnam,
"the reasons they gave were not that the Chinese colonists were foreigners. Rather, their 'excessive punishments and harsh government
had long lost the hearts of the people.'"[38] This story – whether true or
not – reflects the enduring East Asian focus on rule by virtue, or the
responsibility of rule. Put simply, authority and legitimacy cannot be

[34] Kelley, "Vietnam as a 'Domain of Manifest Civility'," 68.
[35] Keith Taylor, "The Literati Revival in Seventeenth-Century Vietnam," *Journal of Southeast Asian Studies*, 18, no. 1 (1987), 14.
[36] Lieberman, *Strange Parallels: Integration on the Mainland*, vol. 1, 381.
[37] Whitmore, "Literati Culture and Integration in Dai Viet," 675.
[38] Alexander Woodside, *Vietnam and the Chinese Model* (Cambridge, MA: Harvard University Asia Center, 1988), 21.

derived from coercive practices. Vietnamese rulers appeared to have taken note of the shortcomings in Ming occupation and worked toward exerting political control with Confucian principles. As Whitmore concludes, Lê Thang Tông (r. 1460–1497) "was crossing a line and moving Dai Viet from a position of separation from the Sinic world to one of explicit participation in it."[39]

Woodside further points out that "by no later than the fifteenth century Vietnamese rulers had joined Chinese and Korean ones in organizing their central administrations around six specialized ministries."[40] Taylor notes that

The fortunes of the Ly and Tran dynasties waxed and waned with the Song and Yuan dynasties ... both sides carefully observed the tributary relationship. Books, medicine, theater, music, weapons, and government policies in the north were easily perceived, understood, and adopted in the south. Disorders and political troubles in the south were monitored and any potential for requiring or enabling intervention was evaluated in the north.[41]

The Vietnamese bureaucracy was now organized into six ministries to make policy, identical to China's Six Ministries. Below them were thirteen provincial headquarters, which in turn administered district offices and the village level, with inspectors traveling the country to monitor the civil service, as was the case in China.[42] This rationalized system of governance covered almost 10,000 villages organized into a "Chinese-style grid," composed of circuits (*đạo*), prefectures (*phủ*), and districts (*châu*), and was "exceptionally penetrating by Southeast Asian standards."[43] There was also a standing army of up to 200,000 troops, a census every three years, and the civil service examinations described previously.[44] Those who passed the exam and became Mandarins were given privileges such as land and special attire, but they were not allowed to own larger estates with serfs, nor were they allowed to retain their own military militias or armed forces.[45]

---

[39] John K. Whitmore, "China Policy in the New Age: Le Thang-tong (r. 1460–1497) and Northern Relations," Paper presented at the annual meetings of the Association of Asian Studies (2005), 4.

[40] Woodside, *Lost Modernities*, 25.

[41] Taylor, *A History of the Vietnamese*, 165.   [42] Karnow, *Vietnam*, 117.

[43] Lieberman, *Strange Parallels: Integration on the Mainland*, vol. 1, 382.

[44] Whitmore, *Vietnam, Ho Quy Ly, and the Ming*, 17.

[45] Nguyen, *Vietnam*, 66.

7.4 Emulation in Vietnamese Society

That the Vietnamese adopted Chinese practices out of genuine emulation and cultural borrowing from the most advanced state is indeed not surprising. Emulation was also encompassing: As in Korea and Japan, Vietnamese copied political ideas, institutions, and norms, as well as science, the calendar, math, social customs, and dress. Indeed, so pervasive was the Sinic influence and so comprehensive was its hegemony that it was nearly impossible to imagine anything different in the ways society was organized. It was simply the way the world was. As Taylor notes, "Books, medicine, music, weapons, and government policies in the north [China] were easily perceived, understood, and adopted in the south [Vietnam]."[46]

The justifications given for emulation centered almost completely on the appropriateness, or desirability, of mimicking the Chinese model. Emulation was further premised on a fundamental acceptance of what was being copied. Scholars in Vietnam often called China the "central efflorescence" or the "domain of manifest civility" (*văn hiến chi bang*) because it was the most complete reflection of the Confucian practices. Literally, the latter phrase means "using texts to rule the country," and implies a country ruled by Confucian ideas. Vietnamese scholar-officials in particular often used China as a model, comparison, or ideal, and historical writings from Vietnam are thoroughly imbued with the use of China as a reference point. One of any number of examples is that of Vietnamese scholar-official Lê Quý Đôn (1726–1784): "Our kingdom calls itself [a domain of] manifest civility [but] compared to writers in the Central Efflorescence [China], we have not produced even one-tenth of what they have. This is profoundly regrettable!"[47] As Kiernan notes, "Vietnamese literature now flourished – in Chinese."[48] In the first few centuries of Vietnamese autonomy, the literati wrote "at least" twenty-five lengthy histories, religious studies, and historical mythologies. "Their inspiration ranged from Buddhism, to spirit veneration, to Daoism and Confucianism. All were written in Chinese."[49]

---

[46] Taylor, *A History of the Vietnamese*, 165.
[47] Kelley, *Beyond the Bronze Pillars*, 34–35.   [48] Kiernan, *Viet Nam*, 133.
[49] Kiernan, *Viet Nam*, 133.

As in Korea and Japan, even Vietnamese clothing was heavily influenced by Chinese styles. Writing in 1225, "a Chinese official noted that the king had a Chinese surname and 'the clothing and food of the people are practically the same as in the Middle Kingdom'."[50] Yet, as Woodside notes, "In Vietnamese and Korean eyes, these ideals and choices existed independently of any perceived ethnic Chinese proprietorship of them."[51] Going beyond the point of simple conscious copying of China, it reflected the realities of the world as it existed. As Womack observes,

The Chinese court innovated and refined its institutions and ideology to face the challenge of preserving central order for the common good [and Vietnamese rulers] faced the same problem, and China provided an agenda of "best practices." ... it should be emphasized that if China were still an active threat, then Vietnam's political task would have been military cohesion, and its intellectual task would have been one of differentiation from China [not emulation].[52]

Expanded Vietnamese centralization and state control using Chinese models was a key for the royal house to expand its control over the 10,000 villages that comprised traditional Vietnam. Rationalizing taxation and land use expanded state revenues and increased the ability of the capital to reward supporters and eliminate opposition. At the sub-provincial level, royal appointees oversaw thirty to seventy villages, where they gathered data, standardized weights and measures, and encouraged better agricultural practices.[53] In contrast to Korea, the geographical size of the Vietnamese state expanded dramatically over time. This great southward advance occurred in the 1300s and 1400s, as Vietnam pushed Champa southwards in a series of battles. Vietnam thus has a more diverse ethnic makeup than Korea or Japan, and a greater geographic area to control.

The idea of centralized, unified political rule in Vietnam was deeply held. By the seventeeth century, the Lê dynasty had fallen into decay, with two rival clans competing for power: The Trịnh in the north and the Nguyễn in the south. From 1627 to 1673, the Trịnh and the Nguyễn clans fought for control of all Vietnam. Yet, even though the Lê king's power was waning, both rival clans retained superficial

---

[50] Kiernan, *Viet Nam*, 165. [51] Woodside, *Lost Modernities*, 25.
[52] Womack, *China and Vietnam*, 132–133.
[53] Whitmore, "Literati Culture and Integration in Dai Viet," 665–687.

loyalty to the Lê dynasty, largely because without firm control of the entire country neither could claim the legitimacy needed to found a new dynasty. Furthermore, as Taylor notes, "preservation of the Le dynasty lessened the possibility of Chinese intervention," since the Chinese had recognized the Lê as legitimate rulers of Vietnam.[54]

Indeed, neither the Trịnh nor the Nguyễn challenged the concept of unified political rule over what is today Vietnam, nor did they reject the increasing Confucianism that the Lê dynasty had begun. They both believed themselves to be the legitimate rulers of all Vietnam, "and retained a strong sense of themselves as ethnic Vietnamese."[55] Just like the *daimyō* of Japan, they did not challenge the idea of Vietnam or attempt to create their own states. That is, the Nguyễn in the south did not hope or attempt to establish a separate state, but rather they sought to succeed the Lê. Beyond modern nationalist interpretations, there exists very little evidence that the rationale for reforms at the time was to prevent Chinese intervention. We also have no evidence that the Chinese would have intervened, or that the Chinese court was engaged in discussions about a military solution.

As late as the nineteenth century, Vietnamese rulers were conducting their business in a classic way. Like all Confucian societies, the Vietnamese royal court wrote annalistic histories. One of the last annals was the 欽定越史通鑑綱目 (The Imperially Ordered Annotated Text Completely Reflecting the History of Viet, referred to hereafter as the "IHV"), originally commissioned and drafted in 1859 and finally published in 1884.[56] The IHV is a classical Chinese-language history of ancient and historical Vietnam in annalistic style.[57] In his decree to the scholars in charge of the IHV in 1856, Emperor Tự Đức explained why it was imperative to compile the IHV at that moment. He noted that

Compiling and revising history is an important task for a country in peace and prosperity. Throughout China's history, the Han Dynasty has 東觀漢記

[54] Taylor, "The Literati Revival in Seventeenth-Century Vietnam," 2.
[55] Whitmore, "Literati Culture and Integration in Dai Viet," 671.
[56] Thanh Giản Phan (ed.), 欽定越史通鑑綱目 [The Imperially Ordered Annotated Text Completely Reflecting the History of Viet] (Taipei: National Library, 1969).
[57] Specifically, the IHV covers the historical records from the Hồng Bàng dynasty (around the twenty-ninth century BCE) of ancient history to the end of the Later Lê dynasty in 1789.

(*The Dong Han Guan Ji*; History of the Dong Han) and the Song Dynasty has 崇文總目 (*The Ch'ungwen Tsungmu*; Ch'ungwen General Catalog), just to name a few. Every dynasty regards the work of history compilation as one vital mission to complete.[58]

The Emperor added that, while most students and intellectuals were quite familiar with Chinese history, they possessed very limited historical knowledge of their own country, which can be largely attributed to the fact that the compilation of Vietnamese history had not been resumed since 1675. He believed this needed to be rectified as "昧於古者何以驗今" (one must understand the past to see the future).[59]

7.5 Vietnam's Foreign Relations

In Chapter 4, we discussed in detail Đinh Bộ Lĩnh's foreign relations with the Song court. From that time on, until the arrival of the French colonizers in the late nineteenth century, Vietnam remained essentially a constant tributary to successive Chinese dynasties. Investiture continued at regular intervals. In 1174, for example, Emperor Lý Anh Tông of Đại Việt received investiture from Emperor Xiaozong of the Chinese Song Dynasty. While the first Ming emperor, Hongwu, cited the Mongols in the north as the primary existential threat that needed to be contained, he also explicitly listed Vietnam (along with Korea, Japan, and twelve other states) in his guidelines for future generations as "not to be invaded."[60] Like Korean relations with Chinese dynasties, the 800-year China–Vietnam relationship lasted, by any standard, for an exceedingly long time.

Vietnam, in addition to Korea, was "widely recognized as [one of] the premier domains of manifest civility after the Middle Kingdom."[61] Vietnam first entered into a tributary relationship with China upon its independence in the tenth century, and from that time on, "Song [Chinese] rulers unquestionably placed the Vietnamese kingdom at the top of a hierarchical system of relationships with leaders along

[58] Phan, 欽定越史通鑑綱目, preface.
[59] Shangqing Wu, "《钦定越史通鉴纲目》评介" [Comments on the "Imperially Ordered Annotated Text Completely Reflecting the History of Viet"], 史学史研究 [*Journal of Historiography*], no. 4 (1998), 65.
[60] Zhiben Chen and Zhaoyou Liu (eds.), 皇明寶訓 [Ancestral Injunctions of the Ming Dynasty], vol. 6 (Taipei: Taiwan Xue Sheng Press, 1986), 487
[61] Kelley, *Beyond the Bronze Pillars*, 182.

the southern frontier."[62] The Lê Dynasty (1427–1789) was considered one of the "most loyal" tributaries of China, and tribute missions and cultural imports and learning were regular and comprehensive.[63]

The China–Vietnam border was clearly demarcated as early as 1079, and "has remained essentially unchanged to the present day."[64] The Vietnamese and Chinese had agreed that "the Quan Nguyen and Guihua prefectures [were] two sides of a 'fixed border' region between the two states."[65] A fifteenth-century Vietnamese map shows the "official [route] for Vietnamese embassies traveling to the Chinese capital of Beijing. Going north from the capital, the map ... moves past the walled city of Lang-son to the great gate on the Chinese border leading into Guanxi Province."[66] When China and Vietnam signed their modern land boundary treaty in 1999, they agreed upon essentially this same historic border.

Recognition of the border, and the stability it represented, is woven through the writings of government officials of the time. The Trấn Nam/Zhennan Frontier Post (or South Holding Frontier Post) was located at the border of Guangxi province and Lạng Sơn defense command. For centuries it was "the main border post between the two domains."[67] As scholar-official Nguyễn Du (1765–1820) wrote in 1813,

The old affairs of Ly and Tran are distant and hard to find
The two kingdoms evenly divide at this lone rampart
But it is close to the Celestial, so one can finally understand the depth of the benevolence we receive
From the [Qing] emperor's palace looking down, this place is as if beyond the scattered clouds
Yet by my ears I can still make out a bit of the imperial tune.[68]

62 James A. Anderson, *The Rebel Den of Nùng Trí Cao: Loyalty and Identity along the Sino-Vietnamese Frontier* (Seattle: University of Washington Press, 2007), 8.
63 Wills, "South and Southeast Asia, Near East, Japan, and Korea," 20.
64 Keith Taylor, "The Early Kingdoms," in Nicholas Tarling (ed.), *The Cambridge History of Southeast Asia* (Cambridge: Cambridge University Press, 1993), 147.
65 Anderson, *The Rebel Den of Nùng Trí Cao*, 145.
66 John K. Whitmore, "Cartography in Vietnam," in J. B. Harley and David Woodward (eds.), *Cartography in the Traditional East and Southeast Asian Societies* (Chicago: Chicago University Press, 1994), 492.
67 Kelley, *Beyond the Bronze Pillars*, 81.
68 Kelley, *Beyond the Bronze Pillars*, 83.

The Vietnam–China border, especially the western areas, was especially difficult to define and patrol, given that the frontier was jungle-covered mountains populated by hill tribes. Indeed, "Qing authorities knew they had all they could do to control territory on their side of the border as it filled up with miners and frontier farmers, frequently encroaching on and clashing with the hill peoples," and "the Qing had regular procedures for the extradition of criminals to Annam."[69] In 1725, Vietnam had moved the border 120 *li* (about 40 miles) northwards into Yunnan, toward promising copper mines. Given the difficulties in dealing with the border, Ertai, an official and confidant of the Qing Yongzheng Emperor, argued that, "If we get the land we won't be able to defend it; if we get the people we won't be able to make any use of them." The Emperor agreed to let Annam keep 80 *li*, while 40 *li* returned to Qing. "The King of Annam sent officials to greet with great ceremony the emperor's edict conceding the territory," and the matter was settled.[70]

The history of Vietnam was as much about civil war and rebellion as it was about dealing with external powers. Perhaps most notable in terms of hierarchy was the pattern of rebellion and intervention in Vietnam. For centuries, the central political task in Vietnam was crafting political unity and dealing with civil war or rebellion; in contrast, China–Vietnam relations were generally unremarkable. The few times that China did intervene in Vietnam followed a pattern: China intervened in Vietnam only when the Chinese court felt the need to restore a fallen dynasty or state (*xing mie ji jiue*; 興滅繼絕). In this sense, every Chinese intervention into Vietnam was deemed necessary and legitimate because the invested rulers had been overthrown by traitors and villains.[71] More importantly, the IHV clearly shows almost every Chinese intervention into Vietnam was requested by Vietnam first.

[69] John E. Wills Jr., "Great Qing and Its Southern Neighbors, 1760–1820: Secular Trends and Recovery from Crisis," Paper presented at the Interactions: Regional Studies, Global Processes, and Historical Analysis, Library of Congress, Washington, DC (2001).
[70] Wills, "Great Qing and Its Southern Neighbors."
[71] Chung-Yu Chen, 清代中葉中國對越南宗藩關係的重建－以「中華世界秩序原理」的角度分析 [Rebuilding the Relationship Between China and Vietnamese During the Middle Period of Qing Dynasty: Analyzing from the view of "Chinese World Order Principle"], Ph.D. dissertation, 2016, Chinese Culture University, Taipei, Taiwan.

There were two major Chinese military interventions in Vietnam after the latter had entered into a tributary relationship with China. Significantly, in both of those interventions, the Chinese were initially invited in by their tributary in order to provide support for the regime against internal rebellion and insurgents. As was discussed in detail in Chapter 4, after the intervention of 1407, the Chinese ultimately decided to attempt to retain control of Vietnam. In 1788, in contrast, the Chinese left immediately. The 1788 Qing intervention was on behalf of the Lê dynasty, which the Qing court had properly invested as legitimate rulers of Vietnam.[72] In the late eighteenth century, rebel leader Nguyễn Huệ (阮惠) began to threaten the Lê court, and the king's mother appealed to Beijing for support. Taylor writes that "the Qianlong emperor was not interested in territorial expansion in the south, but, taking his duty as an overlord seriously, he approved a limited expedition to support Le dynasty forces in taking back their capital."[73] The Vietnamese ruler, Lê Duy Khiêm (黎維), was restored to his palace, where he

fruitlessly urged the Qing to advance against Nguyen Hue. Qing authorities were in the process of preparing to withdraw when ... Nguyen Hue rushed his armies north and pushed the Qing troops into and across the Red River ... Scholars assisting Nguyen Hue quickly negotiated peace with the Qing court, sending apologies, tribute, and appropriate words of submission.[74]

The relevant point is that the initial impetus came at Vietnam's request, rather than from China's ambitions for territorial expansionism.

There were two other Chinese interventions into the domestic politics of Vietnam during the time under study, in 1540 and 1593. In 1540, the Mạc and the Lê had become rival dynasties in Vietnam; the Lê were the properly invested rulers according to the Ming court in Beijing, but the Mạc appealed to China for investiture in their place. Taylor writes, "the question of whether the Le or the Mac were the legitimate rulers of the vassal state of An Nam was ignored until 1537."[75] The Ming court ultimately decided that the Mạc should recognize the Lê as suzerain, which Mạc Đăng Dung, leader of the Mạc regime, rejected. The Ming assembled a 100,000-man army on

[72] Kiernan, *Viet Nam*, 261.   [73] Taylor, *A History of the Vietnamese*, 378.
[74] Taylor, *A History of the Vietnamese*, 378.
[75] Taylor, *A History of the Vietnamese*, 243.

the border and prepared an expeditionary force against the Mạc in 1540. In response, Mạc Đăng Dung and forty of his officials crawled across the border bareheaded and requested to be allowed to submit to the Ming, yielding a small symbolic amount of territory to the Ming. The Ming army withdrew and recognized the Mạc as administrators of their territory, "albeit at a lower status in the scheme of tributary relationships than had previously existed for the Le … it was a small price to pay for Ming recognition and for peace on the northern border."[76]

In 1593, Mạc Mậu Hợp (莫茂洽), the fifth reigning emperor of the Mạc dynasty was killed by the force led by Lê Duy Đàm (黎維潭). Descendants of the Mạc turned to the Chinese court for help in the form of military intervention. After some internal debates, the Ming dynasty decided to neither "reject" the Lê nor "abandon" the Mạc, preferring to stay above the fray. Descendants of the Mạc were subsequently placed in Cao Bằng, and Lê Duy Đàm was recognized as the administrator.[77]

In sum, China and Vietnam engaged in diplomacy with each other on a consistent basis. Far from being isolated and autarkic, the early modern East Asian system developed rules and norms governing trade, border relations, diplomacy, and international migration. Vietnam and China co-existed for eight centuries in an explicit, formally recognized and unequal diplomatic relationship. China did not seek to renege on its commitment to Vietnam, and the unquestioned, unequal relative status between the two sides was the foundation of their stable relations.

7.6 Conclusion

Unlike Korea and Japan, Vietnam had influences from the rest of Southeast Asia, and its ethnic diversity and different cultures were unique. Yet Vietnam, like Korea and Japan, was so heavily influenced by China that the use of Confucian and Sinic ideas and institutions was simply the way things were done. Emulation was not necessarily even a conscious choice. Domestic politics also played an important role in

[76] Taylor, *A History of the Vietnamese*, 244.
[77] Yongchang Zheng, 論清乾隆安南之役:道義與現實之間 [On Qianlong's Annam War: Between Morality and Reality], *Bulletin of History Department at National Ch'eng Kung University*, 22 (1996), 221.

Vietnam's state formation, just as it did in Korea and Japan. Vietnam's rulers borrowed Chinese ideas for domestic legitimacy and prestige, and gaining China's recognition and support helped the rulers across the dynasties cement their political legitimacy. In turn, this centralized the court's power for domestic governance. Adopting and accepting Confucianism, tribute, and investiture all reinforced emulation of Sinic ideas, culture, and civilization in Vietnam's emergence as a state.

8 | *Epistemic Communities and Regional Connections*

How ideas spread, and how diffusion takes place, has often been either overlooked or simply assumed in studies of state formation around the world. Yet in East Asia, this book clearly shows diffusion of ideas about state formation from the hegemon to the periphery. These ideas were carried by actual people, who studied, learned, and interacted with each other across countries. There was an extensive epistemic community in historical East Asia that was central to the creation and dissemination of regional civilization that flowed mainly from China outward, from core to periphery. This epistemic community was composed of Buddhist monks and Confucian scholars. They studied at Buddhist temples and Confucian academies, wrote in a common Chinese language using common styles, and made up the bulk of government officials in each country.

These scholar-officials also staffed the diplomatic missions to other countries. These tribute missions comprised formal diplomatic relations at the time. The role of these epistemic communities was central to the diffusion of Sinic civilization across the region. Holcombe concludes that "through the reunified Sui and Tang dynasties, a degree of shared international aristocratic culture developed throughout East Asia. This was a time when elites in China, Korea, and Japan (as well as northern Vietnam) in some ways had more in common with each other than they did with their own peasants ... in particular, educated East Asians shared a common written language and literary canon. The glories of Tang poetry were as much admired by contemporary elites in Korea and Japan as they were in China."[1]

Confucian academies and Buddhist monasteries used Chinese language and Chinese texts to train scholar-officials across the entire East Asian region. Sugimoto and Swain observe that "Learned men of the fourth and fifth centuries probably knew how to use, if not produce,

[1] Holcombe, *A History of East Asia*, 109.

155

the Chinese-style calendar, used at least simple Chinese arithmetic in fiscal and construction work, and had an everyday knowledge of ills and cures according to Chinese medicine."[2]

8.1 Buddhism

The most influential initial conductors of Chinese civilization were Buddhist monks, who traveled widely and set up temples across East Asia. "Particularly vital to the formation of a shared East Asian cultural community were the connections provided by Buddhism."[3] Yet Buddhism was not simply a religious philosophy. It was also a means for the spread of the influence of Chinese civilization and learning across many disciplines. Thus, Buddhists brought with them Chinese culture, science, and philosophy. Both Korea and Japan actively sought out Chinese Buddhist monks for their teachings in general, as well as their religious teachings.

As one example, in 541, the Korean kingdom of Paekche "requested and received from Southern dynasty China not only copies of the Buddhist *sutras* but also physicians, craftsmen, painters, and specialists in the Confucian Classic *Book of Odes*."[4] As another example, in 552, during a Japanese court debate about whether to accept Buddhism, it was recorded that "'all the Western frontier lands without exception' worship the Buddha, Japan should not alone refuse to join them."[5] Holcombe notes that "Buddhism was the cutting edge of a powerful wave of continental influences that swept across Japan in these centuries." As Lee and de Bary describe it, "The introduction of Buddhism meant the importation not only of the religion but also of an advanced Chinese culture because by nature Buddhism was neither closed nor exclusive."[6]

Hwang writes that

Buddhism's influence also came from the great standing that China enjoyed as the perceived center of high culture. [Korea] sent students, scholars, and clergymen to the Middle Kingdom to gain exposure to advanced Buddhist

[2] Sugimoto and Swain, *Science and Culture in Traditional Japan*, 44.
[3] Holcombe, *A History of East Asia*, 109.
[4] Holcombe, *A History of East Asia*, 77–78.
[5] Holcombe, *A History of East Asia*, 78.
[6] Lee and de Bary, *Sources of Korean Tradition*, 34.

learning ... such activity was not limited to Buddhism, however; other aspects of Chinese culture were eagerly absorbed, including the complicated but impressively ordered set of teaching about government and politics known as Confucianism.[7]

We have already briefly discussed in previous chapters the influence of Buddhists or Confucians from Korea and Japan, who went to China to study and then returned back to their natal lands, bringing with them deep knowledge of Chinese civilization. "Almost imperceptibly, this Buddhist transmission was a lubricant bringing with it other Chinese influences as well."[8] The community was truly interlocked – many Chinese ideas came to Japan through Korea, not directly from China. For example, Buddhism was first imported into Japan in 552, when Korean Paekche kings sent a statue of Buddha and sutras to Japan. Another example of this epistemic community is the Koguryŏ monk Hyegwan, who studied in China for ten years before returning to Koguryŏ. In 625 he traveled to Japan, and he eventually became a key figure in Japanese Buddhism and lived at a key Buddhist temple by Japanese imperial command.

Holcombe points out that "Japanese monks who had been sent to study in China with the early embassies began returning home in the 630s, bringing with them firsthand knowledge ... a coalition developed involving some off these returned masters of Chinese learning."[9] Batten writes that

Japanese sources from the Heian and Kamakura periods are replete with stories of Buddhist monks coming to Japan from China to propagate Buddhist teachings and of Japanese priests making pilgrimages to China for the purpose of study. An excellent example is Ennin, the Tendai monk who spent the years 838–847 in Tang China studying Buddhism and also, not incidentally, acquiring a wealth of up-to-date information on Tang China.[10]

He adds, "At the level of prestige goods and information networks, Japan was fully merged with China and the rest of East Asia no later than the eighth century."[11] The process was similar in Korea. Early in the fourth and fifth centuries CE, Buddhist monks began to bring ideas

---

[7] Hwang, *A History of Korea*, 14.   [8] Holcombe, *A History of East Asia*, 110.
[9] Holcombe, *A History of East Asia*, 115.
[10] Batten, *To the Ends of Japan*, 211.   [11] Batten, *To the Ends of Japan*, 227.

and institutions to Korea from China. "Beginning in the time of King Chinhung (540–576), Silla monks studying abroad began to return home, bringing with them Buddhist images and scriptures … Buddhism was regarded primarily not as a religion but as a political–religious ideology that furthered the secular objectives of the state."[12]

Buddhism was just as influential a religion in Vietnam. As discussed in Chapter 7, Buddhism arrived in Vietnam quite early, and the Buddhist influence was enduring – and linked directly with Vietnam's relations with China. Although there is evidence that Buddhism came directly to Vietnam from India, over the centuries the flow of Buddhist ideas and influences increasingly came from China and was mediated by Chinese modifications of that religious philosophy. For example, King Lý Thái Tông (r. 1028–1054) ordered the sculpting of over 1,000 Buddhist status and 10,000 painted images. He "regularly requested Buddhist texts and materials from the Song."[13] In short, Vietnam was fully integrated into the regionwide community of Buddhist monks and the flow of religious and political ideas.

8.2 Confucianism and Classical Culture

Confucianism was thoroughly intertwined with Buddhism and larger Chinese civilization. The intellectual canon in China was composed of a broad array of texts that today are largely called "Confucian," although the term is as general as that of "Western culture." A better term might be "classical culture" that involves the great texts from ancient China. We use the term "Confucianism" simply for its convenience.

China, of course, was the first to develop and institute a civil service and examination system based on exhibiting mastery of these classical texts. The exam is the most vivid institutional expression of Confucian ideas about the importance of learning and "wise men" for governance. During Phase II of state formation and beyond, there were also Koreans, Japanese, and Vietnamese who sought to study in China in order to learn. Holcombe notes that "Sillans remained probably the most numerous group of foreign students studying in late Tang Chinese schools. Some eighty-eight Sillans are known to have passed

---

[12] Quoted in Lee and de Bary, *Sources of Korean Tradition*, 78.
[13] Lien and Sharrock, *Descending Dragon, Rising Tiger*, 68.

the civil service examination in China during the last century of the Tang dynasty. Several of them served in Tang government office before returning to Korea."[14] For example, Confucian scholars such as Ch'oe Chi'wŏn (857–?) and Sŏl Ch'ong (c. 680–750) emerged to play a major role in importing Chinese civilization to Korea, drafting diplomatic papers and functioning as political advisers.

Ch'oe, for example, passed the Tang civil service examination, held official appointments in the Tang bureaucracy, served as secretary to Gao Pian, and possibly even traveled to Vietnam. Gao was the Chinese military commander who was widely remembered as a famous governor of Vietnam, as discussed briefly in Chapter 7. The multi-ethnic makeup of the Chinese bureaucracy was notable as well: A Japanese, Abe-no Nakamaro, studied in China, passed the examination at the highest levels and became a Tang official. He was head of the Protectorate of Annam from 761 to 767.[15] At least eight imperial officials came from Vietnam as well during the Tang.

Another Sillan monk, Wŏn Kwang (d. 640), studied for eleven years in Tang and upon his return to Korea became an influential member of the Sillan court. In 602, he formulated a highly influential Sillan code of conduct. The first two of the precepts were explicitly Confucian, even using the standard Chinese characters for "loyalty" and "filial piety".[16] Wŏn Kwang wrote, "Here are five commandments for laymen: serve your sovereign with loyalty; attend your parents with filial piety; treat your friends with sincerity; do not retreat from a battlefield; be discriminating about the taking of life."[17]

It is important to note that Buddhism and Confucianism were not seen as rival philosophies or religions – indeed, the entire way in which East Asian religious and political philosophies function is syncretic and inclusive.[18] De Bary et al. note that "Buddhism and Confucianism were able to exist side by side in Japan for a thousand years without any serious conflict."[19] Lee and de Bary emphasize the syncretic nature of Buddhism and Confucianism – these were not oppositional philosophies, but rather deeply intertwined in many of their ideas. Lee and de Bary write that "in the early state, Buddhism helped foster the concept

---

[14] Holcombe, *A History of East Asia*, 113.   [15] Kiernan, *Viet Nam*, 111.
[16] Holcombe, *A History of East Asia*, 110.
[17] *Haedong kosung chon*, 18: 1020c–1021b, from Lee and de Bary, *Sources of Korean Tradition*, 45.
[18] Kang, "Why Was There No Religious War in East Asian History?"
[19] Quoted in De Bary et al., *Sources of Japanese Tradition*, 41.

of the state and aided in the understanding of Confucian political thought. This was possible because in the process of translating scriptures into Chinese, a certain amount of Confucianism was inevitable."[20]

Vietnam was as deeply influenced by Buddhism, Confucianism, and the underlying classical culture, as were Korea and Japan. The interactions between Vietnamese scholar-officials and their counterparts from China, Korea, and beyond are well documented. Kathlene Baldanza discusses an important fifteenth-century history, written by Lê Tắc, a Vietnamese Trần dynasty official who later lived in and served the Yuan court. His book, *A Brief History of Annan*, was a history of the region that "belonged neither to China nor to Vietnam."[21] Lê Tắc wrote: "undeserving as I am, I served the government [Trần] for more than fifty years I have been attached to the royal court [Yuan]. I am ashamed of my foolishness, all that I once studied is muddled and confused ... I will never be able to read all that I want from the past and present."[22] As Baldanza points out, "Le Tac is ashamed neither of his work with the Tran, nor of his even longer service to the Yuan. Rather, he is ashamed only at his inability to recall all that he learned in his youth ... he treats as significant only a third self-identification as a participant in the larger world of classical culture."[23] Indeed, we consistently find writing such as that of eighteenth-century Vietnamese scholar-official Nguyễn Vĩnh, who wrote of his service as an envoy to China that

The only literatus who can expand his capacity to the greatest degree, have his prestige praised at court, and his name honored for all ages in other lands is the envoy. Only someone who has the skill to govern [is] always aware of what is most important ... During the years of the Song dynasty [960–1279] ... the great talents all emerged in the south. It was at this time we came to be called a domain of manifest civility. Now to be able to see with one's own eyes [China] all that one has read in books, is that not the great joy in one's life?[24]

[20] Lee and de Bary, *Sources of Korean Tradition*, 28.
[21] Kathlene Baldanza, *Ming China and Vietnam: Negotiating Borders in Early Modern Asia* (Cambridge: Cambridge University Press, 2016), 15.
[22] Baldanza, *Ming China and Vietnam: Negotiating Borders in Early Modern Asia*, 15.
[23] Baldanza, *Ming China and Vietnam*, 16
[24] Kelley, *Beyond the Bronze Pillars*, 60–61.

Kathlene Baldanza discusses at length a book written by Hồ Nguyên Trừng (1374–1446), a Vietnamese prince who spent twenty years living in China and serving as an official of the Ming Board of Works. Hồ wrote *A Record of the Dreams of an Old Southerner*, which was an account of the achievements of the Trần dynasty (1225–1400), as well as a series of vignettes and poems. We should emphasize that the role of poetry in Sinic civilization was central to revealing education, erudition, and to establishing one's position as an educated member of a larger cultural realm. As Baldanza writes, "the importance of poetry for Ho Nguyen Trung cannot be overstated. For all literati of his time and place, poetry was a tool for displaying one's erudition and even for advancing one's career."[25] The final chapter in the book is a tale about a Vietnamese official escorting a Yuan envoy from the capital back to the border. The two spend ten days on a boat, composing poetry to pass the time. Hồ thus "ends his book with this scene of cross-border amity, expressed through 'brush talks' in the form of classical poetry."[26]

Another example of the cultural power of classical education comes from Korea. One of the most famous folk tales from historical Korea is the *Song of Chunhyang* (춘향가). In this tale, the governor's son of an outlying province falls in love with a commoner. All governors and local officials were appointed from the capital, and the governor was soon recalled back to the capital for another assignment. The son eventually passes the civil service exam with the highest score and is sent back to the original province as an ethics inspector (*amhaeng ŏsa*, 암행어사) in disguise. The new provincial governor is evil and rapacious – and decides to mock this itinerant visitor by asking him to write a poem, fully expecting it to be unsophisticated. However, the son reveals through his use of sophisticated Chinese characters that he is actually extremely well educated, and the poem is a clear indictment of the governor. As it dawns on the local ruffians that this is not the man they thought he was, the son stands up, displays the king's seal, and summons his military escort, who have also been disguised as commoners. They arrest the evil governor and save the day. This entire tale, famous in Korea, is suffused with Sinic references, from the central

[25] Baldanza, *Ming China and Vietnam*, 72.
[26] Baldanza, *Ming China and Vietnam*, 72.

appointment of local officials to the climax of the story being a poetry contest.

A vivid example of the epistemic community that educated scholar-officials participated in, and the cultural exchange that they eagerly sought with each other, comes from a famous meeting in 1597–1598 between Vietnamese and Korean scholar-officials in Beijing. Yi Sugwang (1563–1628) from Chosŏn Korea and Phùng Khắc Khoan (1528–1613) from Vietnam were in Beijing with their respective tribute missions to meet their Chinese counterparts. A detailed discussion between these two scholar-officials provides a vivid picture of the institutionalization of the Confucian state across the region, and the common classical cultural vocabulary that existed. Both were eminent scholars and both had passed the highest levels of the civil service examination. Yi, for his part, was holder of a *chinsa* (進士) degree, the highest and final degree in imperial examination, and what makes one eligible for entry into the Sŏnggyun'gwan (Royal Confucian Academy), the highest educational institution. Yi had continued his scholarly studies and by 1597 had risen to be director of the Sŏnggyun'gwan itself. Phùng was the senior member of the 1597–1598 Vietnamese embassy to China. He also was a *tiến sĩ* (進士, the Vietnamese equivalent of *chinsa*), a very talented literatus and an eminent Lê dynasty official, having most prominently served as vice-director on the board of the secretariat of state.

They met in Beijing in late 1597 as senior members of their respective delegations to China. Both scholars most likely resided in the same hostel, which was regularly used to house foreign delegations. They engaged in "brush talks" using their shared knowledge of Sinic literature to exchange poetry and ideas with each other. As Baldanza points out, "A Vietnamese scholars who performed well would be greeted as a success at home," noting that some of these exchanges were famous as anecdotes well into the nineteenth century.[27] Yi and Phùng discussed politics and culture. When Yi asked Phùng "what is the government system and what are the customs of your state?," Phùng replied "We study the teachings of Confucian and Mencius, *The Book of Poetry*, *The Book of Documents*, rites, and music. We study the essays

---

[27] Baldanza, *Ming China and Vietnam*, quoting Woodside, *Vietnam and the Chinese Model*, 115.

of Tang and Song presented scholars (*tien si*, 進士)."[28] As William Pore points out, when Yi asked about the government of Vietnam, "to Yi, it perhaps was important for its affirmation of one of Vietnam's similarities to Korea: its Confucian heritage."[29] Indeed, the nature of Yi's questions shows that he presumed institutional similarities in Vietnam and Korea.

Yi then asked "do you choose people [for the bureaucracy] on the basis of their poetry and compositions or on the basis of questions and themes? In addition, do you have a military examination?" Phùng's response is worth repeating in detail, because it shows the complexity of the examination system:

We do choose people on the basis of examinations. There is a provincial examination in two parts. The provincial examination is the first stage. In the first part, the examination is on the Five Classics and Four Books. In the second stage, one of the parts of the examination is on evaluating imperial decrees and royal edicts. In the third stage, poetry forms a part. In the fourth stage, the theme requires a response on the best way to rule the country. For the general examination, there are first, second, third and fourth stages. It is like the provincial examinations. In the fifth stage, there is the palace examination, which requires composition and the reply to questions. As for the military examination, the examinees' use of strategy is most important. There are talent competitions in horseback riding, elephant riding and shooting from horseback. Candidates are chosen every five years.

Yi's recollections of these interactions include a question from Phùng, who asks Yi how the Chosŏn government is organized. As Yi recounted in his collecting writings,

The [Vietnamese] envoy asked what the laws and system of our state were. I answered that we are governed by officials and regulations. In accord with the Celestial Empire, our officials are arranged in three ranks and six departments in ascending levels. As for our other laws and systems, they all respect the usages of China. The [Vietnamese] envoy commented, "Korea has long been regarded as a state gifted in the literary arts. My humble state cannot dare to approach its respect."[30]

---

[28] Baldanza, *Ming China and Vietnam*, 182.
[29] William Pore, "The Inquisitive Literatus: Yi Sugwang's 'Brush-Talks' with Phung Khuc Khoan in Beijing in 1598," *Transactions of the Royal Asiatic Society, Korea Branch*, 83, no. 1 (2008), 9.
[30] Translations taken from Pore, "The Inquisitive Literatus," 8.

What is remarkable in this exchange is the connectivity that spans these Sinic-influenced states. Both scholars grew up speaking different languages and lived in vastly different environments, yet they found commonality that needed little to no translation. The bond that connected them – and throughout much of East Asia – was rooted in the mastery of classical culture that drew on Buddhist and Confucian traditions, as well as in their understanding of the important contributions such classical culture had on governance and the writ of the state. Finally, in parting, Phùng wrote a poem to Yi that further reflected their shared cultural linkages:[31]

王道車書共	The Kingly Way has its conformity and universalism,
皇朝志紀編	But in the emperor's realm, the compilation of annals,
詩成聊使寫	The writing of poetry, and even the writings of envoys,
霞燦海雲煙	Are as the radiance of a sunset, sea clouds and mist.

8.3 Tribute Missions

Countries explicitly ranked each other on a hierarchy, and there were explicit expectations, rituals, and rights associated with different places on the hierarchy. The sending and receiving of tribute missions was carefully institutionalized, and countries of higher rank were allowed more frequent missions, and also given greater privileges for those missions. Most explicit were the number and frequency of tribute missions that China allowed other countries to send. Vietnam, the most highly ranked country in Southeast Asia, was allowed frequent tribute missions, and they were of higher quality than other countries were allowed, with greater rights and greater trading privileges, as well.

Initially, Buddhist monks, and over time increasingly Confucian scholar-officials, made up the majority of the personnel on the diplomatic tribute missions that were key sources of cultural transmission from China to Korea, Japan, and Vietnam. Ji-Young Lee's research concludes that "China's neighboring states manipulated external recognition from the hegemon in a form of symbolic politics but in ways that enhanced their legitimacy at home against domestic rivals."[32] Holcombe reports that, "Between the years of 413 and 502, no fewer

---

[31] Translations taken from Pore, "The Inquisitive Literatus," 8.
[32] Lee, *China's Hegemony*, 2.

than thirteen Japanese tribute missions are mentioned in Chinese dynastic histories ... the originally Chinese title 'general' (*jiangjun*) is pronounced *shogun* in Japanese, a word that would have a prominent future in Japan."[33] *Kentoshi* – the Japanese missions to China – were, like all tribute missions, massive affairs. Each mission "usually had four ships ... the largest complement of personnel was that of the seventeenth mission, with more than 600 persons."[34]

Later, between 607 and 894, the Japanese government commissioned twenty official embassies to China. China was, especially for Japan, very far away and hard to reach. Tribute mission would take years to complete, given the technology of the time, and the missions would often spend an entire year in China at the capital. So difficult and slow was communication that it took, for example, three years for news of a major rebellion in Tang China in 755 to reach the Japanese court.[35] In short, "Tributary relations with the Han dynasty and its successors were not 'just' superficial diplomatic contacts. Rather, they actively stimulated state formation in Japan by conferring political legitimacy on Wa chieftains, both directly through diplomatic recognition, and indirectly by providing them access to prestige goods."[36]

Batten notes that "ritualized exchanges were only the tip of the iceberg; diplomatic missions provided myriad opportunities for envoys to observe and collect information about their hosts ... indeed, collecting information was often the primary goal of the mission, such as acquisitions of texts and legal codes."[37] Cultural transmission was fundamentally a function of a regional epistemic community of Buddhist monks and Confucian scholars who eagerly exchanged ideas with each other and for whom China and Chinese learning and culture were the most highly prestigious and desired elements. Informally, through travel and study, and formally, through diplomatic tribute missions, these monks and scholars were the main source of learning and emulation in historical East Asia.

These missions were enormously arduous – travel at the time of the sixth century, or even the sixteenth century, was long and arduous. Even Korean embassy missions would take roughly two months to travel from Seoul to Beijing, often using a complete land route. For

[33] Holcombe, *A History of East Asia*, 87.
[34] Sugimoto and Swain, *Science and Culture in Traditional Japan*, 16.
[35] Holcombe, *A History of East Asia*, 123.
[36] Batten, *To the Ends of Japan*, 156.   [37] Batten, *To the Ends of Japan*, 209.

Vietnamese tribute missions, it was often years. Pore notes that "Phung Khac Khoan wrote that his journey was 13,000 *li* in length and had taken about eighteen months, having begun in the fourth lunar month of 1596 and ended with his arrival in Beijing in the tenth lunar month (Gregorian November) of 1597."[38] The missions would reside in Beijing for months at a time, before returning home.

8.4 Vietnamese Tribute Missions to China

A closer examination of Vietnamese tribute missions serves as a useful case study. From its inception in 968 until the late nineteenth century, tribute missions were a key diplomatic tool of the Vietnamese court. But more than that, these years-long missions served as a key means for Vietnamese scholar-officials to travel to, interact with, and learn from their counterparts in China and from around the region.

During the Ming Chinese dynasty (1368–1644), Vietnam sent seventy-four tributary missions to Beijing, averaging one every 3.7 years (see Table 8.1). Between 1644 and 1839, during the Qing dynasty, Vietnam sent forty-two missions to Beijing, an average of one every 4.6 years (see Table 8.2). Vietnam under the Lê dynasty (1427–1789) was particularly enthusiastic in its embassy missions to China. As Whitmore notes, "besides the standard role of political subordination and contact that these tributary missions undertook, they increasingly brought Vietnamese literati, those scholars committed to the beliefs of the Chinese classical and Neo-Confucian texts, in touch with the Sinic literati world as it actually existed and functioned. This included both administrative and social roles, as well as the literary."[39] In the middle of the fifteenth century, Vietnam sent embassies to Beijing "every year or two," where the new regime "sought recognition, offered tribute, congratulations, and condolences, and explained events that were occurring on the southern border."[40] Vietnamese official Hồ Sĩ Đống (1739–1785) wrote of his time as an envoy on a tribute mission:

I was transferred to take up the post as surveillance commissioner of Hai Duong. Later I received orders to serve as an envoy to the North [China].

---

[38] Pore, "The Inquisitive Literatus," 6.
[39] Whitmore, "Vietnamese Embassies and Literati Contacts," 1.
[40] Whitmore, "Vietnamese Embassies and Literati Contacts," 2.

Table 8.1. *Vietnamese tributary missions to China conducted during the Ming Dynasty*

Reign name	Reign years	Number of tributary missions
Hongwu 洪武	1368–1398	13
Jianwen 建文	1398–1402	0
Yongle 永樂	1403–1424	1
Hongxi 洪熙	1425	0
Xuande 宣德	1426–1435	3
Zhengtong 正統	1436–1449	9
Jingtai 景泰	1450–1456	4
Tianshun 天順	1457–1464	5
Chenghua 成化	1465–1487	10
Hongzhi 弘治	1488–1505	7
Zhengde 正德	1506–1521	5
Jiajing 嘉靖	1522–1566	4
Longqing 隆慶	1567–1572	0
Wanli 萬曆	1573–1620	8
Tianqi 泰昌	1621–1627	2
Chongzhen 崇禎	1628–1644	3
Total	**1368–1644**	**74**

Sources: Yunquan Li, 明清朝貢制度研究 [Study on the Ming and Ching Tributary System], PhD dissertation, Jinan University, Guangzhou (2003), 42; and Tingyu Zhang (ed.), 明史 [History of the Ming Dynasty], 12 vols (Peking: Zhonghua Press, 1974).

Table 8.2. *Vietnamese tributary missions to China conducted during the Qing Dynasty*

Reign name	Reign years	Number of tributary missions
Shunzhi 順治	1644–1661	1
Kangxi 康熙	1662–1722	13
Yongzheng 雍正	1723–1735	3
Qianlong 乾隆	1736–1795	15
Jianqing 嘉慶	1796–1820	5
Daoguang 道光	1821–1839	5
Total	**1644–1839**	**42**

Sources: John K. Fairbank, and S. Y. Teng, "On the Ch'ing Tributary System," *Harvard Journal of Asiatic Studies*, 6, no. 2 (1941), Table 5; and Li, 明清朝貢制度研究, 74.

I recalled when I was studying in the capital the Master [Nguyen Tong Khue] was living in seclusion in his home. I always regretted that I could not study under him. Now I was fortunate to be able to follow in his footsteps and view the [moral] radiance of the Esteemed Kingdom [China] ... This was truly a meeting of the minds.[41]

Kelley ends his extensive research on the writings of the Vietnamese scholar-officials by concluding that

This way of viewing the world as consisting of unequal domains of [Confucian] manifest civility which partook in a common cultural tradition, and this sense of anxiety that some Southern scholars felt at their land's inability to live up to the standard of such a domain, are important to keep in mind ... For while the existing scholarship has accustomed us to think of Southern [Vietnamese] envoys as proud believers in their own (cultural) importance who only "posed" as tribute bearers, in fact ... their minds may have been filled with quite contrary thoughts. Rather than seeking to demonstrate that "Vietnam" was "civilized" so that the "Chinese" would not invade, Southern envoys may have harbored other thoughts and intentions when they journeyed to the North.[42]

Relations between these Sinic states occurred within the same institutions and norms, and the interactions among them were vibrant. Confucian scholar-officials and Buddhist monks viewed themselves as members of the same intellectual, religious, and philosophical community. For example, Vietnamese scholar-official Li Bancun wrote in 1748 that

Chosŏn [Korea] and the Secure South [Vietnam] are especially considered as domains which have established the proper institutions. In the past I perused the *August Dynasty's Collections of Pearl and Jade* and the *Record of Collected Airs from Dongxing*. From these I saw that poetry in Chosŏn is deeply imbued with the ways of the Efflorescence [Confucianism]. My only regret is that I have never seen such a poetry collection from the Secure South.[43]

Lê Quý Đôn, writing in the eighteenth century, noted that

The people of Chosŏn are gentle and respectful. Envoys from our Viet kingdom who journey to Beijing to present tribute often meet with their

[41] Kelley, *Beyond the Bronze Pillars*, 47–48.
[42] Kelley, *Beyond the Bronze Pillars*, 36.
[43] Kelley, *Beyond the Bronze Pillars*, 49.

envoys. . . . The Eastern Kingdom [Chosŏn] is a kingdom of exemplary men who take pleasure in upholding trust and propriety and following [the teachings in the *Classic of*] *Poetry* and the *Venerated Documents*. This all inspires respectful admiration among others.[44]

The distance from Vietnam to Beijing was vast; and these missions would take over a year to make the trip. When the tribute missions entered China at the border, they would first conduct rituals there. They were then eventually escorted to the capital for a series of rituals that took places over the course of weeks. This included the exchange of tribute gifts and letters. They would then typically spend six months in Beijing, exchanging information, holding meetings, and conducting business. Accompanying personnel would interact with their counterparts, and official trade would occur. Trade also occurred at the border, between envoys left there to trade.

Tribute embassies served a number of purposes: They stabilized the political and diplomatic relationship between the two sides, provided information about important events and news, formalized trade, and allowed intellectual and cultural exchange among scholars. Tribute missions were massive affairs, involving hundreds of scholar-officials and supporting staff. Although in theory the number of people allowed on a mission was restricted, this number was also often exceeded. Missions themselves, composed of interpreters, physicians, alternates, messengers, and assistants, could comprise up to 200 people. Wills notes that "the [Vietnamese] Le kings sent regular tribute embassies, were meticulous in the use of seals and terminology, and prepared their own tribute memorials and accompanying documents in quite respectable literary Chinese."[45]

The Vietnamese court would begin the process of sending an embassy by instructing the Ministry of Revenue and the Imperial Household Department to draft an official request for approval to cross the border on a given day. This request would be delivered to the border, and a delegation of "awaiters of orders" would be dispatched to the border to await a response from China. The Vietnamese court would also select envoys and other members of the actual entourage. "A chief envoy journeying to the North to request investiture for the Southern king would have to be an official of at least second rank,

---

[44] Kelley, *Beyond the Bronze Pillars*, 189–190.
[45] Wills, "South and Southeast Asia, Near East, Japan, and Korea."

while the first and second assistant envoys had to be of the third or fourth rank."[46]

Serving on a mission was an immense honor, as is reflected in the following poem composed by scholar-official Nguyen Co Phu for the Vietnamese king in the fourteenth century:

To this distant domain which desires to be transformed official word has come ...

I will sincerely report our fief's efforts when I visit the Celestial Court

The benevolence we bathe in is as if from a golden goblet brimming to the rim

Already the radiance seems so close as I set off to receive his moral blessings

In this distant wilderness we will joyfully maintain this enterprise for ages to come.[47]

Kelley notes that the poem "describes the South's relationship with the North in strikingly unequal terms ... why [would] a Southern official describe the relationship in this manner to his own monarch. Could it be that the Southern elite actually believed in this characterization of their relationship with the North?"[48] Indeed, it is important to take seriously the beliefs of the actors at the time. Viewing the world as unequal was not strange, but instead it seemed self-evident to the people of the time. And thus, that rules and norms developed around an unequal, hierarchic international order rather than one based on equality is also not a surprise.

Vietnamese tribute sent to the Song in 1156 reveals both the character of the relationship and the wealth of Vietnam:

The tribute is extremely rich and all the characters in the letter were written with gold. There were 1200 *taels* of gold wares, half of them decorated with pearls or valuables; 100 pearls contained in gold vases, of which three were as big as eggplants, six as big as the cores of jackfruit, 24 as big as peach pits, 17 as big as palm hearts, and 50 as big as date pits, making a total of 100; there were 1000 catties of aloewood, 50 kingfisher feathers, 850 bolts of gold brocade decorated with dragons, six imperial horses complete with saddles,

[46] Kelley, *Beyond the Bronze Pillars*, 66.
[47] Kelley, *Beyond the Bronze Pillars*, 66.
[48] Kelley, *Beyond the Bronze Pillars*, 72.

plus the regular tribute of eight horses and five elephants. The envoys were quite proud of being able to bring so rich a tribute.[49]

This type of diplomacy reveals the way in which international relations had a formative impact on states throughout the region. Although China was clearly the center, and maintaining stable relations with China was paramount, these states sought information about each other, interacted with each other, and had a set of norms and practices that were recognized and accepted that communicated information about each other's preferences, interests, and goals. As noted previously, being able to read and write in sophisticated Chinese was central to presenting the state in a positive light to China.

Looking at the stability of their tribute relations with stable and effective states in Vietnam and with Siam in the early nineteenth century, the Qing rulers had every reason to believe that their inherited practices were working very well ... a multiplicity of sources of information increased the possibility that the emperor could demonstrate his mastery of the situation.[50]

8.5 Conclusion

There was clearly a wide intellectual community that ranged from Vietnam through China to Korea and Japan. Composed of Buddhist monks and Confucian scholar-officials, these members eagerly sought to interact with each other and exchange ideas and experiences. The diffusion of Sinic ideas and classical culture was carried by these scholar-officials and monks – along with texts and other artifacts.

---

[49] Li Tana, "A View from the Sea: Perspectives on the Northern and Central Vietnamese Coast," *Journal of Southeast Asian Studies*, 37, no. 1 (2006), 88.
[50] Wills, "Great Qing and Its Southern Neighbors."

9 | Who Doesn't Emulate?
The Borderlands of the Central Asian Steppe

The East Asian international system up to the nineteenth century was one of considerable diversity, composed of a number of consequential units. While many societies on the periphery of the Chinese hegemon sought Chinese civilization, others resisted emulating China. The fact that many political units chose *not* to copy Chinese practices but endured and survived throughout the entire time under study is further evidence that emulation was voluntary. For example, religious-ordered "mandala" states in Southeast Asia, such as Siam, regularly used the tribute system to interact with China for purposes of commercial exchange without ever copying Chinese practices.[1] Perhaps the most interesting contrast is with the semi-nomadic, pastoral peoples of the vast Central Asian steppe.

In contrast to the European historical experience, where bellicists claim that war led to mimicry and similar institutions and state-building, in East Asia it was the units most different – the diverse societies on the Central Asian steppe – that did the most fighting. These societies retained their own social, cultural, and organizational ideas and institutions. They generally neither wanted nor appreciated Chinese civilization, whether it was settled agriculture, clear territorial boundaries, or literary texts and governments. The fighting that did occur was rooted in ideological differences, rather than material interests or territorial ambitions. Their long periods of contact and interaction with Chinese states reflected selective borrowing or adaptation of Sinic traditions, and modification of Confucian values was more prevalent than pure emulation.

In this chapter, we show that culture and ideas, more than interests and material incentives, explain the lack of emulation of China by the steppe peoples and their preference to engage with Sinic norms and

[1] Colin Chia, "Social Positioning and International Order Contestation in Early Modern Southeast Asia," *International Organization* (in press).

172

practices on instrumental grounds. What we will observe is that war did not make states in the Central Asia steppe. Rather, it was the political societies that differed from China the most that also had the most trouble crafting stable relations with each other. The scholarly literature on relations between China and the Central Asian steppe over the past 2,000 years is vast, and our purpose here is to simply distill the key points as they relate to state formation. Most important, despite this being clearly where most of the fighting was in East Asia across two millennia, this is not where states formed. Rather, the fighting led to entrenched differences between the two sides. Culture, not material interests, explains this paradox.

9.1 Why All the Fighting?

Fighting along the periphery has been widely documented throughout China's border relations with the semi-nomadic, pastoral peoples of the vast Central Asian steppe. As noted in Chapter 4, Dincecco and Wang point out that "in centralized China ... the most significant recurrent foreign attack threat came from Steppe nomads ... external attack threats were unidirectional, reducing the emperor's vulnerability."[2] Rosenthal and Wong concur: "periodically, the people living beyond the Great Wall mobilized armies that could threaten major disruptions. These types of threats typically brought dynasties to their knees, but they occurred very infrequently and were separated by long periods of stable rule ... rates of conflict were radically different in China and Europe."[3]

But what explains all this fighting? In particular, why was there endemic conflict between China and the borderland peoples, but not among the Sinicized states of China, Korea, Japan, and Vietnam? Why did some polities accept and emulate Chinese civilization, and other marginal societies resist and eschew it? More specifically, why did the peoples of the Central Asian steppe not begin to create state institutions based on the Chinese model, even as they sporadically interacted with each other and ended up engaged in conflict over the centuries?

---

[2] Dincecco and Wang, "Violence Conflict and Political Development over the Long Run," 342.

[3] Rosenthal and Wong, *Before and beyond Divergence*, 162–168.

Relations between Chinese dynasties and the nomads highlight the importance of culture to the outbreak of violence. Material power is one consideration, but just as important, if not more, are the beliefs and identities that serve to define a group or nation. China was able to develop stable relations with other units that adopted similar civilizational identities: States that conducted diplomacy in the Chinese style, and states that were recognizable and legitimate to Chinese. Even though certain traditions and practices were selectively adopted, the consideration largely involved the weighing of costs and benefits or, as discussed in Chapter 2, rational learning. It was thus much harder to establish stable relations with political units that fundamentally questioned China's vision of the world.

It is not surprising that the political units that sought to resist Confucianism and Sinic notions of cultural achievement engaged in more conflict with the Chinese core. Reus-Smit points out that stability in international orders "rests not only on material capabilities, but also legitimacy. [International orders] face two interrelated legitimation challenges: to convert unequal material capabilities into political authority, and complex heterogeneity into authorized forms of cultural difference."[4] Moreover, the fundamental rejection of shared ideas, values, and beliefs would inevitably lead to increasing levels of tension because legitimacy derives from a "congruence between the social values associated with or implied by organizational activities and the norms of acceptable behavior in the larger social system."[5] Over time, the rejection creates "vicious cycles of repression and resistance" as coercive actions by one entity lead to greater resentment among others, especially those with different concepts of governance or means of political organization.[6] Authority relations that underpin the interactions between large, powerful states and their smaller neighbors are thus far more complex and go beyond material considerations alone.[7]

[4] Christian Reus-Smit, "Cultural Diversity and International Order," *International Organization*, 71, no. 4 (2017), 882.
[5] John Dowling and Jeffrey Pfeffer, "Organizational Legitimacy: Social Values and Organizational Behavior," *Pacific Sociological Review*, 18, no. 1 (1975), 122.
[6] David Lake, "International Legitimacy Lost? Rule and Resistance When America Is First," *Perspectives on Politics*, 16, no. 1 (2018), 10.
[7] Huang, *Power, Restraint, and China's Rise*.

Indeed, it may even point to the opposite of Tilly's dictum that "war made the state," where the most fighting occurred between dissimilar units, rather than homogenous, state-like ones. Indeed, neither states nor nomads ever truly changed their view of how best to organize themselves and their societies. The semi-nomadic peoples of Central Asia were playing a different international game by different rules, and thus crafting enduring or stable relations was difficult. The frontier was only turned into a border when other states, such as Russia, began to expand eastward in the eighteenth century, and the nomads were left with nowhere to move.

A number of scholars have made complementary arguments explaining patterns of relations between China and the Central Asian steppe. For example, Jack Hirshleifer argues that societies on the Central Asian steppe responded to the growth of a rich, advanced state nearby with increased raiding, border skirmishes, development of strong warrior cultures, and occasional conquest when some exogenous factor temporarily weakened the richer state.[8] Thomas Barfield points out that when trade was more advantageous, the steppe peoples traded with China; when trade was difficult or restricted, they raided China's frontier towns to get the goods they needed.[9] As Spruyt observes, "The organization of China and the steppe thus worked in parallel fashion."[10] The Chinese weighed the costs of warring with the nomads against the problems of trading with them; likewise, the nomads made similar considerations. Sechin Jagchid and Van Symons write, "When the nomads felt they were getting too little or the Chinese felt they were giving too much compared to the relative power of each participant, war broke out."[11]

Territorial ambitions were not at the forefront of the steppe rulers' minds. Rarely did the Central Asian peoples desire to expand across all of China. As such, "the nomads were generally more of a nuisance than a threat to China."[12] Although the Mongols of the thirteenth

---

[8] Jack Hirshleifer, "The Paradox of Power," *Economics and Politics*, 3, no. 3 (1991), 177–200.

[9] Thomas J. Barfield, *The Perilous Frontier: Nomadic Empires and China* (Cambridge: Basil Blackwell, 1989).

[10] Spruyt, *The World Imagined*, 101.

[11] Sechin Jagchid and Van Jay Symons, *Peace, War, and Trade along the Great Wall: Nomadic–Chinese Interaction through Two Millennia* (Bloomington: Indiana University Press, 1989), 1.

[12] Kang, *East Asia Before the West*, 10.

century clearly wanted to conquer the known world, this was the exception, not the rule. Even the steppe itself was far from as violent as is often depicted. MacKay explains that "the historical steppe was in fact a complex and diverse place ... nor was it inherently violent – war came and went, as we might expect in any region."[13]

The only other foreign conquest of China in its history came from the Manchus in the seventeenth century. But even here, the cause was more the collapse of the Ming empire than the attack of the Manchus. The consensus among historians appears to be that the early Manchus originally had no intention of trying to conquer China. But, as the Ming fell into greater internal disarray, and as eventually the dynasty was toppled from within by rebels, the Manchus pushed on an open door. The fall of the Ming and the rise of the Manchus were separate events. Although one had an influence on the other, they were not directly or causally related.

As Mote writes, "the circumstances of Ming collapse – the capital's finding itself suddenly defenseless against a foreseeable and far from invincible military attack – were not brought about by any general disintegration of government and society ... those circumstances were brought about carelessly ... the fall of the Ming was, in short, caused by an accumulation of political errors."[14] In fact, the founding of the Manchu dynasty was not obviously about conquest or rejection of the existing international order. More prosaic and pressing cost–benefit needs were clearly important to Nurhaci, the Jurchen chieftain who subsequently became the founding emperor of the Qing dynasty. Perdue notes that "As he defeated rival clan leaders ... he incurred responsibilities for provisioning these troops ... the urgent need for grain supplies became a major factor in the expansion of the state."[15] One of Nurhaci's first attacks on Ming frontier outposts, at Fushun in 1618, was prompted by heavy rains and the ruined harvests and the starvation that Nurhaci's people were facing.[16] As Pamela Crossley writes of the creation of the Manchu state and declaration of war against the Ming in the early seventeenth century,

---

[13] MacKay, "The Nomadic Other," 473.
[14] Mote, *Imperial China 900–1800*, 802.
[15] Peter Perdue, *China Marches West: The Qing Conquest of Central Eurasia* (Cambridge, MA: Belknap Press of Harvard University Press, 2005), 117.
[16] Swope, *The Military Collapse of China's Ming Dynasty, 1618–1644)*, 12.

It is probable that Nurhaci's declaration of war against the Ming was motivated less by the prospect of a dramatic increase in distributable wealth than by fears that the current levels would be constricted ... the conquest of Liaodong prepared the way for the creation of the Qing empire, so we are often inclined to associate it with the unlimited energies, hopes, and ambitions that "birth" implies ... Yet there is no point at which either the shape or his campaigns or his proclaimed reasons for them departs much from the consistent goal of protecting and enhancing the economic basis of the wealth his lineage had nurtured ... he achieved those ends, but there is no evidence that he was determined to do much more.[17]

Our purpose here is not to comprehensively delve into two millennia of China's relations with the Central Asian steppe, nor is it to isolate and explain only the outbreaks of violence. Rather, we focus on the broader patterns of border relations that endured over a long period of time: China's relations with the nomads were marked by skirmishing and occasional war, while China's relations with the Sinicized states of Korea, Japan, and Vietnam were marked by relatively stable diplomatic relations. That unipolarity – China's overweening material power and capabilities – was a constant feature in historical East Asia cannot explain both patterns at the same time. Instead, as the rest of this chapter explains, this stark contrast is rooted in ideational grounds. The kind of security relations achieved along the borderlands was indicative of the social interactions, norms, and practices that the rulers and elites on both sides were exposed to. Why some polities emulated China and others did not is as much about cultural ideas as it is power or structural conditions.

9.2 Culture, Not Material Interests

The steppe peoples of Central Asia existed along a vast frontier zone, and the disparate cultural and political ecology of the various nomads and China led to a relationship that, although mostly symbiotic, never resulted in a legitimate cultural or authoritative relationship between the two. These peoples of the steppes had vastly different worldviews and political structures than the Sinicized states; they eschewed written texts and settled agriculture, and fundamentally questioned Chinese ideas of civilization and Confucianism. What centralization that

---

[17] Pamela Crossley, *The Manchus* (Oxford: Blackwell, 1997), 69–74.

existed was mainly due to the personal charisma and strength of the ruler, and Perdue writes that "tribal rivalries and fragmentation were common."[18] As Daniel Rogers points out, "mobility is a hallmark of Inner Asian societies, but, like pastoralism, it is not a unitary concept ... Inner Asian polities were not always clearly centralized under a single ruler, instead traditions of hierarchy were embedded in the aristocratic lineages from which leaders came."[19]

As a result, there was far more complex organization along this vast region than simple roving bands of nomads. Indeed, Rogers underscores that "steppe polities display characteristics of both complex chiefdoms and simple states ... this is a reflection of the 'inapplicability of the terminology of settled societies to the history of pastoral nomads.'"[20] MacKay describes the political ecology as "steppe environmental conditions [that] drove wide-ranging adaptations," while William Honeychurch notes that "pastoral nomadic polities represent alternative forms of complex organization that were different from sedentary counterparts ... but still quite complex in unexpected ways."[21] However, we should not privilege structural or environmental causes too centrally in examining the organization of the Central Asian peoples. There is nothing inherently more conducive to pastoral nomadism in the Central Asian steppe than there was in the Chinese central plain: Under different situations, China could just as easily have not emerged as a central hegemonic state but could have been something entirely different.

The peoples of the Central Asian steppe knew very well what China and Chinese civilization were. And, borne out of cost–benefit considerations, many of the peoples used Chinese-style institutions when it suited their interests. Zhang argues that the interactions between China and the nomads were characterized by "instrumental hierarchy," which was aimed at maximizing units' self-interest by exploiting hierarchical relationships.[22] For example, the Oirats and other

---

[18] Perdue, *China Marches West*, 520
[19] J. Daniel Rogers, "Inner Asian States and Empires: Theories and Synthesis," *Journal of Archeological Research*, 20 (2012), 210, 212.
[20] Rogers, "Inner Asian States and Empires," 242.
[21] MacKay, "The Nomadic Other," 484; and William Honeychurch, "Alternative Complexities: The Archeology of Pastoral Nomadic States," *Journal of Archeological Research*, 22, no. 4 (2014), 277.
[22] Zhang, *Chinese Hegemony*, 8

Mongol tribes actively used tribute missions in their dealings with China, as well as accepting investiture at various levels.[23] Between 1411 and 1424, Arughtai, a powerful Mongol chieftain, sent twenty-seven tribute missions to the Ming court. Even Altan Khan, a descendant of Kublai Khan and the leader of the Tümed Mongols who created the position of the Dalai Lama, was invested as a Ming vassal. The frequency of the tribute pointed to pragmatic interests for instrumental purposes. The titles were prestigious and highly profitable. As Henry Serruys explains, "cultural appeal never was the decisive factor for [the Mongols] ... Tribute presented to the Chinese court was always liberally paid for, and thus essentially constituted a form of exchange, or trade."[24] The higher the rank accepted by a Mongol chieftain, the more ornate the gifts he received in return for the tribute. Moreover, the prestige that came with the invested title enabled the Mongol chieftains to assert even greater control among their followers.

However, accepting some of the norms and institutions of the tribute system for practical and instrumental reasons of foreign relations with China is different from the full-range emulation that Korea, Japan, and Vietnam aspired to. Gaining the status as a tributary of China was a powerful indicator of authority for prestige and legitimacy, but the key distinction between the Sinicized states and the Central Asian steppe groups lies within the fundamental acceptance of the ideas and principles behind the authority of investiture, which only mattered within a society that already viewed and accepted Chinese civilization as legitimate. Put simply, selectively using some of these institutions and norms did not mean that the rulers of the Central Asian steppe were interested in emulating China to organize their societies in similar ways or for similar purposes. Indeed, Rogers points out that "describing the relationship as dependency, however, discounts the growing evidence for independent traditions of authority building and the complex interactions that the steppe pastoralists maintained in all directions."[25] Central Asian societies borrowed *some* ideas from Sinic civilization, but not all. They were not nearly as influenced by Confucianism, with its emphasis on literary texts and formal education, as were Sinicized

---

[23] Zhang, *Chinese Hegemony*, 147.
[24] Henry Serruys, *Sino-Mongol Relations during the Ming, II: The Tribute System and Diplomatic Missions (1400–1600)* (Brussels: Institut Belge Des Hautes Etudes Chinoises, 1967), 19.
[25] Rogers, "Inner Asian States and Empires," 216.

states. Central Asian societies were, however, more deeply influenced
by various strands of Buddhist philosophy and religion. Indeed,
MacKay points out the hybridity of Central Asian polities, noting that
"striking periods of hybridity between East and Inner Asian social
orders occurred during periods of foreign rule in China."[26]
     The evidence leads to the conclusion that these differences developed
not only for material reasons but also for reasons centered on identity
and deeply held cultural beliefs. Culture, beliefs, social organization,
institutions, and politics were all valued and reinforced in their difference. Unlike the agrarian societies of Korea, Japan, and Vietnam, the
peoples of the Central Asian steppe neither desired nor emulated
Chinese civilization. Nomads were willing to trade with the Chinese
and Koreans, but they had no intention of taking on or accepting
Chinese norms and cultures as did Korea, Japan, and Vietnam.
Wright concludes that

> China's failure to solve its barbarian problem definitively before the advent
> of the Manchu Qing dynasty was a function neither of Chinese administra-
> tive incompetence nor of barbarian pugnacity, but of the incompatibility
> and fixed proximity between very different societies, ecologies, and world-
> views. Many statements in historical records strongly suggest that the
> Chinese and the Nomads had clear ideas of their differences and were
> committed to preserving them against whatever threats the other side
> posed.[27]

From this perspective, the difference between Korea's, Japan's, and
Vietnam's relations with China in the late imperial period and China's
relationships with the Manchus, Tibetans, Burmese, Uyghur,
Mongolians, and the chiefdoms of Sichuan and Yunnan is clearer: To
the extent that selectively borrowing occurred by the latter nomadic
and semi-nomadic peoples, there were modifications to suit their local
circumstances and practices. The Manchus, for instance, adopted
Chinese state institutions before they invaded China, and inserted
"local variations within that dominant script [of neo-Confucian ideol-
ogy]."[28] When the Qing dynasty took hold, its rulers were still largely
influenced by its past experiences in the steppes for administration and
governance. As Spruyt explains, "[The Qing emperors'] legitimation
hinged on their ability to tap into multiple narratives and tropes to

[26] MacKay, "The Nomadic Other," 488.
[27] Wright, "The Northern Frontier," 76.   [28] Spruyt, *The World Imagined*, 98.

justify their role. Invoking Confucian traditions was only one means to do so."[29] In contrast, Korea, Japan, and Vietnam shared with China an elite who communicated in the same language, shared a similar sense of right and wrong, were given an education that emphasized their country's ritual role in a global ritual hierarchy, and were able to use this training to maintain their personal access to power.

Identity and deeply held cultural beliefs were just as important as material factors in causing endemic frontier skirmishes.[30] Peoples of the steppe were willing to trade with the Chinese and Koreans, but they had no intention of truly replacing or competing directly with Chinese norms and cultures. Alan Shiu Cheung Kwan argues that "China and the nomads formed an international society for much of their history, one based not on a common Confucian heritage or China's immutable centrality, but on the principle of an adaptable hierarchy based on common diplomatic norms and practices that allowed its members to affirm and contest their status within this hierarchy."[31] In short, explaining endemic warfare between a rich, powerful, territorial state and smaller, mobile polities is relatively straightforward.

9.3 Hybridity, Flexibility, and Localization of Practices

Amid the fighting and tussles between China and the nomadic and semi-nomadic tribes, centuries of interactions along the borderlands also provide additional evidence of rational learning for both sides. Mongol policies and views on primogeniture paralleled Confucian traditions, and the Mongols were quick to adapt and accommodate key aspects of Chinese administrative practices when they took over. Yet at the same time, a century of Mongol influence under the Yuan dynasty (1271–1368) left a surprisingly deep impact on the succeeding dynasty, the Ming (1368–1644), and its state administration. For instance, Mongol laws and forces were ubiquitous in the Ming court.[32] Indeed, we are well aware of the outmoded Sinocentric view that "China" simply absorbed its conquerors and totally changed them. As noted earlier in this chapter, neither the Manchus nor the Mongols

[29] Spruyt, *The World Imagined*, 99.   [30] MacKay, "The Nomadic Other."
[31] Alan Shiu Cheung Kwan, "Hierarchy, Status and International Society: China and the Steppe Nomads," *European Journal of International Relations*, 22, no. 2 (2015), 362.
[32] Spruyt, *The World Imagined*, 99.

were totally absorbed by the Chinese state. What the Mongols did do, however, was utilize many of the Sinic institutions and ideas to rule China and to deal with the states that were also relatively Sinicized. This is not one-way assimilation, but rather hybridity. After all, the nomadic and semi-nomadic groups along China's northern and western borders have co-existed with Chinese states for over six centuries. Through their interactions and familiarity with Sinicized culture, they also brought multiple influences to China. Evelyn Rawski underscores the significance of the peoples in the borderland and steppes in China's imperial formation, explaining:

With the exception of the Ming, north or northeast Asian regimes have ruled North China for over two-thirds of the millennium ending in 2000. The Qing incorporated China Proper into a multi-ethnic empire. The contemporary capital, Beijing, bears the marks of their presence in the names of its streets, the architecture of its palaces, and the Tibetan Buddhist temples that remain as artifacts of Qing imperial patronage, but many walking its streets read only the Chinese writing and ignore the rest. Qing rule, too, bore the marks of its northeast origins.[33]

While fighting and conflict tend to characterize relations between China and steppe peoples, far more interesting was the evidence of adaptability and flexibility that occurred, particularly when such groups as the Khitans, Jurchens, Tanguts, and Mongols took over territory on the Chinese boundaries. Spruyt observes that "the various empires that came to control Central and East Asia mutually influenced each other in practices and disposition," whereby a millennium of interactions led to symbiotic interactions.[34]

A vivid example of the steppe societies' selective adoption of key elements of the Chinese state after conquest is the Mongols. Although the Mongols are often viewed as having simply attempted to conquer everyone, as they began to legitimize and institutionalize their rule, they looked to two elements in particular. The first was to take on the Sinic "Mandate of Heaven," that justified their rule over China, eventually resulting in taking the reign name "Yuan dynasty." The second element was to look for other actors that acknowledged that mandate.

---

[33] Evelyn Rawski, *Early Modern China and Northeast Asia: Cross-Border Perspectives* (Cambridge: Cambridge University Press, 2015), 226.

[34] Spruyt, *The World Imagined*, 101.

Thus, submission, rather than conquest, was often the goal by the mid-thirteenth century.

Mongol–Koryŏ relations exemplify this second observation. After refusing to submit for twenty-seven years, in 1258, the Koryŏ king sent a hostage (crown prince and future king Wŏnjong) to Mongols, and accepted "son-in-law" nation status with the Mongols. With the resolution of relative status, Mongol punitive expeditions stopped immediately in 1259. In fact, the dispatch of the crown prince was a form of paying homage to the new Yuan dynasty in China. And, although this was far from a voluntary process, Wŏnjong was treated well by the Yuan court since Kublai Khan was delighted to achieve something that even Tang Emperor Taizhong could not pull off – the submission of a Korean prince at the Chinese court.

As Sixiang Wang puts it, a "consequential dynamic of Mongol–Koryŏ relations was ... efforts by Kublai's officials to cast the Mongols as heirs to a long-standing imperial tradition."[35] Wang explains that it reflects the concept of *zhengtong* (正統; k: 정통, *chŏngt'ong*), which "tied political authority to a diachronic transmission through a line of previous imperial dynasties [and] points to the repertoire of political technologies tied to this genealogical notion of legitimacy."[36] Koryŏ leaders adroitly played their diplomatic hand with the Mongols, which involved "interpolating Korea into the repertoire of imperial legitimation, which rested on the idea that Korea's submission confirmed imperial legitimacy and that a proper empire ought to preserve Korea's political integrity." After Kublai's accession in 1271, the Mongols explicitly linked their political legitimacy to this tradition, and Koryŏ "appealed to a notion of a moral empire rooted in a common cultural inheritance ... and made common cause with their [Mongol] Confucian-minded officials."[37]

Centuries later, the Manchus also used many of the ideas, norms, and institutions of the Chinese state even while retaining many of their own practices as well. This diffusion process thus reflected modification and localization to new circumstances, with a conscious deliberation of which imported ideas, customs, and traditions to incorporate. MacKay notes that the Qing rule was a "distinctively Manchu

---

[35] Sixiang Wang, "What Tang Taizong Could Not Do: The Korean Surrender of 1259 and the Imperial Tradition," *T'oung Pao*, 104, no. 3–4 (2018), 339.
[36] Wang, "What Tang Taizong Could Not Do," 341.
[37] Wang, "What Tang Taizong Could Not Do," 342.

enterprise," although the Manchus, out of practicality, certainly adopted most of the imperial Chinese institutions and norms for governing China itself.[38] Indeed, Dincecco and Wang write,

> Traditionally, external threats came primarily from Steppe nomads ... Following the Manchu conquest of the Ming Dynasty in 1644, for example, the new Qing government put down a mass rebellion in central China, convincing the local gentry that "they could and should work as partners with the alien dynasty" ... the Ming–Qing dynastic change was not a critical shock to the viability of the imperial system.[39]

The Qing's military organization consisted of elite arrow units that reflected their hunting traditions. It rallied and successfully brought in a multiethnic force that included Han Chinese and Mongols to fight alongside the Jurchens.[40] Understanding the effectiveness of how previous dynasties like the Ming organized their militaries, the Qing court took on board similar military organizational strategies to centralize its power over the aristocracy and quell rebellions.

Elsewhere, selectively adopting existing Confucian rites and rituals was an important consideration for the Qing rulers too. The Manchu rule and takeover from the Ming saw a conscious effort by the former to use such Confucian concepts as merit and virtue to justify their ascendance to power and to argue that the unjust Ming rulers had lost their mandate to govern. But the Qing never engaged in full mimicry or emulation of Confucian traditions. As Spruyt explains, "the Qianlong emperor (r. 1735–1796), under whose rule the Qing Empire reached its greatest territorial extent, still insisted on the use of Manchu language, which remained an important language of imperial administration throughout the Qing dynasty. Additionally, Shamanism continued alongside Confucianism."[41]

All these examples point to flexibility and adaptability in the approach of the nomadic and semi-nomadic leaders toward

---

[38] Joseph MacKay, "Rethinking Hierarchies in East Asian Historical IR," *Journal of Global Security Studies*, 4, no. 4 (2019), 600.

[39] Mark Dincecco and Yuhua Wang, "Internal Conflict and State Development: Evidence from Imperial China," Working paper, University of Michigan (April 2021).

[40] Barfield, *The Perilous Frontier*.

[41] Evelyn Rawski, "Reenvisioning the Qing: The Significance of the Qing Period in Chinese History," *Journal of Asian Studies*, 55, no. 4 (1996), 829, cited in Spruyt, *The World Imagined*, 106.

governance. There were elements of performance and power in the longstanding interactions between the steppe peoples and China, and each side interpreted things for their own benefit. It was not unidirectional civilizing influences flowing from the core to the periphery, but more reflective of a hybridity and adaptation of a common script that governed the borderlands. Such an approach reflects rational learning, where selective elements are adopted for instrumental purposes and logic.

9.4 Conclusion

War did not make the state in East Asia. Rather, the units that did the most fighting over the centuries – China and the peoples of the Central Asian steppe – were quite aware of their differences and determined to preserve them as long and as clearly as possible. And significantly, the fighting over the centuries did not lead to similarity. Despite the fighting, for long stretches of time, the Central Asian steppe peoples had no interest in conquering China. Just as significantly, there was little desire by Central Asian societies to emulate Sinic civilization practices, norms, or ideas. The two sides had clear knowledge of each other and were determined to preserve their differences as long as possible. What this shows is that war, conquest, and states are not nearly as inevitable as the bellicist, European-derived theories would expect.

10 | Conclusion
East Asian Developmental States in the Twentieth Century

Deeply institutionalized and territorially defined states in historical East Asia emerged and developed under the shadow of a hegemonic international system through emulation, not competition. Many of these institutions lasted over 1,000 years in China, Korea, Japan, and Vietnam. The research presented in this book reveals that the bellicist argument linking war and state-making is a partial explanation based on one particular region and time, not a universal theory. This book introduces agenda-setting research that takes a central issue in the discipline – state formation – and opens up entirely new theoretical and empirical avenues for research.

Most importantly, emulation as the basis for state formation has widespread implications for the study of regions other than East Asia. There is likely far more emulation of ideas and institutions that informed state formation than has previously been recognized. In Europe, Latin America, Africa, and indeed in all regions of the world, emulation is probably far more pervasive and influential than current scholarship allows. The extant literature has been largely fixated on the bellicist competition model of state formation, so much so that clear patterns of emulation have been overlooked and undertheorized.

10.1 The Beginnings of a New Model of State Formation and Development

In the case of East Asia, we conclude this book by looking at how the past affects the present with regard to the forces that shape state formation. The influence of premodern ideas and institutions of East Asian states waned with the arrival of the Western colonizing powers. However, what is not often asked is whether there remains any link, no matter how tenuous, between the past and present. It is tempting to treat the transition from historical East Asia to the "modern," contemporary era as a complete rupture, and that nothing from the past remains or matters. This is too simplistic an observation. Between the one extreme of pure modernity

186

and adoption of all Western ideas and the other extreme that views history as a straightjacket lies the reality that ideas and cultural norms persist, institutions and their forms can lie latent, and that decisions and past practices can prove to be a partial guide to the future. It is in this midpoint that all countries – including East Asian countries – exist. The past has an influence, but it is only partial and selective.

The arrival of the Western colonial powers in the nineteenth century upended the East Asian system, both domestic and international. What was considered "modern" changed almost instantly from Chinese ideas to Western ideas. Institutions, norms, and even clothing and dress all changed. The impact of the West on East Asian societies was so powerful and direct that it could appear that nothing of the past remained. It also appeared at the time that the West was vibrant and creative, the East was stagnant and despotic.

However, after a century of chaos and change, the East Asian states began "miraculous" economic growth. Indeed, no matter how it is measured, China, South Korea, Japan, and Taiwan experienced spectacular economic growth over the second half of the twentieth century. Likewise, Vietnam is rapidly developing. It is widely accepted that the East Asian region has been the most successful region in terms of economic development and "catching up" to the West. This occurred despite the wide variety of political and economic systems – Japan's one-party democracy, China's and Vietnam's one-party authoritarianism, and military dictatorships and subsequent multiparty democracy in South Korea and Taiwan. The economic growth in these countries was so remarkable, and the growth occurred under political institutions that were so unlike those in the West, that the growth did not easily fit into existing models of economic development that had been developed to explain the Western experience.

As a result, beginning in the late 1970s, scholars of Asian development challenged the fields of economics, political science, and sociology to move beyond the longstanding dichotomy between a neoclassical free market and centrally planned economy in their study of economic development. Chalmers Johnson was particularly forceful in arguing that Japan's economic growth fit into neither category.[1] Stephan Haggard writes, "Spearheaded by scholars outside the

---

[1] Chalmers Johnson, *MITI and the Japanese Miracle: The Growth of Industrial Policy, 1925–1975* (Stanford, CA: Stanford University Press, 1982).

mainstream of North American economics, this work began by under-lining empirical anomalies: the myriad ways in which the East Asian cases failed to conform to the neoclassical view."[2] In the 1980s, as Japan's economic rise continued, and South Korea and Taiwan became successful developers (e.g., newly industrialized countries, or NICs), the debate over the explanation for their success intensified.

The dependent variable in the case of Asia's development was start-lingly clear: All three countries – and later, China – were experiencing economic development that was historically unprecedented by world standards in both pace and depth.[3] The issue was how to explain this growth. The debate began by focusing on whether state intervention was central to the NICs' economic success: The "state versus the market" debate.[4] In surprisingly little time, it became obvious that the common variable was extensive government intervention into the market. This finding made it clear that the simple dichotomy between a neoclassical free market and a centrally planned economy needed to be modified.

The concept of a "developmental state" emerged from this debate. The period of high growth in South Korea, Japan, and Taiwan is often characterized by relatively depoliticized states that were run by austere technocrats and stern military leaders who focused on national eco-nomic development as a priority. The role of the strong state and the bureaucracy is exemplified in the workings of South Korea's

---

[2] For an overview of the intellectual development of the field, see Stephan Haggard, "Institutions and Growth in East Asia," *Studies in Comparative International Development*, 38, no. 4 (2004), 4. For empirical assessments, see Richard Luedde-Neurath, *Import Controls and Export-Oriented Development: A Reassessment of the South Korean Case* (Boulder, CO: Westview, 1986); and Russell Mardon, "The State and the Effective Control of Foreign Capital: The Case of South Korea," *World Politics*, 43, no. 1 (1990), 111–138.

[3] Robert Wade, "East Asia's Economic Success: Conflicting Perspectives, Partial Insights, Shaky Evidence," *World Politics*, 44, no. 2 (1992), 270–320.

[4] For economic perspectives, see Alwyn Young, "The Tyranny of Numbers: Confronting the Statistical Realities of the East Asian Growth Experience," *Quarterly Journal of Economics*, 110 (1995), 641–680; Paul Krugman, "The Myth of Asia's Miracle," *Foreign Policy* (1994), 62–79; and Helen Hughes (ed.), *Achieving Industrialization in Asia* (Cambridge: Cambridge University Press, 1988). For discussions of statists, see Robert Wade, *Governing the Market* (Princeton, NJ: Princeton University Press, 1990); Alice Amsden, *Asia's Next Giant* (Oxford: Oxford University Press, 1989); and Stephan Haggard, *Pathways from the Periphery* (Ithaca, NY: Cornell University Press, 1990).

developmental state.[5] The existing literature on this subject postulates two major arguments. The first is that the state was largely, although not completely, autonomous from society.[6] The second central tenet follows from the first: Shielded from politics, a technocratic Weberian bureaucracy designed efficient policies and pursued a national agenda of development.[7] In the classic explication of the developmental state, Johnson argued that "in Japan politicians reigned while rulers ruled ... Bureaucrats make most of the major decisions ... and are the source of all major policy innovations in the system."[8]

Central to the concept of the developmental state lies the argument that the organization of bureaucracies has a direct influence on development strategies and success. Scholars argue that autonomous and insulated bureaucracies are more effective, can initiate major policy innovations, and implement their development policies in an objective and rational manner. This "Weberian" bureaucracy is insulated from social demands, internally coherent, relatively uncorrupt, staffed with far-sighted technocrats who put the national welfare above their individual needs, and yet retains ties to the business community with which it interacts quite closely. In many instances this bureaucracy has a single "pilot" agency that takes the overall lead in guiding and leading

---

[5] See Johnson, *MITI and the Japanese Miracle*; Peter Evans, *Embedded Autonomy* (Princeton, NJ: Princeton University Press, 1995); Amsden, *Asia's Next Giant*; Wade, *Governing the Market*; Haggard, *Pathways from the Periphery*; Ziya Önis, "The Logic of the Developmental State," *Comparative Politics*, 24, no. 4 (1991), 109–126; and Chalmers Johnson, "Institutions and Economic Performance in South Korea and Taiwan," in Frederic Deyo (ed.), *The Political Economy of the Newly Industrializing Countries in Asia* (Ithaca, NY: Cornell University Press, 1987).

[6] Ben Ross Schneider, "The Career Connection: A Comparative Analysis of Bureaucratic Preferences and Insulation," *Comparative Politics*, 25, no. 3 (1993), 331–350; Michio Muramatsu and Ellis Krauss, "Bureaucrats and Politicians in Policymaking: The Case of Japan," *American Political Science Review*, 78 (1984), 126–146; and Barbara Geddes, "Building State Autonomy in Brazil, 1930–1964," *Comparative Politics*, 22 (1990), 217–234.

[7] Alice Amsden's celebrated work has emphasized the economic rationale for state discipline over big business by examining "two interrelated dimensions: (a) penalizing poor performers; and (b) rewarding only good ones." Amsden, *Asia's Next Giant*, 15.

[8] Johnson, *MITI and the Japanese Miracle*, 21. See also Bernard Silberman, "The Bureaucratic State in Japan: The Problem of Authority and Legitimacy," in Tetsuo Majita and J. Victor Koschman (eds.), *Conflict in Modern Japanese History: The Neglected Tradition* (Princeton, NY: Princeton University Press, 1982).

development. As Jonathan Hanson notes, "Basic state authority ... has a strong positive effect on [economic growth]."[9] Peter Evans has argued that "the internal organization of developmental states comes much closer to approximating a Weberian bureaucracy. Highly selective meritocratic recruitment and long-term career rewards create commitment and a sense of corporate coherence."[10]

Forty years later, it is clear that the careful study of Asian development, and the theoretical standards that this scholarship has lived up to, has forced scholars to face a myriad of new ideas and issues. The concept of a "developmental state" has now become part of the canon in political economy.[11] New developments in microeconomics, sociology, and anthropology have underlined the role of institutions in East Asia's economic performance. Scholars no longer view markets as the frictionless intersection of supply and demand curves. Instead, markets are being reinterpreted as complexes of principal–agent relationships in which problems of imperfect and asymmetric information, contracting, and credibility are ubiquitous.[12] The smooth functioning of markets requires more than getting policies, incentives, or prices right. Also needed are public and private institutions that facilitate market exchange – everything from the legal system and a clear delineation of property rights, via the public provision of information, to informal institutions that build trust.[13] As Dani Rodrik points out,

[9] Jonathan K. Hanson, "Forging then Taming Leviathan: State Capacity, Constraints on Rulers, and Development," *International Studies Quarterly*, 58, no. 2 (2014), 380.

[10] Evans, *Embedded Autonomy*, 12.

[11] Meredith Woo-Cumings (ed.), *The Developmental State* (Ithaca, NY: Cornell University Press, 1999); and David C. Kang, "Bad Loans to Good Friends: Money Politics and the Developmental State in Korea," *International Organization*, 56, no. 1 (2002), 177–207.

[12] Dani Rodrik, "Getting Interventions Right: How South Korea and Taiwan Grew Rich," *Economic Policy*, 20 (1995), 141–193; Masahiko Aoki, *Information, Incentives, and Bargaining in the Japanese Economy* (New York: Cambridge University Press, 1988); Joseph Stiglitz and Marylou Uy, "Financial Markets, Public Policy, and the East Asian Miracle," *World Bank Research Observer*, 11, no. 2 (1996), 249–276; and World Bank, *The East Asian Miracle: Economic Growth and Public Policy* (New York: Oxford University Press, 1993).

[13] David C. Kang, "Transaction Costs and Crony Capitalism in East Asia," *Comparative Politics*, 35, no. 4 (2003), 439–459; Andrew MacIntyre, "Institutions and Investors: The Politics of the Economic Crisis in Southeast Asia," *International Organization*, 55, no. 1 (2001), 81–122; and Michael Ross,

"the quality of institutions is key" for economic growth.[14] Scholars continue to probe the relationship between development on the one hand and politics, corruption, the international system, and the role of history on the other.[15] As Haggard writes, "In the 1990s, intellectual developments ... provided earlier insights on government intervention with micro-foundations that made them legitimate to the economics profession."[16]

10.2 Linking the Past to the Present

Although the initial focus was on explaining economic growth, an obvious and underlying question was "where do developmental states come from?" Why do some countries develop strong state capacity and others not? In particular, why did the East Asian NICs develop as a region faster than any other region? Why were they the only countries that have managed to close the gap with the West? What are the institutional origins of the capitalist developmental state?

Scholars have adduced a variety of possible answers. The most ambitious of the avalanche of scholarship argued that it was conscious political decisions made by elites in the 1960s. As discussed in Chapters 1 and 2, many scholars working in the rationalist or institutional tradition pioneered by Weingast, Levi, North, and others emphasized choices and constraints on rulers: One way the ruler can communicate a sincere desire to reform is institutional. This strategy involves the voluntary delegation of political authority to disinterested technocrats: a "tying of hands" by political elites that will restrain their ability to interfere for political reasons in the formulation of economic

"Indonesia's Puzzling Crisis," Manuscript, University of California at Los Angeles (2003).

[14] Dani Rodrik, "Introduction," in Dani Rodrik (ed.) *In Search of Prosperity: Analytic Narratives on Economic Growth* (Princeton, NJ: Princeton University, 2003), 10.

[15] Kang, *Crony Capitalism*; Richard Doner, Bryan Ritchie, and Daniel Slater, "Systemic Vulnerability and the Origins of Developmental States: Northeast and Southeast Asia in Comparative Perspective," *International Organization*, 59, no. 2 (2005), 327–361; and Mushtaq H. Khan and Jomo Kwame Sundaram, *Rents, Rent-seeking and Economic Development: Theory and Evidence in Asia* (New York: Cambridge University Press, 2000).

[16] Haggard, "Institutions and Growth in East Asia," 14.

policy.[17] In a political restatement of the developmental state, Robert
Bates and Anne Krueger have argued that delegating authority to a
disinterested and technocratic elite can have a feedback effect. They
argue that sophisticated politicians may possess a response to this
dilemma: The creation of new agencies to which politicians delegate
the responsibility for a particular policy domain. The mission of these
public institutions is to defend the collective welfare rather than the
private political interests of particular politicians.[18] Policies can be
chosen on the basis of efficiency, rather than on the basis of political
calculations. In this manner, rent-seeking behavior is minimized. David
Waldner argues that "coalitional pressures" are key to institutional
formation.[19]

Other scholars have emphasized the role of external threats in
prompting the creation of strong states in East Asia. Richard Doner
et al. contend that "developmental states will only emerge when political leaders confront extraordinarily constrained political environments [and in particular] severe security threats."[20] Johnson and
Jung-en Woo have emphasized the centrality of external threats in
some successful developers.[21]

Yet other scholars began to argue that, although choices at the time
were of course important, recent history has also had an important
influence on the creation and emergence of developmental states. Atul
Kohli, Carter Eckert, and others argue that Japanese colonialism of
Korea (1910–1945) was the key element in producing South Korea's

---

[17] Johnson's discussion of the Japanese developmental state implicitly uses
voluntary delegation of power to the bureaucracy as the basis of the Japanese
success. See Johnson, *MITI and the Japanese Miracle*, 21.

[18] Robert H. Bates and Anne O. Krueger, "Generalizations from the Country
Studies," in Robert Bates and Anne Krueger (eds.), *Political and Economic
Interactions in Economic Policy Reform* (Oxford: Basil Blackwell, 1993), 464.
See also Kathleen Bawn, "Political Control versus Expertise: Congressional
Choices about Administrative Procedures," *American Political Science Review*,
89, no. 1 (1995); Terry Moe, "Politics and the Theory of Organization," *Journal
of Law, Economics, and Organizations*, 7 (1991), 106–129; and Matt
McCubbins and Thomas Schwartz, "Congressional Oversight Overlooked:
Police Patrols versus Fire Alarms," *American Journal of Political Science*, 28
(1984), 165–179.

[19] David Waldner, *State Building and Late Development* (Ithaca, NY: Cornell
University Press, 1999).

[20] Doner et al., "Systemic Vulnerability and the Origins of Developmental States."

[21] See Johnson, *MITI and the Japanese Miracle*, Chapter 2; and Jung-en Woo,
Race to the Swift (New York: Columbia University Press, 1991), Chapters 3–4.

developmental state of the 1960s.[22] Kohli writes that the Japanese transformed a corrupt Chosŏn state into a modern, developmental state, "capable of simultaneously controlling and transforming Korean society [and] created the framework for the evolution of a high-growth political economy."[23] Eckert argues that "from 1876 on Korea saw the emergence of a native entrepreneurial class that eventually turned its attention to industry. Far from stifling such growth, colonialism advanced it ... the Japanese permitted and abetted the developmental of a native bourgeoisie class."[24] As Vu points out, "by turning to history ... move away from proximate causes of developmental success and address deeper links in the causal chain. The goal is not to explain economic growth or build a profile of developmental states, but to account for their structure."[25]

Vu finds the origin of developmental states after colonialism, writing that "this explanation gives primary role to Koreans and Indonesians in the postcolonial period rather than to their colonial masters."[26] Wonik Kim argues that colonialism is the key era, but it is the political economy of the particular type of colonialism that is formative for developmental states. He argues that "the developmental state fundamentally requires relative income equality as the initial socio-economic condition."[27] This builds on Daron Acemoglu et al., who argue that colonialism shapes the character of institutions and, in particular, the income distribution in society.[28]

---

[22] Atul Kohli, "Where Do High Growth Political Economies Come From? The Japanese Lineage of Korea's 'Developmental State'," *World Development*, 22, no. 9 (1994), 1269–1293; and Carter J. Eckert, *Offspring of Empire: The Koch'ang Kims and the Colonial Origins of Korean Capitalism 1876–1945* (Seattle: University of Washington Press, 1991).

[23] Kohli, "Where Do High Growth Political Economies Come From?", 1270.

[24] Eckert, *Offspring of Empire*, 65.

[25] Tuong Vu, "State Formation and the Origins of Developmental States in South Korea and Indonesia," *Studies in Comparative International Development*, 41, no. 4 (2007), 28.

[26] Vu, "State Formation and the Origins of Developmental States in South Korea and Indonesia," 29.

[27] Wonik Kim, "Rethinking Colonialism and the Origins of the Developmental State in East Asia," *Journal of Contemporary Asia*, 39 (2009), 383.

[28] Daron Acemoglu, Simon Johnson, and James A. Robinson, "The Colonial Origins of Comparative Development: An Empirical Investigation," *American Economic Review*, 91, no. 5 (2001), 1369–1401.

10.3 Contrasting Views on the Writ of the State

This debate over East Asian growth is emblematic of the contemporary social science scholarship's focus on constraints rather than capacity. From the perspective of Western social science, the obvious question is: Why did these countries not become predatory or corrupt, despite their obvious extraordinary strength, capacity, and purpose, and despite how deeply intrusive they were in society and business?[29] The perspective – as noted earlier in Chapters 2 and 3 – derived from the Western and European experience, is that rulers are corrupt, and the scholarship begins with the assumption of the "abuse of power." As Weingast puts it, a "government strong enough to protect property rights and enforce contracts is also strong enough to confiscate the wealth of its citizens."[30] In contrast, Alice Amsden observed that "economic success in Korea challenges the assumption ... that government intervention degenerates into 'rent-seeking.'"[31]

This contrasting view reflects Western preoccupation with predation and the "abuse of rule" rather than the "responsibility of rule" that animated state formation in historical East Asia, dating all the way back to the principles behind the Mandate of Heaven. This book has shown how rulers in the region, largely unconstrained by domestic elites, did not devolve into predation or corruption.

The research presented in this book leads to a clear answer for the origins of the strong, capable states that arose in the second half of the twentieth century across East Asia. This answer is rooted deeply in the

[29] Levi, *Of Rule and Revenue.*

[30] Barry R. Weingast, "The Economic Role of Political Institutions: Market-Preserving Federalism and Economic Development," *Journal of Law, Economics, & Organization*, 11, no. 1 (1995), 1.

[31] Amsden, *Asia's Next Giant*, 327. For other specific instances, see Karl Fields, "Strong States and Business Organization in Korea and Taiwan," in Sylvia Maxfield and Ben Ross Schneider (eds.), *Business and the State in Developing Countries* (Ithaca, NY: Cornell University Press, 1992), 126–128; Johnson, "Institutions and Economic Performance in South Korea and Taiwan," 152–155; Önis, "The Logic of the Developmental State," 114; Yung-whan Rhee, Bruce Ross-Larson, and Gary Pursell, *Korea's Competitive Edge: Managing the Entry into World Markets* (Baltimore: Johns Hopkins University Press, 1984); Evans, *Embedded Autonomy*, 51–53; and Ben Ross Schneider and Sylvia Maxfield, "Business, the State, and Economic Performance in Developing Countries," in Sylvia Maxfield and Ben Ross Schneider (eds.), *Business and the State in Developing Countries* (Ithaca, NY: Cornell University Press, 1992), 17.

historical experience of these countries. Developmental states are the modern manifestation of the state formation that began over a millennium ago. These East Asian countries have longstanding tradition and experiences with strong states and stable societies. Although the arrival of the West in the late nineteenth century was an exogenous shock, it did not fundamentally destroy or dissolve these countries, their societies and institutions, or their historical memories. Developmental states did not develop *de novo*. Indeed, viewed through the lens of this book, it is not a surprise that China, Korea, Japan, and Vietnam have strong states and orderly societies: They have had them for literally millennia. The source of economic growth and strong states in East Asia is not confined to the decisions made in the 1960s or even in Japanese colonialism. The source dates farther back in antiquity. As Bruce Cumings points out, "if there has been an economic miracle in East Asia, it has not occurred just since 1960; it would be profoundly ahistorical to think that it did."[32] Haggard further explains, "the problem is deeper. The preoccupation with institutions, and the functionalism in much institutionalist thinking, has obscured more fundamental political and social processes that are themselves determinants of institutional form and quality."[33] However, neither Cumings nor Haggard goes far enough. It was not colonialism, or even the nineteenth or twentieth centuries, that provide the key insights into the historical and cultural origins of the strong, interventionist, developmental states in East Asia.

In fact, there is a deeper ideational cause: The fundamental political and social environment of Confucian East Asian states. It is common to dismiss arguments that identify deeply historical factors as being important for economic growth, and in particular arguments privileging Confucianism or cultural factors. This is probably prudent, because culture and history are broad, multifaceted, and at times a challenge to measure. Showing causality is prohibitively difficult, and indeed many cultural traits might have different or even opposite causal influences depending on other circumstances.

However, in the context of the rich, historical evidence provided in this book, it is fairly clear that the developmental states are the

[32] Bruce Cumings, "The Origins and Development of the Northeast Asian Political Economy: Industrial Sectors, Product Cycles, and Political Consequences," *International Organization*, 38, no. 1 (1984), 3.
[33] Haggard, "Institutions and Growth in East Asia," 56.

contemporary manifestation of the ancient states that evolved over 1,000 years ago. The respect for scholar-officials in the past has become the professional and technocratic bureaucratic elite of today. The examination system based on the Confucian classics of the past has become both the actual civil service examination and is also manifest in the high school and college entrance examinations that are infamous across the region. The dreaded Chinese *gaokao* (高考) higher education exam even uses the ancient term *zhuangyuan* (狀元) to denote the annual high scorer for the college exam. The reliance on the bureaucracy to make competent decisions taking the whole nation into account persists – an emphasis on the "responsibility of rule" and the Mandate of Heaven.

The evidence for emulation as a mechanism for state formation reverberated well beyond East Asia. Indeed, even European modernity was influenced by Chinese and East Asian innovations that were borrowed by the West in the nineteenth century. The Northcote–Trevelyan Report of 1854, which formed the basis of the modern British Civil Service, explicitly drew inspiration from the Chinese imperial examination system, as did the United States' Pendleton Civil Service Reform Act of 1883. European states borrowed some of the most central ideas and institutions of East Asian state formation, and it is just as likely that emulation occurred in other parts of the world. We hope our book is part of a process of incorporating and taking emulation seriously as an argument for state formation that can sit alongside bellicist competition.

Appendix
Major Events in Sinicization, 300–1100 CE

Year	Korea	Japan	Vietnam
second and third centuries CE			Buddhism and Confucianism arrive in Vietnam[a]
372	Buddhism comes to Koguryŏ through Sondo, a monk from former Qin		
372	Koguryŏ founds official Confucian Academy, *Taehak*, the first known center for study of Confucianism in Korea		
373	Koguryŏ promulgates first Chinese-style law codes		
384	Paekche adopts Buddhism		
Late fourth century		Confucian *Analects* introduced into Japan from Paekche Korea	
413–502		Thirteen tribute missions from Japan to various Chinese dynasties	
503	Silla adopts Chinese-style titles such as "king"		
514	Silla adopts Buddhism under King Pŏphŭng.		
520	Silla adopts Chinese-style bureaucratic government, administrative law, legal codes, and seventeen official titles		

(*cont.*)

Year	Korea	Japan	Vietnam
541	Paekche requests from southern China Buddhist sutras, physicians, craftsmen, painters, and the Confucian classic *Book of Odes*		
552		Buddhism introduced to Japan by Korean kings	
570	National conscript military introduced; Silla replaces local military lords with commissioners dispatched from the capital		
602	Sillan monk Wŏn Kwang, having studied in Tang for eleven years, formulates the first code of conduct, based explicitly on Confucian and Buddhist themes.		
604	Silla King Muyŏl adopts Chinese-style nomenclature	Prince Shōtoku promulgates the "Seventeen Injunctions," a new ideology of rule based on Confucian and Buddhist thought, drawing on Chinese rituals and regulations	
607–894		Japanese government commissions at least twenty official embassies to China	
625	Koguryŏ monk Hyekwan studies in China		

(cont.)

Year	Korea	Japan	Vietnam
628		Chinese system of timekeeping and calendar adopted, and a Chinese water-clock constructed	
636	Sillan monk Chajang studies in China		
630s		Dozens of Japanese monks go to study in China	
Mid-seventh century		Complete set of Chinese imperial titles officially adopted in Japan, with accelerated adoption of Chinese-style institutions	
645		*Taika* Reforms based on Chinese administrative and legal codes	
649–650	Sillan Buddhist monk Chajang persuades Queen Chindŏk to adopt Tang-style clothing and Tang calendar and reign periods		
651	More Silla reforms to organize its administration closer to the Chinese model		
661	Korean capital of Kyongju remodeled to imitate Tang capital Chang'an		
663	Silla–Tang alliance defeats Paekche–Yamato forces in the only war involving any two of China, Korea, Japan in over twelve centuries. Five years later, Silla–Tang defeat Koguryŏ, leaving Silla as sole Korean kingdom		

(*cont.*)

Year	Korea	Japan	Vietnam
664		Court titles reformed to be closer to Tang model	
670		Introduction of national tax; farmland allocation; creation of comprehensive administrative hierarchy of provinces and districts throughout the empire; and household registry system. National census to be held every six years, roughly along the lines of the Equal Fields system from China	
671		National Confucian Academy founded, with instruction in Confucian classics, law, calligraphy, mathematics, and Chinese language;[b] attempt to create civil service exams	
681	King Sinmun expands local administration to govern conquered territory; divides country into nine prefectures; reforms national conscript army into nine banners and ten garrisons		

(*cont.*)

Year	Korea	Japan	Vietnam
682	Silla founds Royal Confucian Academy, under the Ministry of Rites		
685	Further centralization of administration: post stations for movement of officials and documents; board of academicians study medicine, law, mathematics, astronomy, and water clocks; King Sinmun divides country into administrative districts based on the Chinese model; Silla capital Kyongju laid out like Chang'an, with geomancy and feng shui	Emperor Tenmu (r. 673–686) reorganizes bureaucracy, creates centralized conscript army based on Chinese models, centralizes tax system	
692–730	Confucian scholars Kangsu and Sŏl Ch'ong import Chinese civilization, diplomatic papers, and political advisers		
694		Chinese-style capital built at Fujiwara-kyō, near Nara. More than design – it is a "spatial dramatization of geomantic order, court power, and theocratic authority"	

(*cont.*)

Year	Korea	Japan	Vietnam
702		*Taiho* Code: administrative and law codes based on the Tang model. Over half who drafted the code come from immigrant families or had participated in embassies to the continent	
eighth century	Over eighty-eight Sillans pass the civil service examination in China; many return to Korea after serving in Tang government office		
712		*Kojiki* (Record of Ancient Matters) – court history written in Chinese	
718		*Yoro* Code compiled – further Tang reforms	
720		*Nihon Shoki* (Chronicles of Japan) written, based on Chinese histories	
724–749		Emperor Shomu has Chinese furniture, stationery, games, liturgical implements, musical instruments, armor and weapons, ceramics, wood and metal work, weaving and dyeing	

(*cont.*)

Year	Korea	Japan	Vietnam
757		*Yoro* Code implemented: "functioned in practice as well as on paper"	
788	Silla introduces first civil service examinations based on Chinese-language education and classics, but only aristocrats can take the exam (in China, commoners can also take exam)		
792		Conscript army lapses because no use for military	
973 and 975			Đinh Bộ Lĩnh sends tribute missions to the Song court; accepts investiture as tributary of China
990–1350			Vietnamese authors produce at least twenty-five official histories, based on the Chinese-style dynastic histories and written in Chinese
1013			National taxation implemented along with household registry

(cont.)

Year	Korea	Japan	Vietnam
1020			Lý Thái Tổ constructs an administrative palace next to the ceremonial palace
1042			Administrative legal codes based on Confucianism implemented
1075			Lý dynasty Vietnamese royal court introduces three levels of examinations to select men educated in Confucian and Chinese classics
1086			Court introduces a higher exam to select a *hàn lâm học sĩ*

[a] Kiernan, *Viet Nam*, 17, 92.
[b] Joseph Wong, "The Government Schools in Tang China and Heian Japan: A Comparative Study," MA Thesis, Australian National University (1979), 86.

Bibliography

Abramson, Marc S., *Ethnic Identity in Tang China* (Philadelphia: University of Pennsylvania Press, 2008).

Acemoglu, Daron, Simon Johnson, and James A. Robinson, "The Colonial Origins of Comparative Development: An Empirical Investigation," *American Economic Review*, 91, no. 5 (December 2001), 1369–1401.

Acharya, Amitav, "How Ideas Spread: Whose Norms Matter? Norm Localization and Institutional Change in Asian Regionalism," *International Organization*, 58, no. 2 (2004), 239–275.

Adler, Emanuel and Vincent Pouliot, "International Practices," *International Theory*, 3, no. 1 (2011), 1–36.

Amsden, Alice, *Asia's Next Giant: South Korea and Late Industrialization* (Oxford: Oxford University Press, 1989).

Anderson, James A., "Distinguishing between China and Vietnam: Three Relational Equilibriums in Sino-Vietnamese Relations," *Journal of East Asian Studies*, 13, no. 2 (2013), 259–280.

   The Rebel Den of Nùng Trí Cao: Loyalty and Identity along the Sino-Vietnamese Frontier (Seattle: University of Washington Press, 2007).

Aoki, Masahiko, *Information, Incentives, and Bargaining in the Japanese Economy* (New York: Cambridge University Press, 1988).

Baldanza, Kathlene, *Ming China and Vietnam: Negotiating Borders in Early Modern Asia* (Cambridge: Cambridge University Press, 2016).

Barfield, Thomas J., *The Perilous Frontier: Nomadic Empires and China* (Cambridge, MA and Oxford: Basil Blackwell, 1989).

Bates, Robert H. and Anne O. Krueger, "Generalizations from the Country Studies," in Robert Bates and Anne Krueger (eds.), *Political and Economic Interactions in Economic Policy Reform* (Oxford: Basil Blackwell, 1993).

Batten, Bruce, "Foreign Threat and Domestic Reform: The Emergence of the Ritsuryō State," *Monumenta Nipponica*, 41, no. 2 (1986), 199–219.

   To the Ends of Japan: Premodern Frontiers, Boundaries, and Interactions (Honolulu: University of Hawai'i Press, 2003).

Bawn, Kathleen, "Political Control versus Expertise: Congressional Choices about Administrative Procedures," *American Political Science Review*, 89, no. 1 (1995), 62–73.

205

Benn, Charles, *China's Golden Age: Everyday Life in the Tang Dynasty* (Oxford: Oxford University Press, 2002).

Berry, Mary Elizabeth, *Hideyoshi* (Cambridge, MA: Harvard University Press, 1982).

"Was Early Modern Japan Culturally Integrated?" *Modern Asian Studies*, 31, no. 3 (1997), 547–581.

Boli-Bennett, John and John W. Meyer, "The Ideology of Childhood and the State: Rules Distinguishing Children in National Constitutions, 1870–1970," *American Sociological Review*, 43, no. 6 (1978), 797–812.

Branch, Jordan, "'Colonial Reflection' and Territoriality: The Peripheral Origins of Sovereign Statehood," *European Journal of International Relations*, 18, no. 2 (2011), 277–297.

"Mapping the Sovereign State: Technology, Authority, and Systemic Change," *International Organization*, 65, no. 1 (2011), 1–36.

Breuker, Remco, "Koryŏ as an Independent Realm: The Emperor's Clothes?" *Korean Studies*, 27 (2003), 48–84.

Brindley, Erica Fox, "Barbarians or Not? Ethnicity and Changing Conceptions of the Ancient Yue (Viet) Peoples (~400–50 B.C.)," *Asia Major*, 16, no. 1 (2003), 1–32.

Buswell, E. Robert, Jr., "The 'Short-cut' (徑截) Approach of K'an-hua (看話) Meditation: The Evolution of a Practical Subitism in Chinese Ch'an Buddhism," in Peter N. Gregory (ed.), *Sudden and Gradual: Approaches to Enlightenment in Chinese Thought, Studies in East Asian Buddhism 5* (Honolulu: University of Hawaii, 1987), 321–377.

Call, Josep, Malinda Carpenter, and Michael Tomasello, "Copying Results and Copying Actions in the Process of Social Learning: Chimpanzees (*Pan troglodytes*) and Human Children (*Homo sapiens*)," *Animal Cognition*, 8 (2005), 151–163.

Centeno, Miguel, "Blood and Debt: War and Taxation in Nineteenth-Century Latin America," *American Journal of Sociology*, 102, no. 6 (1997), 1565–1605.

Blood and Debt: War and the Nation State in Latin America (University Park: Penn State University Press, 2003).

Chan, Hok-Iam, "The Chien-wen, Yung-lo, Hung-hsi, and Husan-te reigns, 1399–1435," in Frederick Mote and Denis Twitchett (eds.), *The Cambridge History of China*, vol. 7, *The Ming Dynasty, 1368–1644, Part I* (Cambridge: Cambridge University Press, 1988).

Chega, Pak, "A Reexamination of the Civil Service Examination System," in Peter Lee (ed.), *Sourcebook of Korean Civilization, vol. 2, From the Seventeenth Century to the Modern Period* (New York: Columbia University Press, 1996).

"On Revering China," in Peter Lee (ed.), *Sourcebook of Korean Civilization, vol. 2, From the Seventeenth Century to the Modern Period* (New York: Columbia University Press, 1996).

Chen, Chung-Yu, 清代中葉中國對越南宗藩關係的重建－以「中華世界秩序原理」的角度分析 [Rebuilding the Relationship Between China and Vietnamese During the Middle Period of Qing Dynasty – Analyzing from the view of "Chinese World Order Principle"], PhD dissertation, 2016, Chinese Culture University, Taipei, Taiwan.

Chen, Zhiben and Zhaoyou Liu (eds.), 皇明寶訓 [Ancestral Injunctions of the Ming Dynasty], vol. 6 (Taipei: Taiwan Xue Sheng Press, 1986).

Chia, Colin, "Social Positioning and International Order Contestation in Early Modern Southeast Asia," *International Organization* (in press).

Cho, Young-mee Yu, "Diglossia in Korean Language and Literature: A Historical Perspective," *East Asia: An International Quarterly*, 20, no. 1 (2002), 3–23.

Collcutt, Martin, "Kings of Japan? The Political Authority of the Ashikaga Shoguns," *Monumenta Nipponica*, 37, no. 4 (1982), 523–529.

Crossley, Pamela, *The Manchus* (Oxford: Blackwell, 1997).

Crowell, William, "Social Unrest and Rebellion in Jiangnan during the Six Dynasties," *Modern China*, 9, no. 3 (1983), 319–354.

Cumings, Bruce, "The Origins and Development of the Northeast Asian Political Economy: Industrial Sectors, Product Cycles, and Political Consequences," *International Organization*, 38, no. 1 (1984), 1–40.

D'Arcy, Michelle and Marina Nistotskaya, "The Early Modern Origins of Contemporary European Tax Outcomes," *European Journal of Political Research*, 57, no. 1 (2018), 47–67.

De Bary, William Theodore, *Confucian Tradition and Global Education* (New York: Columbia University Press, 2008).

De Bary, William Theodore, Donald Keene, George Tanabe, and Paul Valery, *Sources of Japanese Tradition: From Earliest Times to 1600* (New York: Columbia University Press, 2001).

Denyer, Simon, "China's Assertiveness Pushes Vietnam Toward an Old Foe, the United States," *Washington Post*, December 28, 2015.

Department of Asian Art, "Scholar-Officials of China," in Heilbrunn Timeline of Art History, Metropolitan Museum of Art, New York (October 2004), www.metmuseum.org/toah/hd/schg/hd_schg.htm.

Deuchler, Martina, *The Confucian Transformation of Korea* (Cambridge, MA: Harvard University Press, 1992).

Dincecco, Mark and Yuhua Wang, "Internal Conflict and State Development: Evidence from Imperial China," Working paper, University of Michigan (April 2021).

"Violence Conflict and Political Development over the Long Run: China versus Europe," *Annual Review of Political Science*, 21, no. 1 (2018), 341–358.

Dobbin, Frank, Beth Simmons, and Geoffrey Garrett, "The Global Diffusion of Public Policies: Social Construction, Coercion, Competition, or Learning?" *Annual Review of Sociology*, 33, no. 1 (2007), 460.

Doner, Richard F., Bryan K. Ritchie, and Dan Slater, "Systemic Vulnerability and the Origins of Developmental States: Northeast and Southeast Asia in Comparative Perspective," *International Organization*, 59, no. 2 (Spring 2005), 327–361.

Dowling, John and Jeffrey Pfeffer, "Organizational Legitimacy: Social Values and Organizational Behavior," *Pacific Sociological Review*, 18, no. 1 (1975), 122–136.

Dreyer, Edward L., "Continuity and Change," in David A. Graff and Robin Higham (eds.), *A Military History of China* (Lexington: University Press of Kentucky, 2012).

Duara, Prasenjit, "Religion and Citizenship in China and the Diaspora," in Mayfair Mei-hui Yang (ed.), *Chinese Religiosities: Afflictions of Modernity and State Formation* (Berkeley: University of California Press, 2008).

Duncan, John, "Examinations and Orthodoxy in Chosŏn Dynasty Korea," in Benjamin Elman, John Duncan, and Hermann Ooms (eds.), *Rethinking Confucianism: Past and Present in China, Japan, Korea, and Vietnam* (Los Angeles: University of California, 2002).

The Origins of the Chosŏn Dynasty (Seattle: University of Washington Press, 2000).

Ebrey, Patricia and Anne Walthall, *Pre-Modern East Asia: To 1800 – A Cultural, Social, and Political History* (Boston: Wadsworth Cengage Learning, 2014).

Eckert, Carter J., *Offspring of Empire: The Koch'ang Kims and the Colonial Origins of Korean Capitalism 1876–1945* (Seattle: University of Washington Press, 1991).

Economy, Elizabeth, "China: Harmony and War," *Council on Foreign Relations Blog*, February 11, 2011, www.cfr.org/blog/china-harmony-war.

Elman, Benjamin, "Political, Social, and Cultural Reproduction via Civil Service Examinations in Late Imperial China," *Journal of Asian Studies*, 50, no. 1 (1991), 7–28.

Elman, Benjamin, John Duncan, and Hermann Ooms (eds.), *Rethinking Confucianism: Past and Present in China, Japan, Korea, and Vietnam* (Los Angeles: University of California, 2002).

Evans, Peter, *Embedded Autonomy* (Princeton, NJ: Princeton University Press, 1995).

Fairbank, John K. (ed.), *The Chinese World Order: Traditional China's Foreign Relations* (Cambridge, MA: Harvard University Press, 1968).

Fairbank, John K., and S. Y. Teng, "On the Ch'ing Tributary System," *Harvard Journal of Asiatic Studies*, 6, no. 2 (1941), 135–246.

Farris, William, *Sacred Texts and Buried Treasures: Issues in the Historical Archaeology of Ancient Japan* (Honolulu: University of Hawai'i Press, 1998).

Feng, Li, *Early China: A Social and Cultural History* (Cambridge: Cambridge University Press, 2013).

Fields, Karl, "Strong States and Business Organization in Korea and Taiwan," in Sylvia Maxfield and Ben Ross Schneider (eds.), *Business and the State in Developing Countries* (Ithaca, NY: Cornell University Press, 1992).

Fravel, Taylor, "Regime Insecurity and International Cooperation: Explaining China's Compromises on Territorial Disputes," *International Security*, 30, no. 2 (2005), 46–83.

Geddes, Barbara, "Building State Autonomy in Brazil, 1930–1964," *Comparative Politics*, 22, no. 2 (1990), 217–234.

Giddens, Anthony, *Sociology* (Cambridge: Polity Press, 1989).

Giersch, Charles, "'A Motley Throng:' Social Change on Southwest China's Early Modern Frontier, 1700–1880," *Journal of Asian Studies*, 60, no. 1 (2001), 67–94.

Goddard, Stacie, *Indivisible Territory and the Politics of Legitimacy: Jerusalem and Northern Ireland* (Cambridge: Cambridge University Press, 2010).

Goldstone, Jack, "New Patterns in Global History: A Review Essay on *Strange Parallels* by Victor Lieberman," *Cliodynamics*, 1, no. 1 (2010), 92–102.

Gorski, Philip S., *The Disciplinary Revolution: Calvinism and the Rise of the State in Early Modern Europe* (Chicago: University of Chicago Press, 2003).

Gorski, Philip and Vivek Sharma, "Beyond the Tilly Thesis: 'Family Values' and State Formation in Latin Christendom," in Lars Kaspersen and Jeppe Strandsbjerg (eds.), *Does War Make States? Investigations of Charles Tilly's Historical Sociology* (New York: Cambridge University Press, 2017).

Grossberg, Kenneth, "Bakufu *Bugyōnin*: The Size of the Lower Bureaucracy in Muromachi Japan," *The Journal of Asian Studies*, 35, no. 4 (1976), 651–654.

Grzymala-Busse, Anna, "Beyond War and Contracts: The Medieval and Religious Roots of the European State," *Annual Review of Political Science*, 23, no. 1 (2020), 19–36.

"Strangled at Birth? How the Catholic Church Shaped State Formation in Europe," Manuscript, Stanford University (August 2018).

Haboush, JaHyun Kim, *Culture & State in Late Chosŏn Korea* (Cambridge, MA: Harvard University Asia Center, 2002).

Haggard, Stephan, "Institutions and Growth in East Asia," *Studies in Comparative International Development*, 38, no. 4 (2004), 53–81.

Pathways from the Periphery (Ithaca, NY: Cornell University Press, 1991).

Hall, John Whitney, "The Muromachi Bakufu," in Kozo Yamamura (ed.), *The Cambridge History of Japan* (Cambridge: Cambridge University Press, 1990), 175–230.

Han, Enze and Cameron Thies, "External Threats, Internal Challenges, and State Building in East Asia," *Journal of East Asian Studies*, 19, no. 3 (2019), 339–360.

Han, Sheng. *Dongya Shijie Xingcheng Shilun* (The *Studies on the Formation of East Asian World*), 1st ed. (Beijing: Zhongguo fang zheng chu ban she, 2015).

Hansen, Valerie, *Changing Gods in Medieval China, 1126–1276* (Princeton, NJ: Princeton University Press, 1990).

Hanson, Jonathan K., "Forging Then Taming Leviathan: State Capacity, Constraints on Rulers, and Development," *International Studies Quarterly*, 58, no. 2 (2014), 380–392.

Herbst, Jeffrey, "War and the State in Africa," *International Security*, 14, no. 4 (1990), 117–139.

Hevia, James Louis, *Cherishing Men from Afar: Qing Guest Ritual and the Macartney Embassy of 1793* (Durham, NC: Duke University Press, 1995).

Hiep, Le Hong, *Living Next to the Giant: The Political Economy of Vietnam's Relations with China under Doi Moi* (Singapore: ISEAS-Yusof Ishak Institute, 2016).

Hirshleifer, Jack, "The Paradox of Power," *Economics and Politics*, 3, no. 3 (1991), 177–200.

Hoffman, Phillip T. and Jean-Laurent Rosenthal, "The Political Economy of Warfare and Taxation in Early Modern Europe: Historical Lessons for Economic Development," in J. Drobak and J. Nye (eds.), *The Frontiers of the New Institutional Economics* (San Diego, CA: Academic Press, 1997).

Holcombe, Charles, *A History of East Asia: From the Origins of Civilization to the Twenty-First Century* (Cambridge: Cambridge University Press, 2011).

Huang, Chin-Hao, *Power and Restraint in China's Rise* (New York: Columbia University Press, 2022).

Huang, Chin-Hao and David C. Kang, "State Formation in Korea and Japan, 400–800 CE: Emulation and Learning, Not Bellicist Competition," *International Organization*, 76, no. 1 (2022), 1–31.

Hughes, Helen (ed.), *Achieving Industrialization in Asia* (Cambridge: Cambridge University Press, 1988).

Hui, Victoria, "Cultural Diversity and Coercive Cultural Homogenization in Chinese History," in Andrew Phillips and Christian Reus-Smit (eds.), *Culture and Order in World Politics* (New York: Cambridge University Press, 2020).

"Toward a Dynamic Theory of International Politics: Insights from Comparing Ancient China and Early Modern Europe," *International Organization*, 58, no. 1 (2004), 175–205.

War and State Formation in Ancient China and Early Modern Europe (Cambridge: Cambridge University Press, 2005).

Huntington, Samuel P., *Political Order in Changing Societies* (New Haven, CT: Yale University Press, 1968).

Hwang, Kyung Moon, *A History of Korea* (New York: Palgrave Macmillan, 2017).

Jagchid, Sechin and Van Jay Symons, *Peace, War, and Trade along the Great Wall: Nomadic-Chinese Interaction through Two Millennia* (Bloomington: Indiana University Press, 1989).

Jansen, Marius, *China in the Tokugawa World* (Cambridge, MA: Harvard University Press, 1992).

Jiang, Weidong, *Gao Ju Li Li Shi Bian Nian (The Chronicle of Goguryeo History)*, 1st ed. (Beijing: Ke xue chu ban she, 2016).

Johnson, Chalmers, "Institutions and Economic Performance in South Korea and Taiwan," in Frederic Deyo (ed.), *The Political Economy of the Newly Industrializing Countries in Asia* (Ithaca, NY: Cornell University Press, 1987).

MITI and the Japanese Miracle: The Growth of Industrial Policy, 1925–1975 (Stanford: Stanford University Press, 1982).

Johnston, Alastair Iain, *Social States: China in International Institutions, 1980–2000* (Princeton, NJ: Princeton University Press, 2008).

Kain, Roger J. P. and Elizabeth Baigent, *The Cadastral Map in the Service of the State: A History of Property Mapping* (Chicago: University of Chicago Press, 1992).

Kanagawa, Nadia, "East Asia's First World War, 643–668 CE," in Stephan Haggard and David C. Kang (eds.), *East Asia in the World: Twelve Events That Shaped the Modern International Order* (Cambridge: Cambridge University Press, 2020).

Kang, David C., "Bad Loans to Good Friends: Money Politics and the Developmental State in Korea," *International Organization*, 56, no. 1 (2002), 177–207.

Crony Capitalism: Corruption and Development in South Korea and the Philippines (Cambridge: Cambridge University Press, 2002).

East Asia Before the West: Five Centuries of Trade and Tribute (New York: Columbia University Press, 2010).

"International Order in Historical East Asia: Tribute and Hierarchy beyond Sinocentrism and Eurocentrism," *International Organization*, 74, no. 1 (2020), 65–93.

"Transaction Costs and Crony Capitalism in East Asia," *Comparative Politics*, 35, no. 4 (2003), 439–459.

"Why Was There No Religious War in East Asian History?" *European Journal of International Relations*, 20, no. 4 (2014), 965–986.

Kang, David C., and Alex Yu-Ting Lin, "US Bias in the Study of Asian Security: Using Europe to Study Asia," *Journal of Global Security Studies*, 4, no. 3 (2019), 393–401.

Kang, David C., Dat Nguyen, Ronan Tse-Min Fu, and Meredith Shaw, "War, Rebellion, and Intervention under Hierarchy: Vietnam–China Relations, 1365–1841," *Journal of Conflict Resolution*, 63, no. 4 (2019).

Karnow, Stanley, *Vietnam: A History* (New York: Penguin Books, 1997).

Keene, Donald, "Literature," in Arthur E. Tiedemann (ed.), *An Introduction to Japanese Civilization* (New York: Columbia University Press, 1974), 375–422.

Kelley, Liam, *Beyond the Bronze Pillars: Envoy Poetry and the Sino-Vietnamese Relationship* (Honolulu: University of Hawaii Press, 2005).

"Inequality in the Vietnamese Worldview and its Implications for Sino-Vietnamese Relations," Paper presented at the Roundtable on the Nature of Political and Spiritual Relations among Asian Leaders and Polities from the 14th to the 18th Centuries, University of British Columbia, Institute of Asian Research, Vancouver (April 19–21, 2010).

"Vietnam as a 'Domain of Manifest Civility' (Văn Hiến Chi Bang)," *Journal of Southeast Asian Studies*, 34, no. 1 (2003), 63–76.

Kelly, Robert, "A 'Confucian Long Peace' in Pre-Western East Asia?" *European Journal of International Relations*, 18, no. 3 (2012), 407–430.

Keyes, Charles, "The Peoples of Asia: Science and Politics in the Classification of Ethnic Groups in Thailand, China, and Vietnam," *Journal of Asian Studies*, 61, no. 4 (2002), 1163–1203.

Khan, Mushtaq H. and Jomo Kwame Sundaram, *Rents, Rent-seeking and Economic Development: Theory and Evidence in Asia* (New York: Cambridge University Press, 2000).

Khong, Yuen Foong, "The American Tributary System," *Chinese Journal of International Politics*, 6, no. 1 (2013), 1–47.

Kiernan, Ben, *Viet Nam: A History from Earliest Times to the Present* (Oxford: Oxford University Press, 2017).

Kim, Key-Hiuk, *The Last Phase of the East Asian World Order* (Berkeley: University of California Press, 1980).

Kim, Seonmin, *Ginseng and Borderland Territorial Boundaries and Political Relations Between Qing China and Chosŏn Korea, 1636–1912* (Oakland: University of California Press, 2017).

Kim, Sun Joo, "Taxes, the Local Elite, and the Rural Populace in the Chinju Uprising of 1862," *Journal of Asian Studies*, 66, no. 4 (2007), 993–1027.

Kim, Wonik, "Rethinking Colonialism and the Origins of the Developmental State in East Asia," *Journal of Contemporary Asia*, 39, no. 3 (2009), 382–399.

Kim, Young-Soo, *Kŏngukui chŏngch'i: yŏmal sŏncho, hyŏkmyŏnggwa munmyŏng jonhwa* [The Politics of Founding the Nation: Revolution and Transition of Civilization during the Late Koryŏ and Early Chosŏn] (Seoul: Yeehaksa, 2006).

Kiser, Edgar and Yong Cai, "War and Bureaucratization in Qin China: Exploring an Anomalous Case," *American Sociological Review*, 68, no. 4 (August 2003), 511–539.

Ko, Chiu Yu, Mark Koyama, and Tuan-Hwee Sng, "Unified China and Divided Europe," *International Economic Review*, 59, no. 1 (2018), 285–327.

Kohli, Atul, "Where Do High Growth Political Economies Come From? The Japanese Lineage of Korea's Developmental State," *World Development*, 22, no. 9 (1994), 1269–1293.

Krugman, Paul, "The Myth of Asia's Miracle," *Foreign Policy* (1994), 62–79.

Kuo, Ya-pei, "Redeploying Confucius: The Imperial State Dreams of the Nation, 1902–1911," in Mayfair Mei-hui Yang (ed.), *Chinese Religiosities: Afflictions of Modernity and State Formation* (Berkeley: University of California Press, 2008), 65–84.

Kwan, Alan Shiu Cheung, "Hierarchy, Status and International Society: China and the Steppe Nomads," *European Journal of International Relations*, 22, no. 2 (2015), 362–383.

Laam, Truong Buu, *New Lamps for Old: The Transformation of the Vietnamese Administrative Elite* (Singapore: Institute of Southeast Asian Studies, 1982).

Lai, Christina, "Realism Revisited: China's Status-Driven Wars against Koguryo in the Sui and Tang Dynasties," *Asian Security* (in press published online 30 June 2020).

Lake, David, "Escape from the State of Nature: Authority and Hierarchy in World Politics," *International Security*, 32, no. 1 (2007), 47–79.

"International Legitimacy Lost? Rule and Resistance When America Is First," *Perspectives on Politics*, 16, no. 1 (2018), 6–21.

Larsen, Kirk, "Roundtable Discussion of Yuan-kang Wang's *Harmony and War: Confucian Culture and Chinese Power Politics*," *International Security Studies Forum*, 4, no. 3 (2012), 4.

Ledyard, Gari, "Cartography in Korea," in J. B. Harley and David Woodward (eds.), *Cartography in the Traditional East and Southeast Asian Societies* (Chicago: Chicago University Press, 1994).

Posting on *Korea Web*, March 21, 2006, http://koreaweb.ws/pipermail/ koreanstudies_koreaweb.ws/2006-March/005455.html.

Lee, Ji-Young, *China's Hegemony: Four Hundred Years of East Asian Domination* (New York: Columbia University Press, 2016).

Lee, Kenneth, *Korea and East Asia: Story of a Phoenix* (London: Praeger, 1997).

Lee, Ki-Baik, *A New History of Korea* (Cambridge, MA: Harvard University Press, 1984).

Lee, Peter (ed.), *Sourcebook of Korean Civilization*, vol. 1, *From Early Times to the Sixteenth Century* (New York: Columbia University Press, 1993).

Sourcebook of Korean Civilization, vol. 2, *From the Seventeenth Century to the Modern Period* (New York: Columbia University Press, 1996).

Lee, Peter and Theodore de Bary, *Sources of Korean Tradition*, vol. 1, *From Early Times through the Sixteenth Century* (New York: Columbia University Press, 1997).

Levi, Margaret, *Of Rule and Revenue* (Berkeley: University of California Press, 1988).

Lewis, Mark Edward, *Sanctioned Violence in Early China* (Albany: State University of New York Press, 1990).

The Early Chinese Empires (Boston: Harvard University Press, 2007).

Lewis, Martin W. and Kären E. Wigen, *The Myth of Continents: A Critique of Metageography* (Berkeley: University of California Press, 1997).

Li, Tana, "A View from the Sea: Perspectives on the Northern and Central Vietnamese Coast," *Journal of Southeast Asian Studies*, 83–102.

Li, Yunquan, 明清朝贡制度研究 [Study on the Ming and Ching Tributary System], PhD dissertation, Jinan University, Guangzhou (2003).

Lieberman, Victor (ed.), *Beyond Binary Histories: Re-imagining Eurasia to c. 1830* (Ann Arbor: University of Michigan Press, 1999).

Lieberman, Victor, "Local Integration and Eurasian Analogies," *Modern Asian Studies*, 27, no. 3 (1993), 475–572.

Strange Parallels: Southeast Asia in Global Context, c. 800–1830, vol. 1, Integration on the Mainland (Cambridge: Cambridge University Press, 2003).

Strange Parallels: Southeast Asia in Global Context, c. 800–1830, vol. 2, Mainland Mirrors: Europe, Japan, China, South Asia, and the Islands (Cambridge: Cambridge University Press, 2009).

Lien, Vu Hong and Peter Sharrock, *Descending Dragon, Rising Tiger: A History of Vietnam* (London: Reaktion Books, 2014).

Liu, Haifeng, "Influence of China's Imperial Examinations on Japan, Korea, and Vietnam," *Frontiers in the History of China*, 2, no. 4 (2007), 493–512.

Lo, Jung-Pang, "Intervention in Vietnam: A Case Study of the Foreign Policy of the Early Ming Government," *Tsing-hua Journal of Chinese Studies*, 8, no. 1–2 (1979), 154–185.

Lockard, Craig A., "The Unexplained Miracle: Reflections on Vietnamese National Identity and Survival," *Journal of Asian and African Studies*, 29, no. 1–2 (1994), 10–35.

London, Jonathan, "Vietnam Needs Bold Responses to Its China Dilemma," *cogitAsia, Center for Strategic and International Studies, CSIS Asia Program*, March 29, 2016, www.cogitasia.com/vietnam-needs-bold-responses-to-its-china-dilemma.

Lopez-Alves, Fernando, "The Transatlantic Bridge: Mirrors, Charles Tilly, and State Formation in the River Plate," in Miguel Antonio Centeno and Fernando Lopez-Alves (eds.), *The Other Mirror: Grand Theory through the Lens of Latin America* (Princeton, NJ: Princeton University Press, 2001), 153–176.

Luedde-Neurath, Richard, *Import Controls and Export-Oriented Development: A Reassessment of the South Korean Case* (Boulder, CO: Westview, 1986).

McCubbins, Matt and Thomas Schwartz, "Congressional Oversight Overlooked: Police Patrols versus Fire Alarms," *American Journal of Political Science*, 28, no. 1 (1984), 165–179.

McHale, Shawn, "Mapping a Vietnamese Confucian Past and Its Transition to Modernity," in Benjamin Elman, John Duncan, and Hermann Ooms (eds.), *Rethinking Confucianism: Past and Present in China, Japan, Korea, and Vietnam* (Los Angeles: University of California, 2002), 397–430.

MacIntyre, Andrew, "Institutions and Investors: The Politics of the Economic Crisis in Southeast Asia," *International Organization*, 55, no. 1 (2001), 81–122.

MacKay, Joseph, "Rethinking Hierarchies in East Asian Historical IR," *Journal of Global Security Studies*, 4, no. 4 (2019), 598–611.

"The Nomadic Other: Ontological Security and the Inner Asian Steppe in Historical East Asian International Politics," *Review of International Studies*, 42, no. 3 (2016), 471–491.

March, James and Johan Olsen, "The Logic of Appropriateness," in Robert E. Goodin (ed.), *The Oxford Handbook of Political Science* (Oxford: Oxford University Press, July 2011).

Mardon, Russell, "The State and the Effective Control of Foreign Capital: The Case of South Korea," *World Politics*, 43, no. 1 (1990), 111–138.

Mass, Jeffrey, "The Early Bakufu and Feudalism," in Jeffrey Mass (ed.), *Court and Bakufu in Japan: Essays in Kamakura History* (New Haven, CT: Yale University Press, 1982).

Meyer, John, John Boli, George Thomas, and Francisco Ramirez, "World Society and the Nation-State," *American Journal of Sociology*, 103, no. 1 (1997), 144–181.

Millward, James, "Qing and Twentieth-Century Chinese Diversity Regimes," in Andrew Phillips and Christian Reus-Smit (eds.), *Culture and Order in World Politics* (New York: Cambridge University Press, 2020).

Mitterauer, Michael, *Why Europe? The Medieval Origins of Its Special Path* (Chicago: University of Chicago Press, 2010).

Mizokami, Kyle, "China's Scrappiest Enemy is a Familiar Foe," *The Week*, March 24, 2015.

Modelski, George, *Long Cycles in World Politics* (London: Macmillan Press, 1987).

Moe, Terry, "Politics and the Theory of Organization," *Journal of Law, Economics, and Organizations*, 7 (1991), 106–129.

Momoki, Shiro, "Land Categories and Taxation Systems in Đại Việt (11th–14th Centuries)," *The Newsletter (International Institute for Asian Studies)*, 79 (2019), 32–34.

"Local Rule of Dai Viet under the Ly Dynasty: Evolution of a Charter Polity after the Tang–Song Transition in East Asia," *Asian Review of World History*, 1, no. 1 (2013), 45–84.

Mote, Frederick, *Imperial China 900–1800* (Cambridge, MA: Harvard University Press, 1999).

Muramatsu, Michio and Ellis Krauss, "Bureaucrats and Politicians in Policymaking: The Case of Japan," *American Political Science Review*, 78 (1984), 126–146.

Nakai, Kate, "Chinese Ritual and Japanese Identity in Tokugawa Confucianism," in Benjamin Elman, John Duncan, and Hermann Ooms (eds.), *Rethinking Confucianism: Past and Present in China, Japan, Korea, and Vietnam* (Los Angeles: University of California, 2002), 258–291.

Nexon, Daniel H., *The Struggle for Power in Early Modern Europe: Religious Conflict, Dynastic Empires, and International Change.* (Princeton, NJ: Princeton University Press, 2009).

Nexon, Daniel H. and Iver B. Neumann, "Hegemonic-Order Theory: A Field-Theoretic Account," *European Journal of International Relations*, 24, no. 3 (2017), 662–686.

Nguyen, Khav Vien, *Vietnam: A Long History* (Hanoi: The Gioi, 2004).

North, Douglass C., *Structure and Change in Economic History* (New York: W.W. Norton & Company, 1981).

North, Douglass C. and Barry Weingast, "Constitutions and Commitment: The Evolution of Institutions Governing Public Choice in Seventeenth-Century England," *Journal of Economic History*, 49, no. 4 (1989), 803–832.

Önis, Ziya, "The Logic of the Developmental State," *Comparative Politics*, 24, no. 4 (1991), 109–126.

Palais, James, *Confucian Statecraft and Korean Institutions* (Seattle: University of Washington Press, 1996).

"Land Tenure in Korea – 10th to 12th centuries," *Journal of Korean Studies*, 4 (1982), 73–205.

Park, Eugene, *Between Dreams and Reality: The Military Examination in Late Chosŏn Korea, 1600–1894* (Cambridge, MA: Harvard University Press, 2007).

"War and Peace in Historical Korea: Institutional and Ideological Dimensions," in Young-Key Kim-Renaud et al. (eds.), *The Military and South Korean Society* (Washington DC: Sigur Center Asia Papers, 2006), 1–14.

Park, Seo-Hyun, "Changing Definitions of Sovereignty in Nineteenth-Century East Asia: Japan and Korea Between China and the West," *Journal of East Asian Studies*, 13, no. 2 (2013), 281–307.

Sovereignty and Status in East Asian International Relations (Cambridge: Cambridge University Press, 2017).

Parker, Geoffrey, *The Grand Strategy of Phillip II* (New Haven, CT: Yale University Press, 2000).

Perdue, Peter, *China Marches West: The Qing Conquest of Central Eurasia* (Cambridge, MA: Belknap Press of Harvard University Press, 2005).

"Strange Parallels across Eurasia," *Social Science*, 32, no. 2 (2008), 263–279.

"The Tenacious Tributary System," *Journal of Contemporary China*, 24, no. 96 (2015), 1002–1014.

Perry, Elizabeth, "Chinese Conceptions of 'Rights': From Mencius to Mao – and Now," *Perspectives on Politics*, 6, no. 1 (2008), 37–50.

Peterson, Mark, "View of the Frog Out of the Well," *Korea Times*, July 8, 2018.

Phan, Thanh Giản (ed.), 欽定越史通鑑綱目 *[The Imperially Ordered Annotated Text Completely Reflecting the History of Viet]* (Taipei: National Library, 1969).

Philpott, Daniel, "The Religious Roots of Modern International Relations," *World Politics*, 52, no. 2 (2000), 206–245.

Pines, Yuri, *The Everlasting Empire: The Political Culture of Ancient China and Its Imperial Legacy* (Princeton, NJ: Princeton University Press, 2012).

Poceski, Mario, *Introducing Chinese Religions* (New York: Routledge, 2009).

Pollack, David, *The Fracture of Meaning: Japan's Synthesis of China from the Eighth through the Eighteenth Centuries* (Princeton, NJ: Princeton University Press, 1986).

Pomeranz, Kenneth, *The Great Divergence: China, Europe, and the Making of the Modern World Economy* (Princeton, NJ: Princeton University Press, 2001).

Pore, William, "The Inquisitive Literatus: Yi Sugwang's 'Brush-Talks' with Phung Khuc Khoan in Beijing in 1598," *Transactions of the Royal Asiatic Society, Korea Branch*, 83, no. 1 (2008), 1–26.

Powell, Walter and Paul DiMaggio (eds.), *New Institutionalism and Organizational Analysis* (Chicago: University of Chicago Press, 1991).

Rawski, Evelyn, *Early Modern China and Northeast Asia: Cross-Border Perspectives* (Cambridge: Cambridge University Press, 2015).

Reid, Anthony, "An 'Age of Commerce' in Southeast Asian History," *Modern Asian Studies*, 24, no. 1 (1990), 1–30.

Reus-Smit, Christian, "Cultural Diversity and International Order," *International Organization*, 71, no. 4 (2017), 851–885.

   The Moral Purpose of the State: Culture, Social Identity, and Institutional Rationality in International Relations (Princeton, NJ: Princeton University Press, 1997).

Rhee, Yung-whan, Bruce Ross-Larson, and Gary Pursell, *Korea's Competitive Edge: Managing the Entry into World Markets* (Baltimore: Johns Hopkins University Press, 1984).

Robinson, Kenneth, "Policies of Practicality: The Chosun Court's Regulation of Contact with the Japanese and Jurchens, 1392–1580," Ph.D. dissertation, University of Hawai'i (1997).

Rodrik, Dani, "Getting Interventions Right: How South Korea and Taiwan Grew Rich," *Economic Policy*, 20, no. 3 (1995), 141–193.

   "Introduction," in Dani Rodrik (ed.), *In Search of Prosperity: Analytic Narratives on Economic Growth* (Princeton, NJ: Princeton University, 2003), 1–22.

Rogers, J. Daniel, "Inner Asian States and Empires: Theories and Synthesis," *Journal of Archeological Research*, 20 (2012), 205–256.

Rosenstein, Nathan, "War, State Formation, and the Evolution of Military Institutions in Ancient China and Rome," in Walter Scheidel (ed.), *Rome and China: Comparative Perspectives on Ancient World Empires* (Oxford: Oxford University Press, 2009).

Rosenthal, Jean-Laurent and R. Bin Wong, *Before and beyond Divergence: The Politics of Economic Change in China and Europe* (Cambridge, MA: Harvard University Press, 2011).

Ross, Michael, "Indonesia's Puzzling Crisis," Manuscript, University of California at Los Angeles (2003).

Rossabi, Morris (ed.), *China among Equals: The Middle Kingdom and Its Neighbors, 10th–14th Centuries* (Berkeley: University of California Press, 1983).

Schmid, Andre, "Tributary Relations and the Qing–Chosun Frontier on Mount Paektu," in Diana Lary (ed.), *The Chinese State at the Borders* (Vancouver: University of British Columbia Press, 2007).

Schneider, Ben Ross "The Career Connection: A Comparative Analysis of Bureaucratic Preferences and Insulation," *Comparative Politics*, 25, no. 3 (1993), 331–350.

Schneider, Ben Ross and Sylvia Maxfield, "Business, the State, and Economic Performance in Developing Countries," in Sylvia Maxfield and Ben Ross Schneider (eds.), *Business and the State in Developing Countries* (Ithaca, NY: Cornell University Press, 1992).

Schultz, Kenneth and Hein Goemans, "Aims, Claims, and the Bargaining Model of War," *International Theory*, 11, no. 3 (2019), 344–374.

Serruys, Henry, *Sino-Mongol Relations during the Ming, II: The Tribute System and Diplomatic Missions (1400–1600)* (Brussels: Institut Belge Des Hautes Etudes Chinoises, 1967).

Seth, Michael, *A Concise History of Korea* (Lanham, MD: Rowman and Littlefield, 2016).

Sharman, J. C., *Empires of the Weak: The Real Story of European Expansion and the Creation of the New World Order* (Princeton, NJ: Princeton University Press, 2019).

Sharpe, Eric J., *Comparative Religion* (London: Bristol Classical Press, 1994).

Silberman, Bernard, "The Bureaucratic State in Japan: The Problem of Authority and Legitimacy," in Tetsuo Majita and J. Victor Koschman (eds.), *Conflict in Modern Japanese History: The Neglected Tradition* (Princeton, NJ: Princeton University Press, 1982).

Simmons, Beth, "Rules over Real Estate: Trade, Territorial Conflict, and International Borders as Institutions," *Journal of Conflict Resolution*, 49, no. 6 (2005), 823–848.

Simmons, Beth, Frank Dobbin, and Geoffrey Garrett, "The International Diffusion of Liberalism," *International Organization*, 60, no. 4 (2006), 781–810.

Solingen, Etel, "Of Dominos and Firewalls: The Domestic, Regional, and Global Politics of International Diffusion," *International Studies Quarterly*, 56, no. 4 (2012), 631–644.

Solis, Mireya and Saori N. Katada, "Unlikely Pivotal States in Competitive Free Trade Agreement Diffusion: The Effect of Japan's Trans-Pacific Partnership Participation on Asia-Pacific Regional Integration," *New Political Economy*, 20, no. 2 (2015), 155–177.

Spiezio, K. Edward, "British Hegemony and Major Power War, 1815–1939: An Empirical Test of Gilpin's Model of Hegemonic Governance," *International Studies Quarterly*, 34, no. 2 (1990), 165–181.

Spruyt, Hendrik, "Diversity or Uniformity in the Modern World? Answers from Evolutionary Theory, Learning, and Social Adaptation," in William Thompson (ed.), *Evolutionary Interpretations of World Politics* (New York: Routledge, 2001), 110–132.

The Sovereign State and Its Competitors (Princeton, NJ: Princeton University Press, 1996).

"War and State Formation: Amending the Bellicist Theory of State Making," in Lars Kaspersen and Jeppe Strandsbjerg (eds.), *Does War Make States? Investigations of Charles Tilly's Historical Sociology* (New York: Cambridge University Press, 2017).

The World Imagined: Collective Beliefs and Political Order in the Sinocentric, Islamic and Southeast Asian International Societies (Cambridge: Cambridge University Press, 2020).

Standen, Naomi, *Unbounded Loyalty: Frontier Crossing in Liao China* (Honolulu: University of Hawai'i, 2007).

Steele, Abbey, Christopher Paik, and Seiki Tanaka, "Constraining the Samurai: Rebellion and Taxation in Early Modern Japan," *International Studies Quarterly*, 61, no. 2 (2017), 352–370.

Steenstrup, Carl, "The Middle Ages Survey'd," *Monumenta Nipponica*, 46, no. 2 (1991), 237–252.

Stigliz, Joseph and Marylou Uy, "Financial Markets, Public Policy, and the East Asian Miracle," *World Bank Research Observer*, 11, no. 2 (1996), 249–276.

Strange, Mark, "An Eleventh-Century View of Chinese Ethnic Policy: Sima Guang on the Fall of Western Jin," *Journal of Historical Sociology*, 20, no. 3 (2007), 235–258.

Stuart-Fox, Martin, *A Short History of China and Southeast Asia: Tribute, Trade and Influence* (Crows Nest: Allen and Unwin, 2003).

Sugimoto, Masayoshi and David L. Swain, *Science and Culture in Traditional Japan* (Rutland: Charles E. Tuttle Company, 1989).

Sullivan, Michael, "Ask the Vietnamese about War, and They Think China, Not the U.S," *National Public Radio*, May 1, 2015.

Swope, Kenneth, *The Military Collapse of China's Ming Dynasty, 1618–44* (New York: Routledge, 2014).

Taylor, Keith, *The Birth of Vietnam* (Berkeley: University of California Press, 1983).

"The Early Kingdoms," in Nicholas Tarling (ed.), *The Cambridge History of Southeast Asia* (Cambridge: Cambridge University Press, 1993), 137–182.

A History of the Vietnamese (Cambridge: Cambridge University Press, 2013).

"The Literati Revival in Seventeenth-Century Vietnam," *Journal of Southeast Asian Studies*, 18, no. 1 (1987), 1–23.

Taylor, P. J., "Ten Years That Shook the World? The United Provinces as First Hegemonic State," *Sociological Perspectives*, 7, no. 1 (1994), 25–46.

Teiser, Stephen F., *The Ghost Festival in Medieval China* (Princeton, NJ: Princeton University Press, 1996).

Thies, Cameron, "State Building, Interstate and Intrastate Rivalry: A Study of Post-Colonial Developing Country Extractive Efforts, 1975–2000," *International Studies Quarterly*, 48, no. 1 (2004), 53–72.

"War, Rivalry, and State Building in Latin America," *American Journal of Political Science*, 49, no. 3 (2005), 4551–4465.

Tilly, Charles, *Coercion, Capital, and European States, A.D. 990–1990* (Cambridge: Blackwell Publishing, 1992).

The Formation of National States in Western Europe (Princeton, NJ: Princeton University Press, 1975).

Toby, Ronald, "Rescuing the Nation from History: The State of the State in Early Modern Japan," *Monumenta Nipponica*, 56, no. 2 (2001), 197–237.

Vermeersch, Sem, *The Power of the Buddhas* (Cambridge, MA: Harvard University Asia Center, 2008).

Von Glahn, Richard, *The Economic History of China* (Cambridge: Cambridge University Press, 2016).

Vu, Tuong, "State Formation and the Origins of Developmental States in South Korea and Indonesia," *Studies in Comparative International Development*, 41, no. 4 (2007), 27–56.

"Studying the State through State Formation," *World Politics*, 62, no. 1 (2010), 148–175.

Wade, Robert, "East Asia's Economic Success: Conflicting Perspectives, Partial Insights, Shaky Evidence," *World Politics*, 44, no. 2 (1992), 270–320.

Governing the Market (Princeton, NJ: Princeton University Press, 1990).

Waldner, David, *State Building and Late Development* (Ithaca, NY: Cornell University Press, 1999).

Walker, Brett L., *A Concise History of Japan* (Cambridge: Cambridge University Press, 2015).

Wang, Gaoxin, *Er Shi Si Shi De Min Zu Shi Zhuan Shu Yan Jiu (The Studies on the Ethno-Historical Recounts in Twenty-Four Histories)*, 1st ed. (Hefei Shi: Huang Shan shu she, 2016).

Wang, Sixiang, "What Tang Taizong Could Not Do: The Korean Surrender of 1259 and the Imperial Tradition," *T'oung Pao*, 104, no. 3–4 (2018), 338–383.

Wang, Yuan-Kang, *Harmony and War: Confucian Culture and Chinese Power Politics* (New York: Columbia University Press, 2010).

Wang, Zhenping, *Tang China in Multi-Polar Asia: A History of Diplomacy and War* (Honolulu: University of Hawai'i Press, 2013).

Weingast, Barry R., "The Economic Role of Political Institutions: Market-Preserving Federalism and Economic Development," *Journal of Law, Economics, & Organization*, 11, no. 1 (1995), 1–31.

Whitmore, John K., "Cartography in Vietnam," in J. B. Harley and David Woodward (eds.), *Cartography in the Traditional East and Southeast Asian Societies* (Chicago: Chicago University Press, 1994).

"Chiao-Chih and Neo-Confucianism: The Ming Attempt to Transform Vietnam," *Ming Studies*, 1 (1977), 51–92.

"China Policy in the New Age: Le Thang-tong (r. 1460–1497) and Northern Relations," Paper presented at the annual meetings of the Association of Asian Studies (2005).

"Literati Culture and Integration in Dai Viet, c. 1430–c. 1840," *Modern Asian Studies*, 31, no. 3 (1997), 665–687.

"The Rise of the Coast: Trade, State, and Culture in Early Dai Viet," *Journal of Southeast Asian Studies*, 37, no. 1 (2006), 103–122.

"Vietnamese Embassies and Literati Contacts," Paper presented at the annual meetings of the Association of Asian Studies (2001).

Vietnam, Ho Quy Ly, and the Ming (1371–1421) (New Haven, CT: Yale University Press, 1985).

Wigen, Kären, "Culture, Power, and Place: The New Landscapes of East Asian Regionalism", *American Historical Review*, 104, no. 4 (1999), 1183–1201.

Wills, John E. Jr., "Great Qing and Its Southern Neighbors, 1760–1820: Secular Trends and Recovery from Crisis," Paper presented at the Interactions: Regional Studies, Global Processes, and Historical Analysis, Library of Congress, Washington, DC (2001).

"South and Southeast Asia, Near East, Japan, and Korea," in Maurizio Scapari (ed.), *The Chinese Civilization from Its Origins to Contemporary Times*, vol. II (Turin: Grandi Opere Einaudi, (in press).

Wolters, O. W., *Two Essays on Dai-Viet in the Fourteenth Century* (New Haven, CT: Yale University South Asia Studies, 1988).

Womack, Brantly, *China among Unequals: Asymmetric Foreign Relations in Asia* (Singapore: World Scientific, 2010).

China and Vietnam: The Politics of Asymmetry (Cambridge: Cambridge University Press, 2006).

Wong, Joseph, "The Government Schools in Tang China and Heian Japan: A Comparative Study," MA Thesis, Australian National University (1979).

Wong, R. Bin, *China Transformed: Historical Change and the Limits of European Experience* (Ithaca, NY: Cornell University Press, 2000).

Woo-Cumings, Meredith (ed.), *The Developmental State* (Ithaca, NY: Cornell University Press, 1999).

Woo, Jung-en, *Race to the Swift* (New York: Columbia University Press, 1991).

Woodside, Alexander, *Lost Modernities: China, Vietnam, Korea, and the Hazards of World History* (Cambridge, MA: Harvard University Press, 2006).

Vietnam and the Chinese Model (Cambridge, MA: Harvard University Asia Center, 1988).

"Vietnamese History: Confucianism, Colonialism, and the Struggle for Independence," *Vietnam Forum*, 11 (1988), 21–48.

World Bank, *The East Asian Miracle: Economic Growth and Public Policy* (New York: Oxford University Press, 1993).

Wright, David C., "The Northern Frontier," in David A. Graff and Robin Higham (eds.), *A Military History of China* (Lexington: University Press of Kentucky, 2012).

Wright, Mary, "The Adaptability of Ch'ing Diplomacy: The Case of Korea," *Journal of Asian Studies*, 17, no. 3 (1958), 363–381.

Wu, Shangqing, "《钦定越史通鉴纲目》评介" [Comments on the "Imperially Ordered Annotated Text Completely Reflecting the History of Viet"], 史学史研究 [*Journal of Historiography*], 4 (1998), 64–71.

Young, Alwyn, "The Tyranny of Numbers: Confronting the Statistical Realities of the East Asian Growth Experience," *Quarterly Journal of Economics*, 110, no. 3 (1995), 641–680.

Yu, Anthony C., *State and Religion in China* (Chicago: Open Court, 2005).

Zhang, Feng, *Chinese Hegemony: Grand Strategy and International Institutions in East Asian History* (Stanford, CA: Stanford University Press, 2015).

Zhang, Tingyu (ed.), 明史 *[History of the Ming Dynasty]*, 12 vols (Peking: Zhonghua Press, 1974).

Zhang, Yongjin and Barry Buzan, "The Tributary System as International Society in Theory and Practice," *Chinese Journal of International Politics*, 5, no. 1 (2012), 3–36.

Zhao, Dingxin, *The Confucian-Legalist State: A New Theory of Chinese History* (Oxford: Oxford University Press, 2015).

"The Mandate of Heaven and Performance Legitimation in Historical and Contemporary China," *American Behavioral Scientist*, 53, no. 3 (2009), 416–433.

"Spurious Causation in a Historical Process: War and Bureaucratization in Early China," *American Sociological Review*, 69, no. 4 (2004), 603–607.

Zhao, Gang, "Shaping the Asian Trade Network: The Conception and Implementation of the Chinese Open Trade Policy, 1684–1840," Ph. D. dissertation, Johns Hopkins University (2006).

Zhao, Zhibin, *Baiji Li Shi Bian Nian (The Chronicle of Baekje History)*, 1st ed. (Beijing: Ke xue chu ban she, 2016).

Zheng, Lina, *Fuyu Li Shi Bian Nian* 夫余历史编年 *(The Chronicle of Buyeo History)*, 1st ed. (Beijing: Ke xue chu ban she, 2016).

Zheng, Yongchang, 論清乾隆安南之役:道義與現實之間 [On Qianlong's Annam War: Between Morality and Reality], *Bulletin of History Department at National Ch'eng Kung University*, 22 (1996), 209–241.

Index

Acemoglu, Daron, 193
Acharya, Amitav, 29, 115
Amsden, Alice, **189**, 194
Anderson, James A., 72, 80
Annam (Ch. Annan 安南)
  independence from China as the state
    of Đai Cồ Việt, 70
  Sino-Vietnamese border established
    by rulers of the Đai Việt period, 72,
    150
Annam (Ch. Annan, 安南)
  Lê Tắc's *Brief History of Annan*,
    160
  as a Tang protectorate, 159
Ashikaga (or Muromachi) Shogunate
  (1338–1573), 44
  centralized control achieved by,
    126–127
  demise of the *ritsuryo* system during,
    119

Baigent, Elizabeth, 140
Baldanza, Kathlene
  on *A Brief History of Annan* by Lê
    Tắc, 160
  on "brush talks" engaged in by
    Vietnamese scholar-officials, 163
  on *A Record of the Dreams of an Old
    Southerner* by Hồ Nguyên Trừng,
    161
banks and banking
  and the absence of independent
    banks and finance in East Asian
    states, 14, 130
  independent central banks in Europe,
    13–15, 130
Barfield, Thomas J., 175
Bates, Robert H., 192
Batten, Bruce, 65–66, 98, 102, 109,
  113, 117, 129, 157, 165

bellicist thesis of state formation. *See
  also* European state formation—
  bellicist thesis of
Anglo-French warfare, 13–14
the Central Asian steppe as a counter
  example, 4, 58–59, 172–173, 176,
  181, 185
as a complex set of factors specific to
  Europe, not a universal theory,
  4–5, 14–16, 186
and contractualist arguments, 13–16,
  18, 30
and the Japanese shogunal system,
  94, 127
the Korean War of Unification not
  associated with state formation,
  63–64
lack of support in the empirical
  record of Phase I, 36–41
Mongol subjugation of Koryŏ as a
  counter example, 121, 183
the relative absence of bellicist
  pressures in Korea, 87–90
and the role of external threats in the
  creation of, 192
Tilly's (Charles) dictum that "war
  made the state, 3, 12, 175
Vietnamese state formation as a
  counter example, 72, 135
war as neither cause nor effect of
  state formation in East Asia, 60,
  63–64, 94
Benn, Charles, 55
Berry, Mary Elizabeth, 44, 65–66, 96,
  103
Boli-Bennett, John, 28
border negotiations
  clearly territorial polities defined in
  East Asia prior to those in Europe,
  2, 13

criticism of arguments of its
continuity, 21–22, 76–77
Chŏng Yag-yong (18th century)
(Korean scholar-official), 84
Chosŏn dynasty (1392–1910)
border negotiations with the Qing,
80–87
court dress of Ming dynasty officials
emulated by, 124
establishment of Six Ministries
(K. Yukcho), 124
Korean Buddhism during, 50, 52
local rebellions during, 48
military service and standing armies,
92, 132
neo-Confucian practices intensified
during, 119, 122–124
taxation implemented by, 132
tributary relations with the Ming, 65,
81, 121–122
Yi Sŏng-gye's founding of, 129
civil service
the establishment of the examination
system in the Sui–Tang era, 55–56
imperial academy for the study of
Confucian classics established
during the Han, 40
influence of China's imperial
examinations on Japan, 113
influence of China's imperial
examinations on systems in
Western states, 196
institutionalization of the civil service
examination in Vietnam, 140–143
selection process based on merit (not
heredity) established in East Asia
prior to, 2
Sinic references in the *Song of
Chunhyang* (춘향전), 162
colonialism
and income distribution in
developmental states, 193
Japanese colonialism of Korea,
193
Western impact on state formation in
East Asia, 187
Confucianism
administrative legal codes based on
Confucianism implemented by the
Lý dynasaty, 139

Chinese-style government run by
scholar-officials trained in, 41
Confucian Academy at Nara
established, 109
Confucian-Legalist state formation in
China, 20–21, 34, 37
founding of Taehak by the Koguryŏ,
97
as the imperial philosophy of the
Han, 39
National Academy (or Royal
Confucian Academy) established
by Silla, 109
neo-Confucian practices intensified
during the Chosŏn, 119, 122–124
neo-Confucianism during the Song,
45
as one of the three teachings
(*sanjiao*), 47
selective adoption by Manchu Qing
rulers, 184
Sinicization in historical East Asia
facilitated by, 9, 50, 100–101,
105–107, 117, 171
and the stability and endurance of
East Asian states, 60
syncretic nature of, 39, 46, 160
Temple of Literature (Văn Miếu, 文
廟) dedicated to Confucius built by
the Lý dynasty, 141
and Vietnam, 24, 136, 146, 154
corruption and predation
abuse of power as the fundamental
concern of the social contract in
European state formation, 42, 54,
194
exploitation of the small by the large
assumed in international relations
theory, 79
internal rivals proposed as a limit on,
14
lack of predation in East Asia, 14–15,
194
Crossley, Pamela, 177
Crowell, William, 48
Cumings, Bruce, 195
Đai Việt
dynastic rule. *See* Đinh Bộ Lĩnh; Hồ
dynasty [1400–1407]; Lê dynasty
[1427–1789]; Lê Hoàn [黎桓]; Lý

hegemonic international systems (cont.)
European hegemons, 36
political power of, 86
Qin bureaucratic innovations as the
result of hegemony, not its cause,
36–38
Hiep, Le Hong, 68
hierarchic nature of society. *See also*
Mandate of Heaven; tribute order
of international
as an element of the philosophical
approach to rule East Asia, 31, 46
persistence in East Asia of, 34, 86
Hirshleifer, Jack, 175
Hồ dynasty (1400–1407)
Trần ruler deposed by Hồ Quý ly, 89
Hồ Nguyên Trừng (Vietnamese scholar
official), 161
Hồ Sĩ Đống (Vietnamese scholar-
official), 168
Hoffman, Phillip T., 91
Holcombe, Charles, 3, 37, 39, 52, 55,
65–66, 98, 112, 116, 159, 165
Honeychurch, William, 178
Hui, Victoria, 5
on Chinese state formation, 19–20
the state defined by, 11
timeless cultural and political unity of
China criticized by, 22
Huntington, Samuel P., 12
Hwang, Kyung Moon, 116, 157

Jagchid, Sechin, 175
Japan. *See also* Ashikaga (or
Muromachi) Shogunate
(1338–1573); *ritsuryo* system;
Tokugawa Shogunate (1600–1868)
Abe-no Nakamaro's tenure as a Tang
official, 159
Buddhism imported from Paekche,
101, 157
economic growth in the second half
of the 20th century, 187–188
emulation of Chinese models. *See*
Japanese emulation of Chinese
models
imperial bureaucracy established in, 1
nationwide cadastral survey and
population census implemented by,
1, 112, 127, 129

tribute missions to various Chinese
dynasties, 101
Japan in this first wave of Chinese
influence was comprehensively
importing Tang-style institutions,
language and writing systems, and
education, including
Confucianism, Buddhism, Daoism,
geomancy and divination, law,
literature, history, mathematics,
calendrics, and medicine, not to
mention art and architecture.
Indeed, all three Japanese writing
systems – *hiragana*, *katakana*, and
kanji – were derived from Chinese
characters. As de Bary et al. put it,,
104
Japanese emulation of Chinese models.
See also judicial systems and legal
codes—Japan
Buddhism's role in the diffusion of
Sinic ideas and classical culture,
117, 156–157
logic of appropriateness as the
motivation for, 105–107
scale of, 104, 113, 118
during the Tokugawa shogunate,
51–52
Jiang, Weidong, 96–97
Johnson, Chalmers, 187, 192
Johnston, Alastair Iain, 28
judicial systems and legal codes
Confucian-Legalist state formation in
China, 20–21, 34, 37
Mongol laws and forces adopted by
the Ming court, 181–182
judicial systems and legal codes—
Japan. See also *ritsuryo* system
and the *Taiho* Code of 702
108
Taika Reforms, 97, 104,
108
and the *Yoro* Code of 718 109
judicial systems and legal codes—Korea
Chinese style law codes promulgated
by the Koguryŏ, 97
specialists in the Silla board of
academicians, 103
Tang-era legal system implemented
by Silla, 62

For EU product safety concerns, contact us at Calle de José Abascal, 56–1°,
28003 Madrid, Spain or eugpsr@cambridge.org.

www.ingramcontent.com/pod-product-compliance
Ingram Content Group UK Ltd.
Pitfield, Milton Keynes, MK11 3LW, UK
UKHW020354140625

459647UK00020B/2464